Consumer Reports

P9-CRL-553

BEST
TRAVEL
DEALS
2000

DONNA HEIDERSTADT & THE EDITORS OF

NSUMER REPORTS TRAVEL LETTER

Consumers Union • Yonkers, New York

A SPECIAL PUBLICATION
FROM CONSUMER REPORTS

Director, Special Publications	Andrea Scott
Managing Editor	Bette LaGow
Project Editor	Maggie Keresey
Design Manager	Kimberly Adis
Assistant Art Director	Debra Roinestad
Designer	Stephanie Fagan
Page Composition	Jennifer Dixon
Special Publications Staff	Linda Coyner, Robert Markovich, Michael Quincy, Pauline Piekarz, Joyce Childs

CONSUMER REPORTS TRAVEL LETTER

Editor	Laurie Berger
Associate Editor	Robin Peress
Senior Researcher	Wendy Goldman
Editorial Researcher	Diane LaVerdi

CONSUMER REPORTS

Editor	Julia Kagan
Executive Editor/ Director, Editorial Operations	Eileen Denver
Design Director	George Arthur
Managing Art Director	Timothy LaPalme
Publishing Operations Manager	Reed Fox
Retail Sales & Marketing	Geoff Baldwin, Carol Lappin, Angela Guerts
Manufacturing Coordinator	Steve Schiavone

CONSUMERS UNION

President	Rhoda Karpatkin
Executive Vice President	Joel Gurin

Contents

4

Consumer Reports: How We Can Help

Consumer Reports Best Travel Deals is just one of the many smart-shopping resources published by CONSUMER REPORTS. The following is a comprehensive list of our other products and series.

Consumer Reports Travel Letter. A monthly newsletter with solid money-saving information, last-minute deals, web-based travel tips, and more. To subscribe (12 issues, $39), write to P.O. Box 53629, Boulder, Colo. 80322-3629.

Consumer Reports. Published monthly, Consumer Reports magazine provides impartial information on brand-name products, services, health, and personal finance. To subscribe (13 issues, including the annual Buying Guide, $26), write to P.O. Box 53029, Boulder, Colo. 80322-3029.

Consumer Reports Online. The Consumer Reports web site at *www.ConsumerReports.org* carries a wealth of recent information from Consumer Reports. Free areas include useful listings, shopping guidance, and product recalls. Site subscribers pay $3.95 per month or $24 per year ($19 for CR subscribers) for unlimited use of searchable Ratings (including new e-Ratings of e-commerce sites), recommendations, and consumer advice, along with the current issue of Consumer Reports and participation in message boards.

Consumer Reports Special Publications. We publish specialty buying guides on cars, computers, and products for the home, as well as books on finance, drugs, and other issues of consumer concern. Consumer Reports Special Publications are available on newsstands and in bookstores, or through our web store (*www.ConsumerReports.org*).

Consumer Reports on Health. A monthly newsletter devoted to your health and well-being, it covers fitness, nutrition, medications, and more. To subscribe (12 issues, $24), write to P.O. Box 56356, Boulder, Colo. 80322-6356.

Zillions: Consumer Reports for Kids. A bimonthly magazine for kids ages 8 and up, features toy tests, games, and "money smarts." To subscribe (6 issues, $16), write to P.O. Box 54861, Boulder, Colo. 80322-4861.

Consumer Reports by Request. Specially edited reports from Consumer Reports are available by fax or mail. Call 800 896-7788 for an index of what's available. The index costs $1.

Consumer Reports New Car Price Service. Comprehensive reports ($12 each) arm you with the information you need to get your best deal. Call 800 269-1139.

Consumer Reports Used Car Price Service. Find market value and reliability data for most 1983 to 1998 used cars and light trucks. Call 800 422-1079. Reports cost $10.

Consumer Reports Auto Insurance Price Service. Compare the cost of insurance for the coverage you need; find the best price. Now available in Ala., Ariz., Calif., Colo., Conn., Fla., Ga., Idaho, Ill., La., Mich., Minn., Miss., Mo., Nev., N.J., N.M., N.Y., N.C., Ohio, Pa., Tenn., Texas, Utah, Va., Wash., and Wisc. Call 800 944-4104. Reports cost $12.

Consumer Reports Television and Other Media. We produce a nationally syndicated consumer news service appearing in more than 100 markets nationwide. Information from CR is available on TV and radio stations around the country and in columns appearing in more than 50 newspapers.

Travel Strategies 2000

We're welcoming the millennium with a completely updated CONSUMER REPORTS BEST TRAVEL DEALS, which features comprehensive strategies for getting the most for your travel dollar, both here in the U.S. and abroad.

One exciting change in BEST TRAVEL DEALS 2000 is the debut of an entire section devoted to the Internet, which has been rewriting the rules of the travel game. In Part 3, "Travel and the Web," we help you sort through the bewildering maze of sizzling web specials, do-it-yourself reservations, and overpriced packages. We detail the best way to conduct an online search for the travel information you want, from the names of bed-and-breakfasts in far-flung locales to global currency exchange rates. Newcomers to the web will appreciate the primers on browsers and serach engines.

Another new feature in BEST TRAVEL DEALS 2000 is the inclusion of product and service Ratings for which CONSUMER REPORTS is renown. You'll find results of recent tests of luggage and a major survey of airline customers. Travelers who really like to know where they're going will want to check out our Ratings of satellite-based GPS technology for your car.

It's no secret that the cruise industry is booming right now. So we've included everything you need to know to navigate your way to the best deal on the high seas.

Whether you're contemplating a cross-country drive or a trek across the world, this guide details the best ways to travel well for less, from booking airline tickets to securing a great room rate. Thinking of being a little (or a lot) more adventurous on your next vacation? BEST TRAVEL DEALS 2000 helps you find the perfect adventure—and tells you how to stay safe while you're there.

Here's to a year of terrific trips! And for up-to-the-minute information and updates on travel bargains, scams, and super deals, subscribe to the CONSUMER REPORTS TRAVEL LETTER. Our experts make it easy for you to get breaking travel news.

Laurie Berger

Laurie Berger
Editor
Consumer Reports Travel Letter

PART ONE

Planning Your Trip

CHAPTER 1

Before You Book Your Trip

Two keys to an enjoyable trip are choosing the right time

to travel—and the right companion for your journey.

◼

You probably already know *where* you want to go, but *when* you choose to travel can be almost as important as where you travel. Anyone who's ever braved monsoons in Southeast Asia or mud season in Vermont can tell you how off-putting "off-season" travel can sometimes be. But peak-season travel has hassles, too—high prices, large crowds, long lines, and frazzled nerves.

What's the solution? With a little planning, you can schedule a well-timed trip to almost any destination. Consult guidebooks and your travel agent for the seasonal particulars of your destination. And consider the following tips to save both money and aggravation:

Aim for spring or fall. Your reward will be a fantastic combination of moderate savings and generally favorable weather. There are a few exceptions: the Caribbean in September and October, when it becomes "Hurricane Alley," and certain European winter resorts, which often close from mid-April to mid-May before reopening for the summer. For the most agreeable weather, choose dates straddling summer—May/June and September/October are generally excellent times to travel.

Avoid summer crowds. Because summer is time for family travel, popular destinations such as national parks (Yellowstone and Yosemite in particular), theme parks (Walt Disney World and Universal Studios), beach resorts (Cape Cod, Martha's Vineyard), and European capitals (Paris, Rome, and London) are almost always crowded. The U.S. Department of Transportation (DOT) estimates that one third of all vacations by American households are taken in July, August, or September. The result? Scarce, expensive accommodations; oversold planes, trains, and buses; long waits in line.

Ask about August. If you do decide to travel in summer, avoid aggravation with a little research. For example, major European cities may offer limited services during August, when locals take their vacations; the cities may be less crowded, but restaurants, theaters, and small shops may be closed. And Europeans often jam resorts along the Mediterranean and Aegean as well as mountain regions.

Swap hemispheres. Winter in the Southern Hemisphere creates different weather in different places. Temperatures in Tahiti are 70° to 85°, while Sydney, Australia, is a springlike 48° to 60°. Check with your travel agent or a guidebook; destinations closest to the equator will be hot, but you'll be able to ski during July and August in Chile and New Zealand.

Take advantage of "shoulder" season. The shoulder is a very brief period, typically two to four weeks, just before and after peak season. Shoulder rates are listed in brochures for resorts, cruises, or condo rentals—moderate savings with generally good weather conditions. But these rates often sell out quickly.

Don't expect a bargain during the holidays. Traveling during the Christmas or New Year's holidays can be fraught with frustration. Flights to certain popular places—Florida, Mexico, the Caribbean—are often sold out far in advance and can cost double what they do just a few weeks earlier or later. (You'll also run into holiday "blackout" periods, when you can't redeem frequent-flier miles for free travel.) Hotel rooms will also command top dollar.

There are bargains to be had, however. Some airlines and travel agents offer good deals to Europe during the holidays; check ads and call travel agents for quotes. But remember, it can be wet and cold, and some cities, like London, are "closed" on Christmas. Also keep in mind that Easter is a major holiday in the Catholic countries of Europe, when roadways, trains, and resorts will be crowded with locals.

Ask about conventions. You'll want to avoid major conventions that monopolize cabs and dinner reservations. Ask your travel agent or the hotel reservation clerk whether these crowds will be in town when you are. If so, you may prefer another date—or destination.

Be aware of local events. New Orleans during Mardi Gras (mid-February) is a vastly different experience than New

HOLIDAYS ABROAD

Like in the U.S., other countries "shut down" during major holidays. Plan ahead to avoid transportation and service limitations.

When	Where	What
January 26	Australia	Australia Day
February 6	New Zealand	Waitangi Day
April 25	Australia and New Zealand	Anzac Day
May 5	Mexico	Cinco de Mayo
July 1	Canada	Canada Day
July 14	France	Bastille Day
August 15	Italy	Feast of the Assumption
October 8	China	National Day
December-January	Muslim countries	Ramadan

Orleans at any other time of year. Ditto for Pamplona, Spain, during the running of the bulls (early July); Siena, Italy, during the Palio (July and August); London during Wimbledon (late June); or Auckland, New Zealand, during the America's Cup (January). Some unsuspecting travelers who book accommodations months in advance arrive at what they expect to be an idyllic locale only to find it overrun.

Grin and bear "off-season." If a little rain won't ruin your parade, by all means check out the bargains of the off-season. Anyone who reads a Sunday newspaper's travel section has seen the $300 round-trip airfares to Europe advertised from January to March. Other off-season flight bargains are those for Australia and New Zealand as well as South America. Domestically, the airlines cut fares several times throughout the year.

TRAVELING COMPANIONS
Even if you think you know someone well, you'll discover new things about them on the road, away from familiar surroundings, languages, and foods.

The only reliable way to discover if you and another person have compatible—or at least mutually bearable—travel styles is to take a trip together. But advance trouble-shooting can help iron out wrinkles.

Traveling with a spouse or partner. Discuss prior travel experiences—both good and bad—to help plan a great trip.

Agree on the itinerary. If parts of it are unappealing to either of you, investigate other options. Or ask a travel agent, tour operator, or resort manager whether alternate activities are available.

Solve problems before you depart. Voice preferences. Then make sure those choices—whether golf, shopping, bird-watching, or gambling—are doable at your destination.

Decide who is in charge of "travel business." A good rule is whoever handles the bills at home handles money, passports, vouchers, and so on during the trip.

Compromise on different travel styles. One solution could be trading off every other trip on the destination (golf resort or European city), the time of year (warm weather or cool), the type of transport (cruise or fly-and-drive), and accommodations (hotel chain or country inn).

Do your own thing—alone or with others. If your travel styles are strikingly incompatible, once at your destination, each can do his or her thing during the day, from museums, tours, and the pool to tennis, fishing, or a hike. Then you can both enjoy a special evening with a good meal or a moonlight walk.

Joining another couple or couples. Although many couples enjoy the camaraderie, the multiple personalities and preferences involved in such trips can make them a challenge to plan and enjoy. What's the solution?

Start small. Your best bet is a long weekend, or a week at most, at an English-speaking destination with a variety of sights and activities to see whether your interests and travel "styles" are a good fit.

Make it annual. If you find a great group of compatible couples, you can return to the same place (a beach house or golf resort, for instance) or try different cruises or tours.

Be part of a bigger group. You and the other couples still get to share the trip but also have plenty of activities available and other interesting people to meet.

Going it alone. You'll find myriad options for single, divorced, or widowed travelers in all age and price categories. You can set your own pace, choose your own sights, meet other travelers, and forge new friendships. Consider these suggestions:

Mix independent travel with short tours. You can maintain your independent spirit but still join in on group tours, either day tours of a city or attraction or two- to four-day excursions through a specific region. Such a mix varies the pace, allows you to meet people, and often saves some money.

Look into "singles" tours, cruises, and resorts. But be certain whether the point of the vacation will be to share the travel experience—or to hook up with a potential mate. Some "singles" resorts and cruises have wild reputations; ask before you book. Other trips are instead geared to such activities as hiking, biking, diving, and skiing.

Decide whether you'll pay a single supplement. Some tours, resorts, and cruises still charge single travelers 30 to 50 percent more in order to ensure a single room. (The rule in tour, cruise, and resort travel is "double occupancy.") If privacy is important, you may decide to ante up the single supplement. If not, a roommate of the same sex will be assigned.

Of course, the game is "roommate roulette." You could end up with a wonderful person who becomes a future travel companion —or someone who snores, coughs through the night, and generally gets on your very last nerve. Or there's always the chance that you could land a private room without paying the supplement; it's a long shot, but if there are an odd number of singles on the tour or at the resort, somebody gets that extra room.

Taking the children. Whether you decide to take the young ones with you or leave them with a sitter, kids add endless details to the travel picture.

Do you take them or leave them? There are "family" vacations, then there are "Mommy and Daddy" vacations. You might consider alternating one type of trip with the other. Most kids won't feel left out if you're already planning an upcoming trip that includes them. And many kids enjoy the change of pace when spending time with grandparents, aunts and uncles, or other sitters.

Be ready for food fights. When planning a trip to a destination with exotic (as in spicy or unusual) cuisine, remember that kids can be fussy about food. America is the land of convenience foods, but Europe, Asia, and other locales can be surprisingly bereft of the kind of "snacks" kids like.

Food is the No. 1 cause of illness for American travelers

when abroad. And kids can be especially susceptible, not only because of their delicate systems, but because they're typically lax about hygiene. When traveling in areas known for potential gastrointestinal problems, pack plenty of anti-bacterial hand-wipes and don't let your kids eat unsupervised. Chapter 36 has travel health tips.

Get discounts. Most transport—train, bus, cruise ships—offers children's fares at a discount, typically 10 to 30 percent.

Hooking up with friends or siblings. Sharing facilities in close quarters can bring stress to even the closest of friends. Try these tactics to have a smooth trip.

Plan together. If both of you are up front about what you want from the trip, there's less chance you'll clash about details as you travel. Make sure you know beforehand about any requirements, such as no shared toilet facilities, or ailments like motion sickness. Also talk about the itinerary to determine which sights you really want to see and which you're willing to skip. And discuss spending limits.

Pack similarly. Three pieces of luggage or one neat backpack? More formal clothing or casual wear? Agree in advance.

Ask about habits. Your adjustments to room-sharing may be easier if you know in advance that the other person snores, leaves a light on all night, or takes two hours to get ready in the morning. Armed with this knowledge, you can try to adjust to each other's idiosyncrasies and enjoy the trip.

Take time on your own. Traveling together needn't mean spending every minute together. Plan some separate activities, then plan to meet back at the hotel or at a restaurant.

Pay separately. Keeping track of who paid for what can add stress to the trip. You can each pay separately with cash or traveler's checks. When using credit cards, ask hotels or restaurants if they'll divide the bill and charge each card.

CHAPTER 2

Finding Travel Information

Smooth your travel path with travel research. Along with a world of destinations, you'll find a world of advice.

■

The more you know about a destination, transportation, and all travel's little details, the easier your trip can be. And now travelers have a great new tool—the Internet. It's such a good resource, we've devoted an entire section (Part 3) of this book to the web.

Here are some other key sources of travel information, including guidebooks and tourism bureaus.

DESTINATION GUIDES

Guidebooks, which typically cost from $10 to $30, are a repository of helpful, affordable, portable information—the who, what, where, when, and why of destinations. There are about two dozen guidebook series on the market, covering virtually every place in the world.

Guides are now available not only in the travel section of your local bookstore, but in online versions on the Internet. They can give you a great snapshot of a destination. Aside

GUIDEBOOKS AT A GLANCE

OLD RELIABLES: Time-tested guides to help you plan A to Z.
Guide

Fielding   Publishes 58 guides for destinations in Europe, Africa, Asia, and the Americas, as well as special-interest guides covering cruises, dive spots, and other topics. Books highlight art, history, culture, and food.

Fodor's   Fodor's is the largest English-language guide publisher. The company puts out 14 different series, such as photo-filled Exploring Guides; the upscale Gold Series; detailed CityGuides; and backpacker-geared UpClose guides.

Frommer's   This series began with budget-travel guru Arthur Frommer's 1957 guide, "Europe on $5 a Day." (The 1999 edition is entitled "Europe on $50 a Day.")

BACKPACKERS' BIBLES: Young at heart, and into travel's cheap thrills.

Let's Go   The three-decade-old series of budget-geared travel books covers about 30 destinations with more on the way in 2000.

Lonely Planet   Founded in 1973 by a pair of backpacker newlyweds, this series has grown to include more than 200 titles, an information-packed web site, and an award-winning cable TV series.

Moon   The 25-year-old Moon Travel Handbook series has titles for over 70 "adventurous" locations.

Rough Guide   Established in England in 1982 by four friends, the series now totals over 100 guides, filled with practical and often entertaining details. The Rough Guide cable TV show appears on the Travel Channel.

JUST THE BASICS: Not fancy, but they'll show you the way.

Berlitz   The British learn-a-language specialist also publishes about 60 destination guides covering Europe and the U.S., focusing on culture, history—and, of course, language. All have color photos.

Michelin   The French company known for its ratings of restaurants and hotels also publishes over 40 destination guides in its Green Book series, with a focus on sights and historical background.

Open Road   With its motto, "Be a traveler not a tourist," this New York–based series publishes about 50 titles covering four continents (North/Central America, Europe, Africa, Asia). However, the all-text format is somewhat underwhelming.

Passport Travel   This series offers particulars and photos of sights, but has limited hotel and restaurant information.

Rick Steves   Steves, host of the award-winning PBS series "Travels in Europe with Rick Steves," is an authoritative voice on budget travel throughout Europe.

Personality	Choose if you . . .	Avoid if you . . .
Thorough and detailed.	Want historical info and lots of rated lodging and dining options.	Prefer guides with lots of area-specific maps
Serious, straightforward, practical.	Want hotel and dining choices in all price ranges (some reports may lack nitty-gritty facts).	Want a thorough history lesson and lots of cultural specifics—or if you're on a tight budget.
Reliable, time-tested, middle-of-the-road guides, with a recently updated format.	Are someone at any spending level, but especially if you're on a budget.	Seek a truly out-of-the-ordinary, off-road experience.
Irreverent, off the beaten path.	Are a student backpacker on a tight budget (or anyone who favors this travel style).	Want a bathroom in your room or a meal costing over $10.
Adventurous, intellectual, sometimes edgy.	Like to dive into a destination headfirst, taking a guidebook filled with background, history, and reliable recommendations.	Consider shopping your favorite pastime.
Earthy, eco-friendly.	Backpack on a budget.	Don't think of Days Inns or Quality Inns as "expensive."
Opinionated information for the independent traveler.	Value maps, historical facts, and destination particulars.	Want more than skimpy descriptions of hotels and restaurants.
Basic and no-nonsense.	Are interested in a sense of place.	Want hotel and restaurant ratings.
Ratings, ratings, ratings.	Have a tight schedule and want to know what's worth seeing.	Desire more historical details.
Strives to put history and culture into perspective.	Like your background information written in an accessible way; and seek small, offbeat hotels.	Dislike guidebooks with no maps illustrations, or photos.
Concise advice.	Only want the basics.	Love to soak up lots of historical background.
Practical, practical, practical.	Are budget-minded and don't want many surprises along the way.	Prefer to splurge.

GUIDEBOOKS AT A GLANCE *continued*

HISTORY LESSONS: Put art and culture into context.
Guide

Baedeker These compact books, put out by AA Travel Guides, have been around for 170 years. Each comes with a plastic cover and a separate map.

Blue Guides Published by A.C. Black in London and W.W. Norton in the U.S., these are straightforward, with sound historical facts and simple hotel and restaurant listings.

Cadogan Published in London, these guides to global destinations offer helpful, up-front tips on organized tours and specific itineraries. Chapters contain solid historical background and hotel and restaurant listings.

COLOR COMMENTARY: When pictures are worth a thousand words.

Eyewitness These guides are exuberantly colorful and feature more photos than written copy. They resemble the children's learning books of the same name put out by DK Publishing.

Insight Guides This London-based publisher puts out 400 books in three complementary series (Insight Guides, Insight Pocket Guides, and Insight Compact Guides) that cover every major tourist locale.

Knopf A division of Random House, Knopf publishes guides to places considered exotic, alluring, and steeped in art and history.

EAT, DRINK, SLEEP, AND BE MERRY: Where to see and be seen.

Access Published by a division of HarperCollins Publishers, these guides are arranged by city or neighborhood and color-coded (hotel descriptions are blue; restaurants are red). But historical and cultural information may be limited.

Time Out These 20 city-based guides, written by local writers, are modeled after the magazine format of monthlies published in major U.S. and European cities.

from the "sights to see" information and basic requirements and restrictions regarding visas, immunizations, and so on, you can get a real flavor for the locale depending on the guidebook you choose. Many also include helpful maps of mass transit systems, as well as walking-tour routes.

TOURISM BUREAUS

Almost every country and many cities have tourism bureaus to disseminate information on their particular region—scenery,

Personality	Choose if you . . .	Avoid if you . . .
Steeped in antiquity.	Prefer art museums and ancient culture.	Are really looking for in-depth hotel and restaurant descriptions.
Cultured, traditional.	Are interested in serious, scholarly descriptions of art and history.	Want advice on nightlife.
Competent and efficient.	Have an eye for detail and an affinity for history.	Enjoy attractions more offbeat than castles, palaces, and art museums.
A highly polished cultural mosaic.	Have a short attention span for reading guidebooks.	Want background reading rather than stirring visuals.
Colorful and enticing.	Enjoy descriptive text on art and history.	Want money-saving tips and recommendations.
A visual feast, plus some savvy guidance.	Are the sort who savors the finer things in life.	Tend to get lost and need practical contents like maps and directions.
Upscale, with snippets of information.	Want the best hotels, restaurants, and shopping.	Are nonplussed when categories are mixed together for aesthetic effect.
Hip.	Pursue the latest art exhibits and the trendiest neighborhoods and nightspots.	Dislike trendy scenes—and ads in your guidebook.

attractions, lodging, dining—primarily through color brochures and booklets.

Travel agents and either magazine or newspaper ads can all direct you to tourism bureaus. But the Internet is the fastest way to track them down, since most are now online. Or simply dial either 800 555-1212 or 888 555-1212 to request a bureau's toll-free number. If you're planning a last-minute trip, inform the bureau that you need information ASAP. Otherwise expect to get the information in several weeks.

THE INTERNET

When you go online to explore vacation possibilities, you'll join millions of others who've discovered the web's vast travel resources. According to Odyssey, a San Francisco–based market research firm, by January 1999, nearly 60 percent of online households had visited sites related to travel planning, making them the number-one destination of web searchers.

Turn to Part 3, "Travel and the Web" for a guide to finding and utilizing some of the best travel-related web sites.

TELEVISION SHOWS

Another first-stop travel resource is your television. Millions of armchair tourists tune in just for fun, but there's a wealth of information for the serious traveler, too.

The mother lode of travel programming is, aptly, The Travel Channel, with dozens of shows airing 24 hours a day, including "Travel Daily," "Amazing Destinations," "Lonely Planet," "Travels with Mom," and "The Best Places to Kiss." Content ranges from upscale to adventurous, all packed with solid advice on vacations almost anywhere in the world.

Flip to the Discovery Channel or your local PBS station for other shows to pique your wanderlust, including "Great Chefs of the World" (Discovery) or "Nova" (PBS).

PART TWO

Money-Saving Travel Basics

CHAPTER 3

What a Travel Agent Can Do

Why and when you might want to consult a travel agent—and when you're better off on your own.

———————————————— ■ ————————————————

Agents can often expedite the booking process, secure great deals on hotel rooms, and take most of the drudge work out of planning a trip. However, using an agent doesn't mean you can ditch your homework. You want to be able to judge what your agent offers. And a good agent can offer a lot.

Access to information. Agents will know about and have access to sources the average consumer never heard of, giving them a decisive edge in ferreting out travel options. By calling or visiting a travel agent—or more than one if you don't have a steady, trusted candidate—you can gather a wide range of information about your travel possibilities, including:

• **Tour, cruise, and resort brochures.** Most travel agents can supply you with elaborate color brochures detailing itineraries, accommodations, and activities, all from leading travel providers around the world.

• **Resource books.** Many travel agencies have trip-planning resources, such as the *Thomas Cook European Timetable* (a list of every departure and arrival time for every scheduled train in Europe) or Alaskan ferry schedules.

• **Anecdotes and reports from other clients.** A good travel agent is an honest one, willing to relay reports—favorable or not—from others who've been on your proposed vacation.

DO YOU NEED AN AGENT?

If your schedule is already jammed with work and family commitments, finding hours for research may be a problem. (Many busy travelers overcome time squeezes by surfing the web late in the evening for ideas and deals.) Using a travel agent definitely expedites the planning process.

Travel agencies work on commissions from hotel chains and tour companies. And starting in 1995, airlines lowered their commissions to agents, capping them at $50 per ticket. To compensate for lost revenue, many agents now include "override commissions"—and can earn bonus payments for exceeding quotas set by the airlines. As a result, you may pay more for a ticket booked through an agent. But if convenience is important, the trade-off may be worth it to you.

Wholesale ticket brokers, known as consolidators, are another option. Just be forewarned that consolidators may be risky to deal with and ticketing restrictions can be onerous.

You may realize particular savings if you want to stay at a large resort or hotel where the agency may have prenegotiated discounts or you use an agency's airline, cruise, and resort "package deals." However, in Europe or other foreign destinations, tourist hotels that travel agents often recommend are usually more costly than small inns, guest houses, bed-and-breakfasts, or pensions.

A travel agent works with many clients at one time, and even a longtime, trusted agent may not understand your personal needs and preferences as well as you think—and certainly not as well as you do. If you have specific requirements, it may be

MONEY SAVERS

25

worth your time to explore on your own. Ask your agent to investigate your choices. A pro may be able to secure a price or all-inclusive package deal that beats what you could book on your own.

HOW TO FIND A PRO

Most travel agents have begun charging fees for their services—or raising the fees they already impose. But are you getting your money's worth? Shopping for a trustworthy counselor is as important—and challenging—as shopping for any other service provider.

Experts advise first asking friends or relatives for recommendations. Then, do the interviews. To get you started, here's a "hot list" of questions to ask prospective agents:

1. How long has your agency been in business?

2. How long have you been an agent?

3. Are you certified by the Institute of Certified Travel Agents?

4. Do you have any additional training or expertise that makes you knowledgeable about specific destinations or certain types of travel, such as adventure tours or cruises?

5. Do you charge service fees?

6. If so, what is your fee structure? (Ask for a written description and an itemized list of fees.)

7. Are there ever any circumstances under which you waive your fee? (For example, some travel agents will waive itinerary-planning fees if the traveler books the proposed trip through the agency.

8. When you book travel for a family, do you charge a fee for each family member or one fee for the entire group?

9. Do you have any special or preferred-supplier relationships with travel providers? If so, with whom and what is the exact relationship? (Such relationships can be a plus or a minus for travelers. If an agent deliberately avoids an airline because it's paying lower commissions, and that airline is offering the

lowest fare in the market, the traveler is hurt. However, if all things are equal, and a special relationship allows the traveler to be upgraded or taken off a waiting list, such a relationship can be a plus.)

10. Do you get override payments from the carriers you book? If so, how does that influence your choice of airlines for customers?

11. What resources do you use to find the lowest available airfares?

12. Can you guarantee that you are finding me the lowest airfare available in the market? If you find a lower fare after I've booked a ticket, will you let me know? If I find one lower than yours, will you match it and refund the difference to me? Will you also refund the fee I paid for your service?

13. Do you use the Internet to research destinations? If so, do you give clients the information you get? Can you direct me to the best travel sites on the Internet?

14. Have you been to the destination I've booked? How many trips have you booked there before?

15. Do you provide special services, such as advocating on my behalf in a dispute with an airline over frequent-flier miles? Will you keep track of credit I may be owed by an airline for a voided ticket?

16. Will you alert me when you spot an attractive package to a destination I'm interested in?

17. Can you provide recent references?

WHAT TRAVEL AGENTS DO BEST

A savvy travel agent can make planning a trip a lot easier by searching for better bargains on airline tickets and hotel rooms, answering questions about transportation or currency exchange issues, or helping secure travel visas. Even if you use a travel agent only as an order processor, travel is less of a hassle. But a capable agent can do much more.

Get you deals. Large agencies in metropolitan areas generally have the broadest access. And agencies specializing in business travel may have first dibs on some discounts.

Nevertheless, expect your agent to be willing and able to find these bargains: discount airline tickets (from wholesale ticket brokers known as consolidators); discount hotel accommodations (through relationships with large hotel chains, room consolidators, tour operators, and travel-agency consortiums); and discount cruises and package tours (directly from tour and cruise operators or through discount clearinghouses).

Airlines may also offer "rule-bending" adjustments to some select agencies. The agency can then adjust pricing from expensive to inexpensive categories or obtain a waiver on ticket-purchase restrictions.

Facilitate overseas arrangements. An agent with international connections can contact a variety of overseas travel suppliers and set up even the most complicated itineraries for you.

Foreign airline tickets and passes. A pro knows more about ticketing restrictions and options, and can also arrange air passes, such as those for a specific region or country that requires you to purchase a minimum number of flight coupons.

Tour segments. Even when traveling independently, you may want to hook up with a tour for some portion of your trip. A travel agent can research the options, saving you long-distance phone calls.

Ground transportation. You may want to be met upon arrival and escorted to your hotel, especially where the language is unfamiliar and the airport far from the city—such as Istanbul, Beijing, or Tokyo.

Offer advice and recommendations. The best agents follow up to see whether a client enjoyed the vacation or was disappointed by any aspect of it. They also travel themselves and have insider knowledge. Determine whether the agent will share these informative real-life experiences.

Ask agents if they've ever been to your proposed destination, then find out what they did or didn't like—and whether they would return. If answers are general, press for specifics. How many clients have they sent there? Did anyone report any problems? If a tour, cruise, or resort is a fizzle, you need to know.

Your agent should also know the type of guest a specific resort, tour, or cruise attracts and relay this information. If you're in your 20s or 30s, you don't want a cruise where 95 percent of your fellow passengers are retirees. Nor would you want to travel solo to a resort where most other guests are honeymooners.

Pull together a complete itinerary. A pro will arrange your tickets, hotel and rental car vouchers, and tour specifics all together in a neat packet. With this attention to detail, those last-minute "What's the hotel's address?" crises are less apt to happen.

CHAPTER 4

Ways to Make Travel Cheaper

You need to spend money to travel—but maybe not as much as you think. Savvy planning can save hundreds, even thousands of dollars on a trip.

---◼---

Looking for great deals on everything from airfares to car rentals to meals? Here are the key rules to travel by.

Travel off-season. When the travel industry goes "on sale," fantastic bargains can be had. Consider these 1999 deals:

• $300 round-trip to more than a dozen European cities—that's what several airlines offered January through April.

• $999-per-couple fares to Hong Kong, including six nights' accommodation early in the year.

• $799 adult and $399 child fares for a seven-day combination Disney Cruise Line/Walt Disney World Resort vacation in April and May.

In addition to airfares, off-season travel (which varies by destination) will also net you savings on hotel rooms, resort stays, and tours (typically 20 to 30 percent, but sometimes as much as 50 percent) and on some forms of transportation.

Be an informed traveler. By subscribing to travel magazines and newsletters, reading your newspaper's weekly travel section, watching travel television shows, and surfing travel web sites, you'll be among the first to hear about deals. As a regular travel news scout, you'll also spot travel bargains and good values.

Earn frequent-flier miles without leaving the ground. With the many promotions and tie-ins offered by most major airlines, you can earn a ticket without being a "frequent" flier (see Chapter 15).

Beat the airlines at their own game. The key to getting the best deal is to adhere to the airlines' 14-day-advance-purchase, Saturday-night-stay restrictions. And do your research. Becoming familiar with fare structures between your home city and a variety of places on your travel agenda will help you zero in on the best possible travel times and fares.

Book via the web. Booking an airline ticket, hotel room, or rental car is easy—and can bring you savings of 10 to 50 percent.

Several top domestic airlines, including American and Continental, post bargain flights every Wednesday for the coming weekend (and will e-mail news to you if you subscribe). Many rental companies offer 10 to 20 percent discounts to anyone who books online. Leading hotel chains, such as Hilton, Hyatt, and Intercontinental, offer last-minute savings on many of their properties; book on or after Wednesday for the coming weekend at savings of up to 50 percent. Consolidators, cruise lines, and tour companies also use the web to post "deals" and "specials," mostly for last-minute travel.

For more on what's available online and how the web can save you money, turn to Part Three.

Take advantage of currency fluctuations. If you were planning a ski trip last winter, you would have paid as much as $50 a day for lift tickets in major U.S. ski resorts in Colorado, Utah, or Idaho. But north of the border, the weak Canadian dollar meant a day on the slopes could be had for $30 or under. You would have also netted the same 35 to 40 percent savings on hotel rooms, meals, rental cars, and shopping.

As an American traveler, you are almost always able to find favorable currency exchange rates somewhere in the world. By keeping track of exchange rates, then planning travel during times when the rate is favorable, you can reap substantial savings —especially if one of your favorite travel pastimes is shopping.

Find hotel discounts. They'll yield substantial savings on a long trip. But even on a quick weekend getaway, savings of 30 to 50 percent "hands" you money to spend other ways. Savvy travel agents, the web, discount room brokers, and travel clubs are all viable savings channels.

Make lunch your major meal. You may have noticed that prices at many restaurants are typically 20 to 30 percent lower at lunch than at dinner. If you make lunch your main meal of the day, you can sample the city's finer cuisine without blowing your budget. Make dinner lighter fare—in a small café, for example.

Use ATMs when available. Savings sometimes equal 5 to 15 percent over exchanging traveler's checks or cash at foreign exchange booths. Most major American banks, and some smaller ones as well, are connected to the Cirrus and Plus systems, which link thousands of ATM machines worldwide. You can withdraw money from your bank account at any machine with the Cirrus or Plus logos, following your familiar withdrawal procedure. Most international ATMs offer an "English" option. You'll be given the amount you request in local currency —usually at the best exchange rate without a transaction fee or, at the most, be charged a nominal amount.

CHAPTER 5

The Best Time to Book Bargains

Timing counts if you're after a real travel deal. Airfares and hotel room rates are seasonal—and knowing where and when to go "off-season" can save you as much as 50 percent.

———————————— ■ ————————————

Many of the world's vacationers want to travel during the same few months. You don't need a degree in tourism to deduce that high demand generates higher prices.

If you'd rather not pay top dollar, avoid travel during the peak seasons: July, August, and September and, depending on your destination, the major holiday periods surrounding Christmas, New Year's, and Easter.

The key phrase to remember if you're a fan of travel bargains is "off-season." How much will you save? Plenty. Keep some basic guidelines in mind when planning.

OFF-SEASON BENEFITS

Off-season is simply the time when most other tourists stay home —and when rates go down to lure in business. Opportunities vary by region and season, of course, but travel scheduled in the low season usually costs less.

33

Lower airfares. Reduced fares can be the largest perk. Time your trip to catch airfare "sales" and you can almost always save 30 to 50 percent—sometimes as much as 65 to 70 percent. Savings depend on the region and the route.

Intercontinental. These routes, linking the U.S. with Europe, Asia, South America, and the South Pacific, have at least two seasonal price levels, usually called high and low, which are limited only to Economy Excursion fares. Some routes have only one seasonal fluctuation each year; others may have several. In addition, several U.S. to Europe and U.S. to South Pacific fares

TRAVEL SEASONS

Peak season means top dollar and heavy crowds. Off-season nets the best deals along with uncrowded locales. Shoulder season is a great compromise; some savings and relatively few fellow tourists.

Destination	Peak Season	Off-season	Shoulder
Western U.S.	June–Aug. Jan.–March (ski)	Nov.–Dec.	Sept.–Oct., April–May
Florida	Dec.–April	July–Oct.	Nov.–Dec., May–June
New York/Boston	June–Sept., Dec.	Nov.–March (except Dec.)	April–May, Oct.
Hawaii	Dec.–March	April–June	NA
Alaska	June–Aug.	NA	May, Sept.
Canada	June–Sept.	Nov.–March (except ski areas)	April, Oct.
Europe (cities)	May–Sept.	Nov.–March	April, Oct.
Europe (Riviera) and Greece	May–Aug, Dec.	Nov.–March	April, Sept., Oct.
Russia/Scandinavia	June–Aug.	Nov.–April	May, Sept., Oct.
The Caribbean/Mexico	Dec.–April	June–Oct.	Nov., May
South America	Varies greatly by destination; consult guidebooks.		
Asia (China/Japan)	June–Sept.	Dec.–March	April, May, Oct.
Southeast Asia	Varies greatly by destination; consult guidebooks.		
Australia/South Pacific	Dec.–Feb.	June–Aug.	Sept.–Oct., March–May
Africa	Varies greatly by destination; consult guidebooks.		
India	Oct.–March	April–Sept.	NA

have an intermediate "shoulder" level. Shoulder fares usually cover a period of several weeks between in-season and off-season. In most instances, your round-trip fare is determined by the day you start your trip. You may return at any time permitted by the ticket's length-of-stay restrictions, although in a few cases the round-trip price varies by your return date as well.

Domestic. Fares within North America are generally not called seasonal, but they often vary through seasonal promotions. Airlines also adjust the number of seats assigned to various price categories to change their yield without changing the advertised fare levels. And some low fares can be blacked out during periods of highest demand. (On some routes, fares vary by week, day, or even hour.)

Rail deals. Amtrak, the private U.S. intercity rail passenger system, uses multiple rates for each route in its system and some vary seasonally. VIA Rail, Canada's passenger rail system, also offers off-peak rates on many routes. Eurailpasses are not priced seasonally, but savings are always available to two or three people traveling together. (See Chapter 26 for pricing information.)

Cheaper car rentals. In some countries, several of the major car-rental companies adjust rates seasonally. They also offer special U.S. promotions during slow seasons.

Bargain hotel rooms. Seasonal price changes are common in the Caribbean, the main European beach destinations (French and Italian rivieras, Greek Islands, Spanish coasts), Hong Kong (most big tourist hotels), the major South American vacation areas (Bariloche, Rio), the prime U.S. winter vacation areas (Arizona, Florida and adjacent states, and Hawaii), and in many U.S. summer-vacation areas (lakes, mountains, coasts). Low-season rates may be less than half the peak rates. But note that special local festivals or conventions push up rates.

Reduced resorts. Seasonal adjustments in resort hotel rates vary greatly according to destination. Some have only one high and low season per year, whereas others have several. Most resort brochures list prices for the various rates. Generally, rates will be highest in warm-weather locales, such as Florida and the Caribbean, when travelers wishing to escape their own winter weather generate the heaviest demand.

More affordable cities. Hotels in major cities rarely adjust their prices by season, but some make seasonal adjustments by promoting special rates as part of airline packages. Tour operators offer reduced-rate promotions in major European cities during the colder winter months and during August, when locals leave for vacation and business grinds to a halt.

On the down side, half-price coupon and travel-club deals may be available *only* during the off-season. On the up side, you can bargain with certain hotels during low-occupancy seasons. Make an offer; many times the hotel will accept it rather than see the room go empty.

HIGH-VALUE SEASONS

In many places, spring and fall shoulder seasons deliver the best mix of weather and prices. Those time periods can be relatively short, such as in Quebec, or quite long, as in the Greek islands. Australia's winter (our summer) offers a long season of good value and mild weather.

Major tourist areas, mobbed in high season, are uncrowded and far more accessible in shoulder season. You can even enjoy weather-dependent activities, with reasonable luck. But check guidebooks or call tourist offices before you schedule. There may be so few off-season visitors that key attractions and visitor services may be closed or operating on reduced hours.

WEATHERING THE SEASON

Know what weather you'll face when booking either a peak-season excursion or an off-season bargain—it can make the difference between a satisfying trip and a washout.

Rainy season. When traveling to specific tropical or

subtropical regions—Southeast Asia, the South Pacific, Africa, and India in particular—pay careful attention to guidebook and travel-agent guidelines on "wet" and "dry" seasons.

WORLD WEATHER

Below are the average daily temperature ranges for 30 major tourist destinations around the world in each of the four seasons. The first number is the average daily high in degrees Fahrenheit, the second is the average daily low.

City	January	April	July	October
Acapulco	85/70	87/71	89/75	88/74
Amsterdam	40/34	52/43	69/59	56/48
Anchorage	22/5	48/22	65/50	48/22
Athens	54/42	67/52	90/72	74/60
Bangkok	89/68	95/77	90/76	88/75
Barcelona	56/42	64/51	81/69	71/58
Beijing	35/15	68/44	89/71	69/44
Bombay	83/67	89/76	85/77	89/76
Buenos Aires	85/63	72/53	57/42	69/50
Chicago	30/13	65/34	84/61	71/37
Denver	44/15	66/29	89/56	73/31
Hong Kong	64/56	75/67	87/78	81/73
Honolulu	80/65	84/68	88/73	88/71
Jerusalem	55/41	73/50	87/63	81/73
Lima	82/66	80/63	67/57	71/58
London	44/35	56/40	73/55	58/44
Los Angeles	65/47	68/51	76/61	76/55
Moscow	21/9	47/31	76/55	46/34
Munich	33/23	54/37	72/54	53/40
Nairobi	77/54	75/58	69/51	76/55
New Orleans	62/43	82/56	91/73	84/54
New York	38/26	65/40	84/67	70/46
Papeete	89/72	89/72	86/68	87/70
Paris	42/32	60/41	76/55	59/44
Rio de Janeiro	84/73	80/69	75/63	77/66
Rome	54/39	68/46	88/64	73/53
San Juan	80/70	82/72	85/75	85/75
Stockholm	31/23	45/32	70/55	48/39
Sydney	78/65	71/58	60/46	71/56
Tokyo	47/29	63/46	83/70	69/55

Although temperatures typically don't vary by all that much, "wet" season is definitely more humid than "dry" and characterized by heavy rains that can last several days. Monsoons are also a hazard. Translation: Your dream vacation could be ruined—or at the very least, soggy. If you want a bargain, consider visiting very early or very late in the dry season.

Hurricane season. Technically, hurricane season in the Caribbean, Florida, and along the East Coast begins in July and runs through early November. But the greatest concentration of devastating storms occurs from August to October. Resorts and cruise lines will typically offer discounts during these months to lure bargain hunters. Beware: Being caught in a major storm can be a frightening and potentially deadly experience. Should you decide to risk it, choose a date at either extreme—either July or November. Tropical storms also strike in the Pacific and Indian oceans, where they're known as typhoons and cyclones, respectively. Consult guidebooks for travel timetables to all tropical destinations.

Heat. Peak travel periods for many tourist destinations are the summer months. Unfortunately, in some places summer brings unbearable temperatures (90 degrees and above)—for instance, in Spain, Greece, Morocco, Egypt, India, Southeast Asia, the Middle East, Southern China, and parts of the Caribbean. In the U.S., the Southwest, particularly Arizona and Nevada, and the Southeast (Florida, Georgia, and Louisiana), can also have sweltering weather in July and August, as can Texas and Oklahoma. When you couple heat with large crowds, the result can be extremely uncomfortable conditions, even dangerous for travelers with medical conditions.

Cold. Freezing temperatures can be equally distressing, especially if you're unprepared. And certain regions are inaccessible during many of the coldest months, including Alaska, parts of Scandinavia and Russia, the Himalayas, and northern China and Japan. In the Southern Hemisphere, southern Chile and

MONEY
SAVERS

Argentina experience their freeze during July and August—their winter. Again, consult guidebooks to avoid the ultra-cold months of your destination.

BOOKING OFF-SEASON AIRFARE

Most bargain airfares, available for a limited number of seats, are advertised for only a few weeks leading up to the earliest departure dates. Usually you must book by a certain date and travel by a certain date, typically within two months.

Call fast—and be flexible. If you can, have a selection of several travel dates. When first choices are not available, ask the ticketing agent (or your travel agent) to search the days just before or after your preferred dates. You may also get a bargain by flying in the very early morning or very late at night.

Call after midnight. Many airlines' reservations computers clear out all unconfirmed, nonpurchased reservations at midnight. If you call a few minutes later, you may be able to snatch up the dates you want. But remember to call when it's after midnight in the airline headquarters' time zone—for example, Eastern time for Delta and Central time for American.

CHAPTER 6

Qualifying for Special Discounts

Can you get something for nothing—or nearly nothing? Yes, if you're a senior, a member of certain travel-related organizations, or pay a small one-time or annual fee.

◼

Here's a guide to the kind of discounts you can expect if you're in certain groups:

SENIOR DISCOUNTS

AARP. Your 50th birthday confers eligibility for the American Association of Retired Persons (AARP). The cost of just $8 per year—including free membership for a spouse—includes money-saving travel benefits: discounts of 10 to 30 percent on hotels; car-rental savings; bus-tour reductions; and discounted cruise and airline vacation packages. Mention your membership when booking to see if you're eligible for a discount.

Assorted senior organizations. Other seniors' organizations also offer travel perks, including member discounts: Catholic Golden Age, Mature Outlook (a travel club), National Alliance of Senior Citizens, National Association of Retired Federal Employees, and several airline clubs.

Airlines. Even without being a member of AARP or any other organization, seniors can reap savings on airfares, typically 10 percent on virtually any published fare. (See Chapter 14.)

Hotels. Most major hotel and motel chains offer modest 10 to 15 percent standard discounts off rack rates for seniors. Be sure to ask when you reserve. (For more information, check out Chapter 19.)

National parks. One of the greatest bargains for seniors is the Golden Age Passport. For a one-time $10 fee, anyone age 62 or older can purchase the pass, which allows unlimited lifetime access to all the country's national parks. (Normally, park entry fees range from $2 to $20 per car per visit.)

CHILDREN'S DISCOUNTS
Young travelers are also eligible for price breaks. All major modes of transport, including airlines, trains, and buses, offer some discounted fares for children.

EMPLOYEE DISCOUNTS
Many U.S. corporations offer their employees special coupons for everything from theme park admissions to movie tickets to airfare price breaks. Check with your human resources department. In addition, as an employee you may be eligible for "corporate" rates at many leading hotels—even for non-business travel. Simply reserve at that rate and show your corporate I.D when checking in.

TRAVEL CLUB DISCOUNTS
A few decades ago, really cheap airline tickets were available only through travel clubs—complete with membership cards, "dues," and other clublike features. But a savvy traveler, club member or not, can get such bargains as consolidator airfares, hotel-room broker discounts, cruise discounts, or online promotions.

Still, some key travel-club services are available only to

members. Annual dues range from moderate to stiff. Some clubs cover an entire family or household, others include just one individual.

Full-service clubs. These organizations cater to frequent travelers and bargain hunters and generally offer multiple services to members. Look for one that offers at least three of the following six benefits:

Hotel discounts. Half-price hotel programs are offered by most of the listed full-service clubs. You get a discount off the rack rate (standard price) at thousands of hotels whenever they expect to be less than 80 percent full. Many full-service clubs also promote smaller discounts at several large hotel chains.

Airfare discounts. A few clubs include one or more discount airline coupons with their annual membership packet, which cut up to $125 off the cost of the ticket, depending on price. However, coupons are usually heavily restricted. A few clubs sell discounted consolidator air tickets.

Dining discounts. Most full-service travel clubs feature dining programs. Discounts at participating restaurants are usually a mix of percent off (25 percent off an entire check, up to 50 percent off a single item) and two-for-one deals.

Last-minute cruise and tour deals. Several clubs include participation in programs that provide last-minute details on tours, cruises, and airline tickets through travel agencies. Travel Alert and Travel Advantage are two. A few clubs run their own last-minute programs. Just about every club promises big cruise discounts. But cruise discounting is so widespread that you can find a deal through almost any full-service or discount agency. So don't pay dues just to get a cruise option.

Travel-agency rebates. Most clubs run an in-house travel agency that rebates some of its commission on any travel service. The average rebate is 5 to 10 percent of the total price, given either as a refund check or a charge-card credit.

Emergency road service. Clubs with a focus on motorists provide emergency assistance or towing.

Travel clubs also have other goodies: vacation rentals (villas and condos), car-rental discounts (but comparable discounts are available elsewhere), and a grab bag of other offers that can even include movie tickets.

Special-interest clubs. Dozens of clubs cater to narrower interests, perhaps targeting travelers looking for expensive hotels and resorts, upscale vacation rentals, singles-matching organizations, or deals at golf courses or tennis resorts.

Automobile clubs. AAA offers an array of deals: 10 to 25 percent discount on hotel rates, 10 percent on limited dining options, 5 to 20 percent on Hertz rental cars, 25 percent on Aloha Air, and 10 percent on Amtrak.

MONEY SAVERS

Resources for Disabled Travelers
Ways to smooth the road

Persons with disabilities can check *www.projectaction.org,* a web site run by Project Action of National Easter Seals. An important part of the site is a database providing information on handicapped-accessible transportation services nationwide.

Select the state and the city you're planning to visit; you then get a list of resources, including public transit, taxis, van rentals, airport shuttles, and travel agencies, all of which cater to persons with disabilities, plus names of hotels with shuttle services for the disabled. Links are provided to entries that have their own web sites.

Though the site is well organized and easy to use, the listings are not totally complete. Still, it's a valuable trip-planning tool.

PART THREE

Travel and the Web

CHAPTER 7

The Lowdown on Online Travel

The Internet is a powerful travel-planning tool. With a little know-how (and patience) you can research and book almost every aspect of almost any trip.

■

The Internet is emerging as the "new travel agent," allowing anyone with a computer and adequate spare time to gain virtually the same access to worldwide travel information as seasoned travel agents. In fact, millions of Americans are already researching and booking trips via the web. Online travel ranks among the fastest-growing e-commerce categories, with transactions predicted to reach $15 billion in 2000, according to the Forrester Online Travel Report—this is a 500-percent increase over the $3 billion of sales in 1998.

A WEB TRAVEL CHECKLIST

Once you start exploring travel sites on the Internet—and be warned, there are literally hundreds of thousands—you'll be able to plan a trip from A to Z. Typically, a site is an extension of an established travel business, be it an airline, hotel chain, travel agency, or cruise broker. Some sites, such as the major travel supersites (see Chapter 8), are web-only enterprises designed specifically to serve travelers who want to book trips without a travel agent. Still others are set up by foreign governments or tourist bureaus to disseminate information about a certain region's sights and accommodations.

Here's an overview of the major categories. You'll find details on a specific category in Chapters 8, 9, and 10.)

Travel supersites. These one-stop trip-planning meccas allow you to compare airfares, hotel room rates, and rental car rates, as well as research hundreds of destinations. Be aware that the web is a dynamic place, with sites merging and changing often. As of late 1999, Expedia and Travelocity were the two biggest supersites.

Travel providers. You can scout prices, even view photos.

Hotels and resorts. All the large hotel chains have web sites, as do most major resorts. These generally provide descriptions—and more important, photos—of properties.

Bed-and-breakfasts. There are sites with hundreds of listings, as well as sites put up by individual establishments.

Rental properties. The classifieds have gone digital. Peruse online listings for the right villa or ski house.

Book flights and explore special deals.

Airlines. Leading U.S. airlines and most foreign carriers have web sites where you can check schedules, book flights, and, in some cases, manage frequent-flier accounts.

Rental cars. These are the biggest companies on the web and may sometimes offer discounts for booking online.

Trains and buses. Check schedules and buy tickets and passes on Amtrak, Greyhound, and others.

Travel information. Find everything from weather info to other travelers' tales.

Guidebooks. All the major guides, from Frommer's and Fodor's to Lonely Planet, have an online presence.

City guides. What will you do once you get there? The web can offer good ideas.

THE WEB

WEB DISCOUNTS

Hotel and rental car sites offer discounts of 10 to 20 percent for online bookings. Some airline sites offer web-only discount airfares, either posted on the site or e-mailed to those customers who sign up for the special service.

Mapping sites. Not sure how to get there? These sites will map out a route for you—direct or scenic.

Weather reports. Polar fleece or cotton? A slicker or a sarong? Surf sites to discover the weather that awaits you.

Currency exchange. If you're quoted a rate in a foreign currency, these sites will do an instant conversion.

Health and safety advisories. When traveling overseas, it's now easy to consult advisories posted by such agencies as the Centers for Disease Control and Prevention, the World Health Organization, and the U.S. State Department.

Personal experiences. Enthusiastic travelers—and sometimes travelers whose enthusiasm has waned—share experiences on personal web sites, chat rooms, or in forums found at some of the supersites or guidebook sites.

Destinations. Can't make up your mind? Surf for inspiration.

Tourism bureaus. Such sites are helpful for travelers trying to pin down sights and accommodations.

Theme parks. The major U.S. destinations—Walt Disney World, Six Flags, Universal Studios, SeaWorld—all have sites packed with information about attractions and upcoming events.

National parks. Research fees, maps, and campsite reservations.

Travel discounters. The web can be your ticket to bargains.

Travel agencies. Now in on the online action, the major agencies post airfares and special deals on their sites.

Cruise brokers. Some are established cruise names; others are web-only outfits. The cruise lines all have sites as well.

Discount room brokers. This business is well-matched to the web. With a few clicks, you can compare room rates in dozens of cities—but the true bargains are harder to find.

WEB PROS AND CONS

Before you take the plunge into online travel research and booking, be aware of the idiosyncrasies of this new travel tool.

What's good. The web can be outstanding for ease of use, convenience, and number of choices. You can compare almost anything online—destinations, airfares, hotel rooms, or rental car rates, and you can research at any hour of the day (or night). Many hotel sites post photos of a property's public areas and guestrooms. Many tourism sites (and some guidebook sites) serve as "electronic brochures," with beautiful color pictures of destinations and sights.

You needn't make appointments with agents, and most sites will mail tickets and vouchers directly to your home.

What's not. Arranging travel on the web also has drawbacks, such as wasting time or getting out-of-date prices.

Many people who use the web to research travel—both beginners and experienced searchers—can get so wrapped up in the endless links that a lot of time is wasted.

And web content is not always up-to-date. (Look for a "last

THE WEB

Online Auction Alert
Don't get scammed

According to the National Consumers League, auctions are the number-one category of Internet fraud—and that includes the auctioning of airline tickets and frequent-flier miles. Look out for "sellers" claiming they have miles that are about to expire. Once they receive money from an eager bidder, they can claim the airline won't let them sell the miles. Other scenarios to avoid are people selling "nonrefundable but transferable" tickets or too-good-to-be-true travel packages.

You can protect yourself. Always ask for more details before sending money, and verify flight and/or sailing times with travel vendors to ensure the seller's on the up and up. Hold payment in an Internet escrow account until you get what you paid for (*I-Escrow.com* provides this service).

updated on . . ." notation, usually at the top or bottom of the site's home page.) Even more maddening are old prices. You find a great deal on a hotel room and e-mail a request for a reservation, only to be told that prices have increased since the web page was last updated. You can either accept the increase —or refuse to do business with any online travel provider not keeping its site (and prices) current.

Do enough researching and booking online and you're sure to send an inquiry that yields no response—frustrating and all too common in the online travel field.

Security issues. While major travel-related sites—airlines, hotel chains, car-rental firms, large travel agencies—all have secure servers that allow you to type in credit card and personal information (name, address, phone number) without worry, other sites are not so vigilant about protecting credit data and privacy. Before offering any information, look for a privacy/security statement on the site—and read "Staying Secure," in this chapter.

Browser Basics
What you need to get around the web

To utilize the ever-expanding travel resources of the web, you'll need access to both a computer and a web browser. Most new PCs come fully equipped with a browser—either Microsoft Internet Explorer or Netscape Navigator. Both allow you to roam from site to site, viewing both text and photos. Some sites may require you to download an application known as a plug-in, which will allow you to view video or hear audio clips. Follow the link provided by the site and complete the downloading process.

To surf the web, you must also sign up with an Internet Service Provider. For a set monthly fee (typically about $20) you'll get an e-mail account and unlimited access to the Internet. For specifics on this and other technology-related topics, check "Consumer Reports Home Computer Buying Guide 2000," available in March for $9.99.

Consider the source. Most well-known names in travel are on the web. But *anyone* can put up a site. So if the name is not familiar, use the site for information only until you check further.

WHERE TO START

When anyone first ventures online for a trip-planning quest, the initial experience is apt to be one of overwhelming confusion and exasperation. Novice surfers may not know the right places to go—or those to avoid. Our four-step approach can make your web foray easier and more rewarding.

1. Check supersites and guidebook sites. Just as you'd first read guidebooks or gather brochures, visiting similar reputable travel sites is a good first step on the web. Such sites (see Chapters 8 and 9) are a vast repository of reliable—and generally up-to-date—information on hundreds of destinations. If you have a place picked out, you can determine specifics (where to stay and eat, what sights to see), then quickly and easily compare airfares and hotel-room rates. Large sites also generally have links to other travel sites (either affiliated or reviewed by experts). Once you have a general feel for your destination, you can print out any pertinent info to read later, then move on to the next step.

2. Conduct a search. Some of the best travel information (and bargains) on the web can only be found by conducting a search—either general or quite specific. ("Travelers, start your engines" has details.) A search allows you to find sites all over the world containing information on a topic as broad as, say, "New Zealand," or as narrow as "Auckland bed-and-breakfast." The former will turn up any site—probably in the tens of thousands—that contains the term New Zealand. The latter will net a listing of any site with both Auckland and bed-and-breakfast—probably still a few hundred links, but definitely more manageable. Or if you'd like to research a specific city or hotel, simply type in the exact name, click, and see what pops up. If the hotel has its own web site, you might be able to see photos and even reserve online, saving yourself the cost of an overseas phone call or fax.

3. Send out inquiries. Initial research done, it's time to begin the reservation process. Most hotel, rental car, and tour sites have either one-click e-mail links, which easily allow you to send a reservation inquiry, or detailed reservation forms (make sure they're secure). You type in the required data, click on "send," and wait to see if your request is accepted. With either option, you'll be notified by e-mail.

And remember, reputable sites generally let you reserve online (which means keying in your credit info and personal data) or provide the information by a toll-free number, either by

Travelers, Start Your Engines
Search engines: The key to successful web hunts

Conducting a web search isn't exactly a science, but some basic rules make the process a whole lot easier and rewarding.

Search engines are interactive sites that check out other sites, then index them by subject or key word so anyone using the engine can link to appropriate web pages. When you type in a key word or phrase, the engine probes its database for all possible links—which could be thousands or just a few, depending on the topic and the breadth of your particular search.

Choose your engine. Literally hundreds of search engines populate the web, with about a dozen used most often.

AltaVista (*www.altavista.com*)
AOL Netfind (*www.aol.com/netfind*)
Dogpile (*www.dogpile.com*)
Excite (*www.excite.com*)
Google (*www.google.com*)
HotBot (*www.hotbot.com*)

Infoseek (*http://infoseek.go.com*)
Lycos (*www.lycos.com*)
MSN (*http://home.microsoft.com*)
Northern Light (*www.northernlight.com*)
Yahoo! (*www.yahoo.com*)
Webcrawler (*www.webcrawler.com*)

phone or fax. Never send your credit-card number via e-mail on an insecure site.

4. Print out confirmation statements. Once you've received confirmation about a flight, hotel room, cruise, tour, or rental car, print out the e-mail and keep it until you receive your tickets or vouchers. Some travel web sites—including some airlines that issue e-tickets—consider the confirmation e-mail to be a valid voucher and will not send another one via regular mail. Confirm if this is the case. If you have not received your tickets or vouchers in the promised amount of time, call the company's toll-free number with your confirmation e-mail in hand to investigate the delay. It's best to do business only with companies that list a customer-service number on their web sites.

THE WEB

Compare engines. To get a feel for engine performance (how quickly various ones respond, how many results they deliver, and the depth of their descriptions), do the same search (say, "Singapore hotels") on several engines and compare the results. You'll eventually find yourself returning to the engine that consistently delivers the best links.

Be specific. The more specific you are, the better your chances of finding useful links. The most useful are usually sorted at the top of the list, but sometimes it's worth clicking through a few pages of links to find offbeat or minor but interesting ones. You can type in a word (Prague, for example), a group of words (Paris restaurants), or a phrase (frequent-flier program) and see what happens.

Check the "help" button. Most search engines use different syntax and different rules; for example, some work better if the phrase is inside quotes ("New York City subway") whereas others prefer you to use terms such as "and" or "or" or "not."

Bookmark sites. Bookmark any link you might want for future reference. Simply click on "favorites" in Explorer or "bookmarks" in Navigator and follow instructions.

If you feel at all uncomfortable booking on the web, you can still reap many online benefits. Simply do your research, then print out or write down details of the flights, fares, hotels, tours, or cruises. Take the details to a travel agent, who should then be able to book through traditional means. And because you've done the research, you'll know exactly what you're getting.

Staying Secure
Protecting your credit card data

Anytime you make a transaction on the web—be it financial or divulging personal information such as your address or phone number—make sure the site is reputable and secure. Look for these indicators:

Secure server. A security symbol should automatically appear whenever you are asked for sensitive information, such as a credit card number. You'll see an "s" in the site's URL (the *http://* in the address changes to *https://*) and/or a small lock icon on the screen that changes from an unlocked to a locked position.

Customer service number and mailing address. Don't patronize a site without a physical address—not a P.O. box—and a telephone number (preferably toll-free). Also look for an entry on the site that details the company's background; it might be a link that says "About Us" or "Company History." Basically, know who you're dealing with.

Independent seals of approval. Some sites are approved by either the Better Business Bureau online (*www.bbbonline.org*) or an independent web site monitoring organization called TRUSTe (*www.truste.org*).

Your own judgment. If a site makes promises that are just too good to be true—say a week-long, all-expenses-paid vacation at a Caribbean resort for $199—be skeptical. Scam artists inhabit the web, just like anywhere else.

CHAPTER 8

The Travel Supersites

One-stop online travel specialists offer easy comparison tools, direct links to thousands of sites, special promotions, and editorial content designed to stimulate your wanderlust.

———————————— ■ ————————————

The supersites are an ideal launching point for anyone interested in planning and booking a trip via the web. Expedia and Travelocity both provide a sizable overview of transportation, lodging, and dining options for almost any trip. A host of newer sites also showcase helpful (and fun) features that might tempt you.

HOW "ALL IN ONE" ARE THEY?

One-stop web shopping is a nice promise, one that supersites pretty much deliver—if their adequate but not always comprehensive offerings happen to meet your needs. They're best at certain services.

Web site links. These links will probably be the most useful tools. Although your own web search may turn up the same ones, on the supersites they're sorted—and sometimes reviewed for content and usefulness.

Airfare comparisons. Trip planners find fare information one of the best and most useful of the supersites' features. Both sites offer relatively easy-to-use "fare finders," which will deliver quotes of the lowest fares on all major airlines to most destinations worldwide.

Hotel finders. The rate comparisons are handy, but depending on the site, listings may skew toward budget and tourist hotels or those in the first-class and deluxe category—but rarely both.

Rental-car finders. Make a supersite your first pricing stop. Just plug in your destination, arrival/departure details, and car class and you'll get a breakdown of the best rates from the top rental-car competitors.

Last-minute deals. If you've got a flexible schedule, you can grab some great travel deals, highlighted on the supersites.

Frequent-flier mileage tracking. Track your miles in one place (you'll need to register with the supersite for this service).

Fare minders. Just plug in a few cities to which you'd like a good airfare, and the site will notify you via e-mail when a low fare becomes available.

Flight tracking. If you've got a flight number and a date, you can check the arrival and departure status of flights on major carriers.

Destination details. Most countries and all the major tourist cities are covered, but information may be sparse on some out-of-the-way locales.

Weather reports. The supersites generally link to one of the major web weather sites; you can often get three- to five-day forecasts for most destinations worldwide.

Travel news. Is an airline under investigation by the FAA? Could civil unrest on what you thought was an idyllic Pacific island overthrow your vacation? The supersites promise to deliver timely news aimed at keeping you informed and safe in your wanderings.

THE BIG PLAYERS

Expedia and Travelocity are well-established sites dedicated exclusively to travel and worth exploring and comparing. They offer a similar selection of services; your preference will depend on which format and destination guides you like best. Here's an overview:

Expedia *(www.expedia.com)*. Microsoft's travel site has a simple, easy-to-use interface and is packed with plenty of visual treats and text about destinations worldwide.

Home page. When you arrive at Expedia you can immediately book a flight, reserve a room, or rent a car. Simply click and follow the instructions (you'll be asked to register and set up a user name and password). You can also explore Expedia's "Fare Compare" feature to see what other Expedia customers are paying on the most popular routes.

Deals. If you're in the mood for a last-minute getaway, check the ever-evolving specials.

Places to go. Choose a 360-degree video clip of a few dozen locales around the world, from Chicago to India to Australia. Or enjoy a "Slide Show" of color photos from travel photographers; locales rotate throughout the year.

Best places. Along with profiles of cities and destinations, you'll get tips on travel planning.

"Travel Postcard." Send an e-card to a friend featuring one of several dozen locations.

Currency converter. Wondering how many dollars that 300,000-lire hotel room will cost? The converter is a convenient way to find out.

Weather. Expedia links to MSNBC's weather map, where you can research four-day forecasts for cities worldwide.

Worldwide links. Anticipate lots of links—in a quick test, we were offered 12 links for information about New Zealand, four for Tasmania, and three for Easter Island.

Interests and activities. Expect information on such topics as

THE WEB

57

business travel and family travel, as well as "Insider Advice" from a half dozen travel experts.

Travelocity (*www.travelocity.com*). Although this site generally matches its competitor feature for feature, if you lack an up-to-date version of Internet Explorer or Netscape Navigator, you could face lots of annoying error messages. (This could change, however, as Travelocity merged with a third travel supersite, Preview Travel, in late 1999 and was set to introduce a new combined web site in early 2000.)

Home page. Clearly indicated links take you through the steps of finding/booking a flight, finding/renting a car, and finding/reserving a hotel room.

Destinations. Content is provided by Lonely Planet guides, geared to those who want history, background, and, perhaps, budget accommodations.

Vacations and cruises. Along with the rundown of special trips and cruises, the site features a "Cruise Critic," based on the Fielding's ratings of ships sailed by major cruise lines.

Special deals. Expect a generous listing—many for Caribbean cruises.

Travel tips. Here you'll find information on how to use the site's "Best Fare Finder," as well as its currency converter and an airline-by-airline list of baggage restrictions.

Weather. Will it rain in Spain? Will Paris be sizzling? Click on links to maps and forecasts.

Flight status. You can check the departure and arrival status of any flight around the world.

MORE BIG SITES

Recently, a few more travel sites featuring fare finders, hotel room finders, and other tools for do-it-yourself travelers have sprung up on the web. Most, however, won't allow you to book online at their site.

Concierge.com (*www.concierge.com*). Developed by publishing giant Condé Nast, this site (formerly Epicurious Travel) features editorial content from *Condé Nast Traveler* magazine, along with a variety of useful and entertaining sections and links. The bargains link features a different specially selected deal each week, while the booking link sends you to Expedia for the actual transaction. Hotel and restaurant reviews are by Fodor's, and there are also links to weather, maps, bed-and-breakfasts, beaches and resorts, and romantic getaways—all filled with suggestions. Under photos, you'll find "Virtual Tours" (slide shows) of places around the world, and along the bottom of the home page, you'll discover helpful features such as the airport guide and a "Traveler's Bookshop."

Trip.com (*www.trip.com*). A bit hipper than others, Trip.com is not as deep in content. The usual trip planner section allows you to research and book airfares and hotels. But its destination guides, for example, fall short of the competition in content and range of covered locales. The "Traveler's Newsstand" and "Marketplace" are both helpful in theory but don't always deliver the information you want. Basically, this site still needs to fill in the blanks.

One effective feature, however, is the "Flight Tracker," which allows you to track any flight as it takes off, flies, and lands, using either a real-time onscreen map or regularly updated text—say, "153 miles SW of LaGuardia."

Biztravel.com (*www.biztravel.com*). A very clean, easy-to-follow home page makes this site a breeze to navigate. Features include a weekly briefing for business travelers that includes information on new flights added to a carrier's schedule or hotel-policy changes, for instance. You'll also find flight tracking, frequent-flier mile tracking, and links to other related sites, from the COC Travel Information site to OANDA, a currency-converter.

And, despite its name, you can also plan family vacations here as well.

THE WEB

CHAPTER 9

Individual Travel Sites

Here's a guide to more than 100 sites, from destination definitions to ticket brokers, that will help you research and book right at home.

───────────────────── ■ ─────────────────────

Once you begin exploring the web, you'll be amazed at how many sites have a travel connection—and how many more you'll stumble upon through an endless array of links. Since feeling overwhelmed is not uncommon, we've compiled a handy guide so you can sample some of the major sites.

GUIDEBOOKS

Most of the major guidebooks have web sites. The following four are particularly complete.

Frommer's (*www.frommers.com*). Geared to the budget-minded, this site contains a wealth of destination information and money-saving tips.

Fodor's (*www.fodors.com*). Going a bit more upscale, this online guidebook has a handy "Miniguide" feature that lets you devise custom guides for any of 99 destinations.

Lonely Planet (*www.lonelyplanet.com*). Anticipate irreverent and indispensable advice for the adventurous traveler, plus great color photos of a variety of destinations.

Rough Guides (*www.roughguides.com*). This is the only guidebook site posting the entire text of its print guides. Lively and well-written, the content covers over 10,000 destinations.

AIRLINES

Whether you're looking for the best airfare or are loyal to one carrier, here is a selection of domestic airline sites to check out for special fares and frequent-flier news (for international airline and low-fare-carrier site addresses, see the Resource Guide at the end of the book):

Alaska Airlines (*www.alaska-air.com*)
American (*www.aa.com*)
America West (*www.americawest.com*)
Continental (*www.continental.com*)
Delta (*www.delta-air.com*)
Northwest (*www.nwa.com*)
Southwest (*www.iflyswa.com*)
TWA (*www.twa.com*)
United (*www.ual.com*)
US Airways (*www.usairways.com*)

CONSOLIDATORS AND BROKERS

Discount sources of airfares and hotel rooms are now easily accessible via the web, with sites listing the latest deals. You can book online or call a toll-free number to reserve.

1-800-USA-Hotels (*www.1800usahotels.com*). The site lists rooms in 11,000 hotels in 1,500 cities.

AirTreks.com (*www.airtreks.com*). This consolidator specializes in around-the-world tickets.

Central Reservation Service (*www.reservation-services.com*). You can surf for rooms in 10 U.S. cities, including New York, New Orleans, San Francisco, and Miami.

Cheap Tickets *(www.cheaptickets.com)*. Its fares for tickets on major airlines are tough to beat—but be aware there are no refunds or exchanges.

Click-It! *(www.travelweb.com/TravelWeb/clickit.html)*. Take advantage of last-minute savings (up to 50 percent off) on hot properties from Hilton, Intercontinental, and Sheraton.

Hotel Reservations Network *(www.hoteldiscount.com)*. A large selection of rooms in most price categories are discounted for properties in 32 cities.

Lowestfare.com *(www.lowestfare.com)*. Meet another consolidator with a growing web business.

Places to Stay *(www.placestostay.com)*. You'll find rooms in more than 7,000 hotels around the world—as well as in several U.S. national parks.

Priceline *(www.priceline.com)*. Like to gamble? At this site, you submit a bid for an airfare or hotel room and indicate the days you're traveling/staying. If it's accepted, you "win"—but you can't choose your airline or departure time.

Quikbook *(www.quikbook.com)*. You can book in 200 hotels in seven major U.S. cities, such as Atlanta, Boston, and Los Angeles.

HOTELS, MOTELS, AND RESORTS

All the major hotel, motel, and resort chains are online. Features vary by site; some simply list properties, rates, and specials, while others allow you to reserve online. Here are 25 of the best known:

Best Western *(www.bestwestern.com)*
Clarion *(www.clarioninns.com)*
Club Med *(www.clubmed.com)*
Comfort Inns & Suites *(www.comfortinns.com)*
Courtyard by Marriott *(www.courtyard.com)*
Days Inns *(www.daysinn.com)*
Econo Lodge *(www.choicehotels.com)*

Embassy Suites *(www.embassysuites.com)*
Four Seasons *(www.fshr.com)*
Hilton *(www.hilton.com)*
Holiday Inn *(www.holiday-inn.com)*
Howard Johnson *(www.hojo.com)*
Hyatt Hotels and Resorts *(www.hyatt.com)*
Inter-Continental Hotels & Resorts *(www.interconti.com)*
Marriott *(www.marriott.com)*
Motel 6 *(www.motel6.com)*
Quality Inns *(www.qualityinns.com)*
Radisson *(www.radisson.com)*
Ramada *(www.ramada.com)*
Ritz-Carlton *(www.ritzcarlton.com/splash.htm)*
Sandals Resorts *(www.sandals.com)*
Sheraton *(www.sheraton.com)*
Travelodge *(www.travelodge.com)*
Walt Disney World *(www.disneyworld.com)*
Westin *(www.westin.com)*

THE WEB

RENTAL CARS

Web sites have made it extremely easy to compare rates and reserve a rental car anywhere in world. You'll probably want to begin your search with a "rental-car finder" at one of the travel supersites (see Chapter 8). After you've found the best rate for your destination, check the company's own web site to see if there are any specials or online savings before you book.

Alamo *(www.goalamo.com)*
Avis *(www.avis.com)*
Budget *(www.drivebudget.com)*
Dollar *(www.dollar.com)*
Hertz *(www.hertz.com)*
National *(www.nationalcar.com)*
Payless *(www.paylesscar.com)*
Thrifty *(www.thrifty.com)*

TRAVEL AGENCIES AND TOUR OPERATORS

Even your local travel agency may have—or be planning—a web site. Larger regional and national operations are plentiful on the web.

American Express *(www.americanexpress.com/travel)*. Explore the travel services operation of the credit-card giant.

Austravel *(www.austravel.com)*. If you want to go "down under," investigate these specialists on travel to Australia, New Zealand, and the South Pacific.

Carlson Wagonlit Travel *(www.carlsontravel.com)*. Find specials on cruises, packages, and holiday getaways.

Central Holidays *(www.centralh.com)*. This concern organizes and operates mostly European tours.

Contiki Tours *(www.contiki.com)*. Contiki conducts tours exclusively for those under age 35.

Empress Travel & Cruises *(www.empresstrvl.com)*. This one's a large East Coast travel agency.

Liberty Travel *(www.libertytravel.com)*. Browse through another large East Coast travel agency's offerings.

Perillo Tours *(www.perillotours.com)*. Perillo is an established Italian tour specialist.

SpaFinders *(www.spafinders.com)*. Need a time-out? You'll discover spa reviews and links to hundreds of spas worldwide.

Swain Tours *(www.SwainAustralia.com)*. Swain is known as an Australian tour operator.

Uniglobe *(www.uniglobe.com)*. Myriad domestic and international vacations and cruises.

Uniworld *(www.uniworldcruises.com)*. Considering a waterway vacation? Here's a river cruise specialist.

TOURISM BUREAUS

Most tourist destinations have tourism bureaus that disseminate information on sights and accommodations. Check this partial list for your destination; if you don't find what you're looking

for, you can probably locate it by using a search engine (try
HotBot or Google). Just type in "South America tourism" if
you're intested in a wide range of options, or "Brazil tourism"
to narrow your search:

Austria *(www.anto.com)*
Arizona *(www.arizonaguide.com)*
Bahamas *(www.bahamas.com)*
Bali *(www.indonesia-tourism.com)*
Bermuda *(www.bermudatourism.com)*
Cayman Islands *(www.caymanislands.ky)*
Colorado *(www.colorado.com)*
Costa Rica *(www.tourism-costarica.com)*
Florida *(www.flausa.com)*
Grenada *(www.grenada.org)*
Hawaii *(www.gohawaii.com)*
Honduras *(www.hondurasinfo.com)*
Hong Kong *(www.hkta.org)*
Ireland *(www.shamrock.org)*
Israel *(www.goisrael.com)*
Italy *(www.italiantourism.com)*
Jamaica *(www.jamaicatravel.com)*
New Mexico *(www.newmexico.org)*
New Zealand *(www.purenz.com)*
New York City *(www.nycvisit.com)*
Outer Banks (North Carolina) *(www.outerbanks.com)*
Oahu *(www.visit-oahu.com)*
Palm Springs *(www.palm-springs.org)*
Panama *(www.panamatours.com)*
San Diego *(www.sandiego.org)*
San Francisco *(www.sfvisitor.org)*
Scotland *(www.scotland99.com)*
Singapore *(www.singapore-usa.com)*
Spain *(www.okspain.org)*
Trinidad and Tobago *(www.VisitTNT.com)*

THE WEB

CRUISE LINES AND CRUISE BROKERS

To comparison shop among cruise lines, visit cruise company web sites. You probably won't be able to book online (only Carnival, Renaissance, and Royal Caribbean were selling online in 1999), but you'll be directed to a toll-free number or your travel agent. You may also want to visit the sites of several cruise brokers—but always do some investigative research before booking. Several cruise brokers have gone under in recent years—taking clients' deposits or entire payments with them.

American Hawaii Cruises (*www.cruisehawaii.com*)
Blue Lagoon Cruises (Fiji) (*www.bluelagooncruises.com*)
Carnival Cruises (*www.carnival.com*)
Celebrity Cruises (*www.celebrity-cruises.com*)
Cruise.com (*www.cruise.com*)
Cruises Inc. (*www.cruisesinc.com*)
Crystal Cruises (*www.crystalcruises.com*)
Cunard (*www.cunardline.com*)
Holland America (*www.hollandamerica.com*)
Norwegian Cruise Line (*www.ncl.com*)
Princess Cruises (*www.princess.com*)
Radisson Seven Seas (*www.rssc.com*)
Renaissance Cruises (*www.renaissancecruises.com*)
Royal Caribbean (*www.royalcaribbean.com*)
Seabourn Cruises (*www.seabourn.com*)
Silversea (*www.silversea.com*)
Star Clippers (*www.starclippers.com*)
Windjammer Barefoot Cruises (*www.windjammer.com*)

ADVENTURE TRAVEL

Yearning for a little outdoorsy adventure? These companies specialize in travel to exotic locales:

Abercrombie & Kent (*www.abercrombiekent.com*). They're known for exciting—but pricey—jaunts, mainly to Africa, the Amazon, the Arctic, and other hard-to-reach-destinations.

Adventure Travel Society (*www.adventuretravel.com*). This organization can provide a list of adventure outfitters (although it won't recommend one over another).

American Wilderness Experience (*www.gorp.com/awe*). Research and book a variety of outdoorsy trips.

Backroads (*www.backroads.com*). Get away from it all by camping, hiking, biking, and more.

Butterfield & Robinson (*www.butterfield.com*). Want to see the continent a different way? European luxury biking and walking tours are on offer here.

Call of the Wild (*www.callwild.com*). They specialize in wilderness trips for women.

Dvorak Expeditions (*www.dvorakexpeditions.com*). Look into river-rafting, kayaking, and fishing trips.

Geographic Expeditions (*www.geoex.com*). Walking and trekking tours in Asia, Africa, and Latin America.

Go Ski (*www.goski.com*). Check out the slopes and accommodations at over 2,000 resorts worldwide.

Marine Expeditions (*www.marineex.com*). Cruises to exotic locales—the Amazon, the Arctic, Antarctic, the Falkland Islands, and more—are on the agenda.

Mountain Travel Sobek (*www.mtsobek.com*). Search for adventures like hiking, trekking, small boat cruising, African safaris, and sea kayaking.

Outdoor Adventure River Specialists (*www.oars.com*). Plan for family rafting adventures on the West Coast.

Outward Bound (*www.outwardbound.com*). You'll experience challenging wilderness experiences.

Sierra Club Outings (*www.sierraclub.org/outings*). Expect North American and international backpacking adventures.

HEALTH AND SAFETY ADVISORIES

International travel planning involves more than booking and packing. You need to be in the know about immunizations, visas,

THE WEB

and possible trouble spots before you go, sometimes well before you go, as is the case with certain immunizations. These web sites have the details.

Centers for Disease Control and Prevention (*www.cdc.gov*). The Travelers' Health area has such information as necessary vaccinations and recent epidemics around the globe.

Cruise Ship Sanitation Report (*www2.cdc.gov/nceh/vsp. uspmain.asp*). This site details cruise sanitation reports.

Traveldocs.com (*www.traveldocs.com*). This visa agency details entry requirements and visa fees for myriad countries.

Travel Health Information Service (*www.travelhealth.com*). Though an independent site, it also provides links to CDC information.

U.S. State Department Travel Warnings & Consular Information Sheets (*http://travel.state.gov/travel_warnings. html*). Look to see if your travel destination holds any perils.

WEATHER
You can get three- to five-day forecasts for almost any place on earth at these three sites:

CNN Weather (*www.cnn.com/WEATHER*)
MSNBC Weather (*www.msnbc.com/news/WEA_Front.asp*)
The Weather Channel (*www.weather.com*)

CURRENCY EXCHANGE
No matter where you're headed, you'll want to know how far your U.S. dollars will go. Here's a currency conversion site:

Universal Currency Converter (*www.xe.net/ucc*).

LANGUAGES
Need to know a few key words of French in a flash? Want to wrap your tongue around a tougher language—say, Swahili? Check out these two language specialists who've set up shop on the web:

Berlitz (*www.berlitz.com*). The familiar language "teacher" sells its books, tapes, and CD-ROMs online.

Travlang (*www.travlang.com*). Learn to say hello (and lots more) in over 70 languages.

WHAT TO DO

In addition to the "destination" guides on the travel supersites, visit these sites to see what's happening where you're going:

CitySearch (*www.citysearch.com*). Cruise through up-to-date entertainment and dining options for 37 major U.S. cities and five cities abroad.

Excite Travel (*www.excite.com/travel/destinations*). Get the lowdown on entertainment and dining in dozens of cities.

Festivals.com (*www.festivals.com*). Review event listings from all around the world.

Time Out (*www.timeout.com*). The guidebook and magazine publisher's site details the goings-on in 30 world cities.

TRAVEL MAGAZINES

Preview these sites before subscribing:

Arthur Frommer's Budget Travel (*www.frommers.com*)

Condé Nast Traveler (*www.travel.epicurious.com*)

Escape (*www.escapemag.com*)

Islands (*www.islands.com*)

National Geographic Adventure (*www.nationalgeographic.com/adventure*)

National Geographic Traveler (*www.ngtraveler.com*)

Travel Channel (*www.travelchannel.com*)

Travel & Leisure (*www.travelandleisure.com*)

Travel Holiday (*www.travelholiday.com*)

DESTINATIONS

Specific places also have web sites where you can get the lowdown on features and facilities:

THE WEB

Walt Disney World (*www.disneyworld.com*)
The Grand Canyon (*www.thecanyon.com*)
SeaWorld (*www.seaworld.com*)
Six Flags (*www.sixflags.com*)
Universal Studios (*www.universalstudios.com/unitemp*)
U.S. National Parks (*www.nps.gov*)
Valley Forge (*www.valleyforge.com*)

BED-AND-BREAKFASTS

If charming, romantic accommodations are what you want on your travel agenda, you can use a search engine to track down establishments all over the globe (type "Big Sur bed and breakfast" or "Amsterdam bed and breakfast"), or you can try these bed-and-breakfast broker sites:

Bed-and-Breakfast Channel (*www.bbchannel.com*). This site lists over 23,000 establishments around the world.

Bed-and-Breakfast Inns (*www.bedandbreakfast.nu*). You can anticipate many American listings on this site.

In Italy Online (*www.initaly.com*). Investigate unique, economical lodgings around Italy.

TRAINS AND BUSES

If you prefer to travel via ground transportation, you'll find all the details you need at these rail and bus sites:

Amtrak (*www.amtrak.com*). Check schedules and buy tickets.

Greyhound (*www.greyhound.com*). Leave the driving to them, but check timetables and buy tickets or passes online.

Rail Europe (*www.raileurope.com*). You've landed on your one-stop site for all things relating to European train travel, such as Eurailpasses and national passes.

MAPS

Do you know how to get there? If not, the web can help. These map sites are free and can even plot the route for you:

CyberMaps (*www.delorme.com/cybermaps*)
MapQuest (*www.mapquest.com*)
Rand McNally (*www.randmcnally.com*)

RENTAL PROPERTIES AND HOME EXCHANGES

When a regular hotel room won't do—for an extended stay or for a family escape—check these sites for potential rentals or home swaps:

Hideaways International (*www.hideaways.com*). Eye hundreds of rentals in Europe, Mexico, the U.S., and the Caribbean.

International Home Exchange (*www.homeexchange.com*). List your home or scout out others looking to swap with you.

VacationSpot.com (*www.vacationspot.com*). Review thousands of rental properties around the world.

THE WEB

TRAVEL GEAR

When you're getting ready to pack, gear up by visiting these travel-oriented web retailers:

E-bags (*www.ebags.com*). The site is packed with every shape and make of luggage.

L.L. Bean (*www.llbean.com*). Shop for rugged travel wear as well as backpacks.

REI (*www.rei.com*). Browse through an excellent array of adventure-oriented gear.

Tilley Endurables (*www.tilley.com*). This Canadian company offers a selection of quality travel apparel, including their famous hats.

TravelSmith (*www.travelsmith.com*). Their specialty is clothes and accessories to take on the road.

CHAPTER 10

Newsgroups and Forums

Want other travelers' opinions about the places they've been and the sights they've seen? Newsgroups and forums let you "hear" from people all over the world.

———————————— ■ ————————————

Guidebooks are great for a general overview of a region or country. But they aren't always up-to-date on specific details—especially about the political climate or new health concerns.

As a result, newsgroups and forums are proving extremely popular with travelers of all ages and backgrounds—but especially with adventure travelers planning extended jaunts through countries, across continents, or even around the world. The web offers literally thousands of travel newsgroups and forums to peruse, some general, others quite specific.

OPINIONS AND MORE OPINIONS

Both newsgroups (specific online areas where surfers voice and read opinions) and forums (generally, communities set up within an established travel or lifestyle web site) allow anyone with a web browser to post or read observations about any topic imaginable. You'll find some views quite useful—but much may be off-target for your interests.

In the travel area, newsgroup and forum users discuss a wide array of topics—where to stay, how to get the best airfares, the safety of a given locale, bad-weather repercussions, recommended restaurants or local guides, sights worth seeing (or skipping). Plenty of opinions are offered. Remember, none of the "speakers" is an expert. You'll find just real people relating their experiences. And tastes vary widely, of course: One person's idea of a wonderful vacation is trekking through a mosquito-infested rain forest and sleeping in dingy cabins; another wants to be waited on hand and foot at a resort.

That in mind, seek a newsgroup or forum that matches your travel style and budget—which means clicking on and wading through an awful lot of opinions. These tips get you started.

THE WEB

Surfing for Cruisers
Getting news and reviews

Before shelling out thousands of dollars on a cruise, check the Internet for cruise reviews from experienced travelers. The Usenet cruise newsgroup (*rec.travel.cruise*) is the place to go for unbiased or unfiltered opinions. (You can access newsgroups through your Internet service provider or an online service such as America Online.)

If you prefer information organized and presented in a user-friendly fashion, check out the CruiseOpinion site (*www.cruiseopinion.com*). The passenger reviews we read on CruiseOpinion seemed thoughtful and well balanced. But beware, CruiseOpinion also *sells* cruises, which may affect the selection of reviews. For example, not every review is posted and most are positive reports, though there is the occasional negative assessment.

Cruise.com (*www.cruise.com*) also offers access to cruise ship reviews. But instead of hosting its own forum, it serves as a gateway to web sites with their own forums, including CruiseOpinion, Fielding Worldwide (*www.fieldingtravel.com*), Sea Letter (*www.sealetter.com*), and Cruise Fun (*www.cruisefun.com*).

Newsgroups. To find a simpatico travel-oriented newsgroup, try checking out two master lists, Deja.com and Liszt, which catalog a wide selection of groups by such categories as topic or destination, so you can more easily locate your areas of interest.

Deja.com (*www.deja.com*). Both the communities (newsgroups and chat rooms) and deja forums areas offer plenty to explore. And there are lots of travel-oriented sections.

Liszt (*www.liszt.com/news*). Simply type in "travel" and you'll get dozens of newsgroups, some quite specific.

Forums. Forums are a bit easier to hunt down—and sort through—since they're generally somewhat better organized. You'll find forums on most major travel and lifestyle web sites. Go to the sites below and click on links that say either "Forums" or "Communities" or "Discussions."

Concierge (*www.concierge.com*)
Excite (*www.excite.com*)
Expedia (*www.expedia.com*)
Fodor's (*www.fodors.com*)
Frommer's (*www.frommers.com*)
Go.com (*www.go.com/community/travel*)
Lonely Planet (*www.lonelyplanet.com*)
Preview Travel (*www.previewtravel.com*)
Rough Guides (*www.roughguides.com*)
Senior.com (*www.senior.com/travel*)
Travelocity (*www.travelocity.com*)
Trip.com (*www.trip.com*)

PART FOUR

Airfare Know-How

CHAPTER 11

Good Deals on Airfares

For many travelers, snagging the best airfare is more than just an exercise in smart shopping; it's a challenge to beat a system perceived as unfair and capricious.

———————————————— ■ ————————————————

Airfare can gobble a sizable chunk of your travel budget—especially for a family of four or more. So it pays to know how to get the most air miles for your dollar. The good news is that the U.S. airline industry is highly competitive, with regular "fare wars" that yield big bargains for savvy travelers.

DECODING AIRLINE LINGO

Some people will sacrifice a little time and convenience for economy—say, accepting a three-hour layover in return for saving $200. Others want nonstop or nothing. To find the best deal on the flight you want, it helps to know what airline industry descriptions mean.

Nonstop. The plane makes no stops between its departure city and its destination city: one takeoff, one landing.

Direct. Frequently mistaken for nonstop, "direct" just means you don't change planes. But you will make a stop. For example, on a direct flight from New York to Dallas, the plane may stop in St. Louis, then continue on to Dallas. (In this case, you'll see St. Louis/Dallas on the departure information board.) The stop—or stops—can add anywhere from 30 minutes to two hours to a flight's time.

Connection. More common than a direct flight is a connecting flight, which means changing planes, usually at a "hub" city, where thousands of other travelers are also scurrying to make connections. Time allotted to make a connection varies by flight and individual airline schedules, but usually you'll have between 30 minutes and an hour. Be wary of booking a flight with a very tight connection (less than 30 minutes); a late arrival could make you miss the connecting plane.

Layover. If the airline cannot get you on a connecting flight in an appropriate amount of time (generally under two hours), you'll have a layover. You sit in the terminal a few hours until the next scheduled departure to your destination, or if you arrive too late for your connecting flight, you may have an overnight layover—at your own expense.

Hub. Over the past two decades, as more airlines turned to short-hop trips and connecting flights to fill planes and boost profits, hubs have grown in importance. Each airline has its own hub cities, where it schedules flight connections to maximize passenger capacity. If you fly a particular airline regularly, you'll get to know its hub, whether it's Dallas for American, Atlanta for Delta, or St. Louis for TWA.

Full fare. Also called an "unrestricted" fare, this is the top ticket price, the standard airlines use to make their discount claims. Leisure travelers rarely pay full fare, since they can book ahead to meet the advance purchase restrictions, but business travelers are often stuck with full fare, either because of last-minute booking or not staying over a Saturday night.

Discount fare. Also called a "restricted" fare (because it entails numerous restrictions), the term discount fare covers any number of sale fares that the airline offers travelers who can book ahead and meet such requirements as length of stay and day of departure. These are the "sale" fares airlines advertise in newspapers and on television.

Excursion. The lowest fares major airlines offer on a given domestic route, these are also known by the trade names Super Saver or Max Saver.

Apex. Sometimes called Super Apex, this is the cheapest economy excursion fare on an international flight.

Economy/coach class. This class, accounting for more than 75 percent of all seats on most scheduled flights, is the only one offering bargain airfares. For a good price, you sacrifice comfort (seats are smaller and more cramped than in luxury classes) and service (food and other amenities are meager).

Business class. On airlines offering business class, you pay a premium (much more than coach, less than first class) for more comfortable seats and better service. As a member of a frequent-flier program, you may be able to upgrade to business class on certain flights for a nominal amount of miles—or even for free, if seats are available and you have "elite" status.

First class. Almost all regularly scheduled flights on U.S. airlines offer some first-class seating, from just four to eight seats (on some smaller short-hop routes) to the entire front section of a 747 on transcontinental or international flights. Most first-class tickets are prohibitively expensive, but you can upgrade using frequent-flier miles. Or you may occasionally be "bumped" to first class if economy/coach is overbooked—and you're in the right place at the right time.

Round-trip. The vast majority of airline tickets are round-trip, meaning the passenger flies from City A to City B and later returns from City B to City A. Virtually all discount tickets require round-trip travel.

One-way. One-way ticketing is possible, but it's usually very expensive, except on certain low-fare carriers. Those needing a one-way ticket (you're moving to a new city, say, or flying back home after having driven to a destination) usually resort to a discount round-trip ticket, then discard the return portion. Or they fly a low-fare airline.

Multi-leg. This itinerary involves three or more flight segments: from City A to City B, then from City B to City C, and finally from City C back to City A, all on different dates. Airfare depends both on the routes and the dates you fly.

Advance-purchase requirement. Discount fares generally entail an advance-purchase requirement—typically 14 or 21 days for domestic flights, 30 days for international flights. Many low-fare carriers do not require advance purchase.

Midweek departure. The lowest advertised discount fares often require a midweek departure: You must travel Tuesday (sometimes Monday) through Thursday. Departing on Friday, Saturday, Sunday (sometimes Monday) costs more.

Length of stay. All but the most costly unrestricted tickets have length-of-stay requirements. They vary by airline and route, but generally range from a minimum of three days to a maximum of 30 days—meaning you can't return sooner than three days or later than 30 days after your departure date.

Saturday-night stay. A stay-over in your destination of at least one Saturday night is almost standard on all discount fares. Business travelers, who prefer to depart and return during the workweek, pay higher fares for that convenience.

Nonrefundable. Read the fine print in airfare ads—most discount fares are nonrefundable. If you must cancel the trip, you won't get your money back. However, most discount tickets are exchangeable, so you can generally rebook at a later date for a service fee (typically $35 to $50).

Code-share. With the recent alliances forged between the world's airlines, many more scheduled flights are, in airlinese, "code-share." Two (or occasionally three) airlines sell seats for the flight, but just one airline actually operates it. For example, a

AIRFARES & AIRLINES

79

domestic airline may have code-share agreements with a variety of European partners. So if you book a trip from New York to Paris through the domestic line, it issues a ticket with its name and flight number. But you'll have to check in at the partner's terminal, because that carrier actually operates the flight and owns the plane. At check-in, you will see both the domestic and the European carriers' flight numbers posted on the departure board.

Code-share flights may not faze you—unless you fly a certain carrier based on its service and safety record. Always ask when booking an overseas flight whether it is a code-share flight and which partner operates the plane. Also check what each code-share partner is charging for the same flight; chances are that one of them is selling seats for less.

Operator. The operator is the airline that runs the flight and, usually, issues the ticket. But in code-share situations or in some short-hop regional flights, the operator may be another airline altogether. For example, most major airlines have affiliate regional carriers that operate flights to secondary markets: You may book a flight from New York to Cincinnati on Delta, with a connecting flight to Indianapolis operated by Comair, an affiliated but separate airline.

Interline ticketing. When one airline cannot get you where you want to go, your travel agent may book an interline ticket. You'll travel one segment on one airline, then switch to another airline for the next segment. Quite common on overseas flights, an interline ticket may also be necessary on some domestic routes. Depending on the individual airline agreements, either your luggage will be transferred from one flight to the other or you'll need to claim and recheck your bags.

Equipment. Whenever you book a flight, whether through a travel agent, via the web, or directly with an airline, you should be able to identify the equipment—the type of plane. Equipment may or may not matter to you. Some people prefer to avoid certain types of planes because of their crowded seat configurations. Or they may want to avoid smaller turbo-props (propeller- rather than jet-engine-driven planes) because of their safety records in certain weather conditions.

On-time performance. How often does a scheduled flight arrive at its destination on time? Depending on the airline and the route, on-time performance can range from 10 percent to 99 percent. A flight's on-time performance record should be available when you book. Some Internet low-fare finders and most airline web sites offer these stats.

TIPS FOR GETTING THE BEST AIRFARE

Airlines use a complex pricing structure resulting in dozens of different ticket prices for various seats on the same flight. Differences can be as little as a few dollars or as much as a few hundred.

These tips can help you find bargains:

Act fast on sale fares. You see a terrific fare advertised in the newspaper, clip the ad, then call the airline later in the day, only to find the low fare is sold out. What's up?

The truth is, those advertised fares are extremely limited. An airline may offer no more than 10 percent of its coach/economy seats (or none on some flights) at the lowest advertised prices. So while American travelers have enjoyed an almost steady

FARE-SALE CALENDAR

Here are the times of year the airlines have more bargain seats available. If you can time your trip to match these tight-travel times, you're more apt to get a good deal.

Destination	Bargain Days
Domestic	Late May/June, August, November
Europe	Late November through March
Caribbean	May through September
Asia	December through March
South America	Varies by destination
Australia	June through August

stream of domestic airfare sales over the past few years, *truly* cheap seats are hard to find. Typically, the purchase window is quite small—some sales last just one day—although buyers usually have several months to complete travel at the sale prices. Sale fares are usually advertised early in the week in major newspapers. You *can* get a head start by having a travel agent check the computer reservation system over the weekend, where all new fares, including some never advertised, show up first. A sale fare on a major airline, whatever type, is tough to beat. Here are some you're likely to see:

Straight-fare reductions. Domestic sale fares can run as much as 50 percent below regular coach-excursion fare (though 30 to 40 percent reductions are more common). Typical transcontinental sale fares hover around $350 to $400.

Free or low-cost companion tickets. Buy a ticket and a companion may travel with you for free, or at a discount of 30 to 50 percent.

A ticket to one destination yields a free ticket to another. In these more limited sales, you generally buy a long-haul ticket, such as one to Europe or Asia. The free ticket covers a short-to-medium-haul domestic route.

Be resourceful. Did you miss a good deal? These tactics can still help you grab a good fare.

Check another carrier. Competitors will almost always match sale fares. However, the airline that started the fare war will probably have the most sale seats.

Travel at nonpeak times. Flights very early in the morning, at midday, late at night, or during midweek will have far more sale seats available. If low fares are still sold out, try calling the reservation number after midnight or in the early morning, after the airlines reservation systems drop all nonconfirmed reservations, freeing up some cheap seats. Airlines will also on occasion reevaluate their pricing, then release some higher-priced seats at low prices.

Beat the clock. What if you've missed an advertised sale's midnight deadline? Call directory assistance in a major city in an earlier time zone for the airline's local reservation number (not the 800 number). If it hasn't struck midnight in Los Angeles, for example, the sale's still on there.

Keep looking. Once you've paid, watch for even better fares. Nonrefundable tickets can almost always be reissued for a lower sale price. Despite the $50 or so per ticket reissue charge the price difference could still be worthwhile.

Get reductions for hubbing. On a few long-haul routes, some lines offer a lower fare if you connect through one of the line's hubs rather than taking a nonstop flight. Hubbing does add about two hours to each one-way trip and poses the risk of a missed connection and lost baggage, but it may save hassle by allowing you to use an airport closer to your home. Secondary airports—such as Burbank or Oakland in California or Bradley in Hartford, Conn.—don't have nonstop transcontinental flights; but you can fly to a mid-country hub, then change for your final destination, avoiding the drive to a more distant major airport, such as LAX or JFK.

WHOSE HUB IS IT ANYWAY?

Making a connection with any of the major U.S. airlines? Here's where you'll probably change planes.

Airline	Plane change
American	Chicago, Dallas, Miami
America West	Las Vegas, Phoenix
Continental	Cleveland, Houston, Newark (N.J.)
Delta	Atlanta, Cincinnati, Dallas
Northwest	Detroit, Memphis, Minneapolis/St. Paul
TWA	New York (JFK), St. Louis
United	Chicago, Denver
USAir	Charlotte, Pittsburgh

RISKY TACTICS

The adroit use of loopholes in ticket-buying rules can also cut your costs substantially—but does involve some risks.

Back-to-back tickets. Sometimes called a "nested" ticket, back-to-back ticketing is a popular strategy, but you invite cancellation if you're caught. Essentially, this procedure lets travelers avoid the Saturday-night stay that the cheapest coach excursions normally require. (Back-to-back tickets still must comply with all the other restrictions.)

Here's how it works: Instead of buying one expensive round-trip ticket with no Saturday-night-stay requirements, travelers buy two cheap round-trip excursions, each of which does require a stay—one originating in their home city, the other originating in the destination city. They use the "going" portion of the first ticket to get to the destination and the "going" portion of the second ticket to return home. Since the two tickets are separate, the airline presumably can't tell how long the traveler stays at the destination.

Back-to-back tickets save money whenever the cheapest coach excursion is less than half the unrestricted round-trip fare. If you hit upon a fare war, the savings can be even larger.

In the simplest version of the strategy, a traveler actually takes just one round-trip, throwing away the "return" portion of both round-trip tickets. But back-to-back tickets can save far more if used for two trips (the "return" coupons of both provide the second trip). The major limitation is that the traveler must typically take both trips within 30 days, the maximum stay allowed on many of the cheap excursions.

Airlines say that back-to-back tickets violate their rules. For a while, they tried to police them through ticket audits. But passengers quickly figured out how to get around that barrier (by buying the two tickets on different airlines or from different travel agencies), and some airlines have apparently stopped trying to monitor back-to-back ticketing.

So the best advice on this ploy is caution. Even if a traveler buys the two round-trip tickets on two different airlines, a violation is easy to spot. Not showing up for the return portion of a round-trip could be viewed as evidence of an intent to bypass airline ticket rules, and such no-shows would be easy to track. So rather than using the risky back-to-back maneuver, fly a low-fare line that doesn't apply the onerous Saturday-night stay requirement.

Hidden-city ploys. Occasionally, you can save by overshooting your mark: A traveler headed from A to B buys a cheaper ticket from A to C by way of B, then gets off the plane (or doesn't catch the connecting flight) at B, the real destination. You can't check baggage to the intermediate city; luggage will automatically be checked to the ticket's final destination.

This trick works best on one-way tickets. While you might use the "going" portion of a round-trip ticket to New York for a trip from San Francisco to Cincinnati, you'd run a big risk on your return. Airlines may issue boarding passes for both flights of a connecting itinerary when you check in for the first flight. Showing up at the departure gate in Cincinnati with a ticket to San Francisco (rather than a boarding pass) for what is supposed to be a connecting flight will immediately arouse the agent's suspicion.

Airlines have been checking for hidden-city ticketing, a violation of their rules. If you're detected, you or your travel agency may receive a bill for the difference between what you actually paid and the higher cost of the shorter flight.

On round-trip tickets, your return space may also be canceled. And if you check in for the final destination of a through flight and get off at an intermediate stop, you could delay the flight several hours while the airline investigates the "loss" of one passenger. Bottom line: too risky to be worthwhile.

Frequent-flier coupons. An entire underground industry has developed to broker frequent-flier awards, which purchasers

AIRFARES & AIRLINES

85

primarily use for upgrades. A broker buys the award from a frequent flier, then sells it to someone else at a profit. If you see a discount agency's newspaper ad for "Business and First Class, up to 70 percent off," figure they're selling frequent-flier awards.

Buying such an award isn't illegal, but it's dicey. Airlines are scrutinizing frequent-flier awards more carefully; an award purchased from a broker may not be honored. Furthermore, airlines allot so few premium-class seats for frequent-flier travel that you'll have a tough time using any coupon you buy. Bottom line: Don't buy someone else's coupons unless you enjoy taking financial risks.

CHAPTER 12

Consider a Consolidator

True "discount" tickets are those that cost less than an airline says they should. Money-saving consolidators are one of the best sources of these travel deals.

■

Big airlines frequently tout their lowest prices as "discount" fares. But in fact, these are really list prices for extremely limited tickets. A *real* discount ticket is one that costs less than the airline's set rate. To get such a true discount, you must turn to a consolidator ticket, a genuine travel bargain.

WHERE TO FIND TICKETS

Why are these discount tickets available? Even the lowest advertised fares don't always fill planes. Rather than offer discounts openly—and invite retaliatory cuts from competitors—many airlines unload some seats discreetly through consolidators. These tickets are available through three main sources.

Consolidators. Welcome to the airline industry's equivalent of factory-outlet stores. These specialized travel agencies have contracts with one or more airlines to distribute discount tickets. Some deal directly with the public, while others are strictly wholesalers, selling their airline tickets only through other travel agencies.

Discount agencies. These sell consolidator tickets (or other discounted travel services) to the public. Many have their own consolidation contracts with some airlines, then buy other airlines' tickets from wholesalers. They may also specialize in a single type of travel service—air, cruises, or hotels. To find a discount agency, check newspaper travel sections for small, all-print ads with listings of discount airfares.

Full-service travel agencies. Besides selling a broad range of travel services to the public, these agencies also counsel clients and provide other customer services. Any full-service agency can obtain consolidator tickets for clients. However, some agents prefer not to—consolidator tickets aren't in the travel agency computer reservation systems, require extra work, and may pay a smaller commission than advertised-fare tickets.

WHAT'S THE FARE?

Consolidators handle discount tickets in two ways:

Net fares. Some consolidators contract with an airline to buy tickets at a specified net rate for each route. That price remains fixed even when the airline's advertised fares change. Consolidators add their markup, then sell to the public or other agencies. A net-fare ticket normally shows no dollar figure in the "fare" box. Such tickets may not earn frequent-flier mileage credit, and can't be upgraded with frequent-flier mileage. And during a short-term price war, the airline's advertised fares may drop below net fares.

Overrides. Other consolidators negotiate an override (an extra large commission) with an airline, a big chunk of which is passed on to the customer. As fares change, prices for those tickets fluctuate. The airline's advertised fare usually appears in the "fare" box. Such tickets may earn frequent-flier mileage and be eligible for a frequent-flier award upgrade.

Like many outlet stores, consolidators rarely mention brand (airline) names in ads or promotions. But when you call (or check the consolidator's web site) about specific fares and schedules, names are available.

HOW MUCH DO YOU SAVE?

Savings depend on where and when you go.

International. The biggest consolidator discounts arise on tickets to Asia, Europe, and Latin America—typically 20 to 30 percent off list, sometimes more. Governments must still approve fares on many international routes, so airlines prefer to discount through consolidators instead of frequently changing their list prices.

In the summer, when the airlines' advertised fares to Europe nearly double the winter ones, consolidators provide their best European deals—like 30 percent off a ticket to London or Paris. Fare wars can slash advertised fares below typical consolidator prices. And in the off-season, even the best consolidator prices are no lower than the airline's regular fares.

Advertised fares to Asia and Latin America vary little by season, so discounts tend to be consistent year-round.

Domestic. With deregulation, U.S. airlines are free to adjust prices as often and as fast as they want. That pricing freedom has eliminated much of the need for back-door discounting through consolidators, meaning the best advertised fares—the big airlines' cheapest coach excursions and low-fare airlines' regular rates—are almost always below the best consolidator prices, especially during a fare war.

FRONT-CABIN DISCOUNTS

Whereas the discount market focuses mainly on coach/economy tickets, some agencies handle business and first class. Even when you find a premium-seat discount, however, it's usually no more than 20 percent, and often less. That may represent a

AIRFARES & AIRLINES

sizable dollar savings but seldom brings the premium-ticket cost even close to low coach/economy prices.

An agency advertising large business- and first-class discounts may actually be a coupon broker that resells frequent-flier awards, very different from a discount ticket and a "deal" that poses risks—like not being able to use your ticket. See Chapter 11 for more on this risky ploy.

LIMITATIONS AND RISKS

Consolidator tickets do have certain drawbacks:

Limitations. Consolidator tickets have some restrictions— some acceptable, others that might ask too much of even the most bargain-hungry traveler.

They're inflexible. If your flight is canceled or delayed, the airline isn't obligated to transfer you to another airline (though occasionally they may do so). And you can get a refund only through the discount agency—if at all.

They often entail trade-offs. You may have to fly an airline you dislike, follow an inconvenient schedule, or take an indirect route with extra stops. You may not receive frequent-flier mileage, be allowed to reserve a seat before you arrive at the airport, or be eligible for special meals.

Choices may be limited. You might hear that only undesirable airlines sell tickets through consolidators, but many of the world's top airlines do it—at least some of the time. Bottom-dollar transatlantic tickets can be on minor airlines, but you can usually fly a major line for only a bit more. Specify which airlines you prefer—or refuse to fly—when you check prices.

Risks. Consolidator tickets have a reputation for being risky, but that indictment is too broad. Once you have a valid ticket and confirmed reservation, you should have no trouble. The risk is in buying the ticket: Too many discount agencies engage in sloppy or dishonest practices, such as:

Bait-and-switch tactics. Most common among discount

agencies, these include not being able to deliver tickets for promised fares or highlighting fares based on a low figure that applies to only a tiny number of seats.

Deceptive advertising. Agencies sometimes advertise list-price charter fares as discounts, deceptive because while charter fares are usually lower than major-airline fares, they're certainly not discounted. Charters are cheaper for good reasons: They're usually jammed; they fly less frequently than scheduled-airline flights; check-in is much more difficult; and a mechanical problem can be a huge headache.

Ticket ownership. The biggest risk to consumers is the fact that consolidators don't own the tickets at the time of sale. The assumption is that consolidators buy seats cheaply in bulk for resale; in truth, they almost never actually buy and take title to a ticket until they have a customer's money in hand.

After receiving payment, a consolidator may find that the airline has no more seats at the promised fare. The consolidator must then ask the customer for more money (for a seat at a higher fare), switch airlines, or put the customer on a waitlist (perhaps without notification) rather than giving a firm reservation. Or a consolidator who's short on cash may keep the customer's money and wait until the last minute to buy the ticket—at best delaying delivery, at worst failing to provide the promised flight at the agreed-to price.

BUYING YOUR TICKET

The safest way to buy a consolidator ticket is through a regular full-service travel agency. If anything goes wrong, you can lean on the agency for a fix. True, buying directly from a discount agency saves money by cutting the extra commission for the full-service agency. If you go that route, beware.

Do your homework. Determine the major lines' lowest advertised fare to your destination for your specific travel dates. Also check out low-fare search engines on the web and look into charter fares. These are all benchmarks for assessing a consolidator deal.

Comparison shop. Check prices among several discount agencies, making sure a discounted fare covers your itinerary. For each quote, find out about any limitations, such as required stops or connections.

Weigh trade-offs. If a consolidator ticket yields no frequent-flier credit, see if the discount is big enough to offset the value of that lost credit (figure about two cents per mile).

Think local. Deal with a discount agency in or near your home city. If anything goes wrong, you have convenient access to small-claims court for redress.

Charge it. Buy with a credit card. If you don't get your ticket in good time or if something's wrong with it, you can get your money back through a chargeback (bill-cancellation) claim.

CHAPTER 13

Low-Fare Airlines and Charters

Both these options offer good savings for savvy travelers.

But they come loaded with limitations and trade-offs.

Know what you're getting before you book.

———————— ■ ————————

Low-fare airlines and charter carriers offer inherently more stable pricing and fewer restrictions. Although each also has its weak points, either one might work for travelers seeking a good bargain above all else.

THE LOWDOWN ON LOW-FARE AIRLINES

Forget meal service and bonus miles. Low-fare airlines deliver the basics only—a low-cost trip to your destination and savings in your pocket.

Actually, you don't even have to fly one of these carriers to cash in. By providing cheap flight alternatives, low-fare airlines help drive ticket prices down across the board—saving consumers an estimated $6.3 billion on airfares in a single year, according to the U.S. Department of Transportation (DOT).

The downside is that these lines are a precarious lot. Between 1978 and 1992, approximately 42 new airlines began service.

Of those, 40 failed—if not killed outright by the big guys, at least swallowed up by them.

Still, a lucky few seem to have staying power: Southwest, the granddaddy of the low fare, has been going strong for 28 years, operating more than 2,500 daily flights in 54 cities; American Trans Air has been operating for 26 years; AirTran, Frontier, and Vanguard are also nestled into comfortable market niches.

Low-fare airlines can face a serious competitive disadvantage on bonus benefits like frequent-flier programs (many have none at all). And the giants often undercut low-fare airlines by flooding the market with cheap seats on competitive routes.

But a low-fare line may still give you a smooth flight. Consider the pros and cons.

THE UPSIDE OF LOW-FARE CARRIERS

The first advantage is obvious: great low fares. And there's even more to like about low-fare airlines:

No or few restrictions. With no restrictions such as advance purchase, length of stay, or Saturday-night stay, they're a good choice when making last-minute travel plans.

One-way fares. Cheap prices don't depend upon your buying a round-trip ticket.

Affordable options. Some low-fare carriers have brought reasonable fare choices to cities or regions where a major airline dominated—and imposed sky-high prices.

THE DOWNSIDE OF LOW-FARE CARRIERS

Low-fare lines offer few of the amenities the majors do, and often follow different rules when it comes to boarding and baggage handling. Know what to expect.

No advance seat assignments. Low-fare airlines don't usually assign seats in advance, so get to the gate early for the best crack at the seat you want. And most low-fare carriers offer coach class only; a few offer business and first class.

No replacement planes. Low-fare fleets are smaller than those of the majors and far less flexible; these airlines can't roll another plane up to the gate if the first plane has been grounded for emergency maintenance.

A less-comfortable experience. Seats tend to be narrower, spacing tighter, and the planes older.

Scarce food. Meals seldom exist, although you usually get snacks and beverages. Consider packing your own provisions.

Few interline baggage agreements. Since many low-fare carriers lack interline baggage agreements with other carriers, you must usually claim your baggage and personally check it in for the next leg of your trip.

Possible default. Buy travel insurance. Many low-fare carriers have gone belly-up. And charge tickets; refunds are easier.

FACTS ABOUT CHARTERS

You've probably flown a charter if you've taken a tour or group package to a Caribbean resort (such as Club Med) or to Europe. Charter airlines operate on select routes and schedules that are "chartered" by tour operators, and most don't sell tickets directly to the public.

Scheduled isn't really the opposite of *charter*. Conventional and charter airlines must both operate on schedules, as best they can. "Wholesale" is a more accurate term for charter lines, while those operators that sell directly to the public are "retail" lines. However, the industry has used the chartered/scheduled terminology for more than 50 years.

Some small airlines also operate what amounts to scheduled service under charter rules—starting up a charter line requires less red tape than launching a scheduled line. And a few former charter lines (such as Germany's LTU) still operate like charters, although they now hold scheduled-line certificates.

The main distinction between a charter flight and a flight on a scheduled airline is a legal one. With a charter, the customer's

AIRFARE & AIRLINES

contract is with a tour operator, not an airline—and the operator is financially responsible for getting passengers to the destination and back. The tour operator charters planes and crews from one or more airlines that actually operate the flights.

When things go well, you seldom notice the distinction between the two types of flights. But when a problem arises with a charter, the tour operator must solve it—such as finding a substitute airline. And when travelers are left stranded at a destination, it's usually because a tour operator went bust and couldn't pay an airline for the return trips.

THE LOW-FARE LINES

Does a low-fare carrier go your way? Here are the basics on 14 around the country.
(See Resource Guide for reservation numbers.)

Airline	Home base	Daily flights	Routes
Access Air	Des Moines	12	Des Moines to New York/La Guardia and Los Angeles.
Airtran Airways	Atlanta	270+	Serves most of East Coast, South, and parts of the Midwest.
American Trans Air	Indianapolis	150	Midwest to Florida, the West Coast, Cancún, San Juan, and New York.
Delta Express	Orlando	170	East Coast or near Midwest to Orlando.
Frontier Airlines	Denver	84	Major and secondary U.S. cities.
Metrojet	Arlington, Va.	184	East Coast, Chicago, and Florida.
Pro Air	Detroit	34	Detroit to East Coast and Florida.
Shuttle America	Hartford, Conn.	44	Handful of northeast routes, such as Hartford to Buffalo.
Southwest Airlines	Dallas (Love Field)	2,500	The West Coast, South, and Midwest; limited in the Northeast.
Spirit Airlines	Ft. Lauderdale (as of 2000)	70	West Coast to New York, Detroit, Florida.
Sun Country Airlines	Minneapolis/St. Paul	15	Midwest, Texas, Florida, the Caribbean, and East Coast.
Tower Air	New York (JFK)	15	Miami, San Juan, West Coast, Athens, Paris, and Tel Aviv.
United Shuttle	Los Angeles	462	Most routes in western U.S.
Vanguard Airlines	Kansas City	72	Denver, Dallas, Chicago, and Atlanta.

CHARTER PLUSES

Charters have good points and bad. Here are the good:

The right price. A charter is usually cheaper than a scheduled line for any given trip. Even when a scheduled line seems to have a price advantage, it may offer just a few seats at the advertised fare, whereas most charters sell all their seats at the same low price. A charter seat may be your only low-fare alternative when scheduled lines sell out their entire allotment of low-priced seats.

Fewer restrictions. Charter tickets have many fewer restrictions than the cheapest tickets on the major airlines, often a particular appeal of domestic charters. The minimum advance-purchase period usually depends on how long it takes to complete the paperwork, and the minimum stay depends on how often the charter line flies a particular route. A few charter operators do, however, offer restricted fares (advance-purchase or minimum-stay) at slightly lower prices than their walk-up fares. And some impose a maximum-stay limit on their lowest fares.

A better route. Because charters may operate where regularly scheduled airlines don't, a charter flight may be the only way to fly between certain cities without making either a stop or a plane change at a hub airport.

A possible premium option. A few charter lines offer both optional seats (and often food service) equal to what you'd find in business class. While a charter's premium seat is more expensive than one of its economy seats, the premium charter seat is still much less expensive—on average, about 60 percent less—than a business- or first-class seat on a scheduled line. A premium charter seat is often the only reasonably priced alternative to a jammed coach/economy seat.

CHARTER MINUSES

But be aware of the bad points too.

Not always cheaper. Charters aren't always your cheapest way to fly. Within the U.S., scheduled low-fare airlines increasingly

AIRFARES &
AIRLINES

match or beat charter prices. Even major scheduled lines may offer lower prices during fare wars. And the major lines' advertised winter fares to Europe are usually low enough to discourage charter competition in that season. Discount tickets from consolidators often undercut charter fares as well.

Less-frequent flights. Many charter programs operate only one weekly "back-to-back" trip: The plane loads up with vacationers, ferries them to their destination, and picks up the previous week's group for the trip home. Unless the flight days correspond with the beginning and end of your vacation, a charter could cut away several days at your destination. Some programs, however, offer more frequent service. Even on weekly programs, you can usually stay additional weeks (sometimes for an additional charge).

Odd schedules and potential delays. Charter carriers own fewer planes, so schedules are tight and flights may arrive or depart at odd hours. Any significant delay of a single flight can throw a charter line's schedule out of whack for days.

Difficulty rescheduling. If your flight is canceled or significantly delayed, the tour operator is the only one who can reschedule. Charter airlines don't have "interline" agreements with each other or with scheduled lines, so a charter line can't sign your ticket over to another line. Nor will you be able to switch flights.

Extreme crowding. Unless you book a premium seat, a charter virtually guarantees a cramped trip. Seating on charter flights isn't necessarily worse than on a scheduled flight, but it's hardly ever better. Most charter flights operate close to full; one reason charters are relatively cheap is that each flight is nearly 100 percent booked, rather than the 70 percent or so on scheduled airlines.

Long check-in lines. Charter lines normally use other airlines or independent airport-service organizations to handle check-in, boarding, and baggage claim. Many apparently skimp on those services, judging by the three-hour check-in lines often seen for charter flights.

No computer listings. Charters are not listed in the computer reservation system used by agents. So some travel agents dislike booking charters because of the extra work required.

Tough refunds. If you must cancel a flight, you may have a hard time getting a refund, and your ticket may not be as easily "exchangeable" (rebookable for a fee) as a coach/economy excursion ticket on a scheduled line. Ask about refunds and exchanges any time you consider a charter. If a ticket isn't exchangeable, you can protect yourself with trip-interruption insurance. But factor in the cost of that insurance—typically $5.50 per $100 of coverage—when you compare ticket prices.

AIRFARE & AIRLINES

CHAPTER 14

Cashing in on Special Fares

Many travelers automatically qualify for a reduced fare. Special fares are available for seniors, children, or someone headed to a relative's funeral.

———————————————◾———————————————

Some status fares cut a percentage off a fare available to anybody. Others are priced independently, and may or may not be good deals, depending on other alternatives.

Be prepared to prove your eligibility when you buy your ticket and again when you travel: Proof of age is required for senior, child, and youth fares; an official school ID to get a student fare; and a funeral or death notice or some equivalent documentation to qualify for a "compassionate" fare. Since status fares are "published," you can buy tickets from an airline or through a travel agency.

DEALS FOR SENIORS

Airlines offer older travelers a variety of discounts. In most cases, the minimum age for eligibility is 62, although some programs set it at 65.

Senior coupons. These are one of the best buys in travel. A qualifying senior can buy a round-trip to anywhere in the lower 48 states (some lines include adjacent points in Canada and the Caribbean) for no more than $298. (For a long-haul flight, that's less than even the best sale fares and less than half the lowest non-sale coach excursion.) You can fly to Alaska or Hawaii for two coupons each way (one coupon to Alaska on United). However, there are no senior coupons for travel to Europe, Asia, or other overseas destinations. Coupons are sold in groups of four.

The "Special fares roundup" shows the eight major U.S. airlines that sell senior coupons and their prices (as of late 1999 and subject to change). Each coupon is good for a one-way trip. Connecting flights are permitted on a single coupon, as long as you don't stop over at a connection point. Each traveler must have a separate coupon book—a couple can't use one four-coupon book to take a single round-trip together.

The pros. For a confirmed seat, you must book at least 14 days in advance, but you can also travel standby. Since round-trip travel isn't required, there's no minimum-stay requirement. Senior coupons also earn frequent-flier miles.

The cons. Senior coupons are valid for only a year after they're issued. So if you can't take at least two round-trips a year, coupons are not a good deal. And as with most promotional fares, seats are limited.

The payoff. Coupons are a good deal whenever the cheapest alternative round-trip airfare exceeds the coupon cost ($274 to $298, depending on the airline), almost always the case on long-haul routes and often true for shorter trips. But always check the low-fare competition before buying coupons.

Senior clubs. Three of the major airlines run senior clubs.

United Silver Wings Plus. Open to travelers age 55 and over, this club offers a variety of deals rather than a standard schedule of benefits. The most consistent bargains in the past few years have been a series of zoned fares, which generally beat even good sale fares, and, for all but the longest trips, win out over senior coupons, too. Membership costs $75 for two years or $225 for lifetime. Members must also pay an extra fee ($25 to $50) to take advantage of some promotions. Call 800 720-1765 for more information, or check the web site at *www.silverwingsplus.com.*

Delta Skywise. This program offers domestic zone fares for travelers age 62 and over, and for as many as three of their companions of any age. Blackouts apply around certain holidays. Membership costs $40 a year for the primary member, plus $25 for a companion. Call 800 325-3750 to enroll or check *www.delta-air.com/skywise.*

SPECIAL FARES ROUNDUP

Special fares on North American airlines

Airline	Senior	Youth/student
Air Canada	10% off	Standby on some routes
Alaska	10% off	—
America West	10% off or published discount; $548 for 4 coupons	Eligible for companion fares
American	10% off; $596 for 4 coupons	—
American Trans Air	10% off	—
Canadian	10% off	—
Continental	10% off; $579 for 4 coupons, $1,079 for 8	Published discount on some routes
Delta	10% off; $596 for 4 coupons	$229 for 4, $412 for 8 shuttle coupons
Midwest Express	10% off	Unpublished discount on some routes
Northwest	10% off; $560 for 4 coupons	—
Southwest	Published discount on some routes	12–22 eligible for your fare
TWA	10% off; $548 for 4 coupons; $1,196 for 8 coupons	$548 for ages 14–24 for 4 coupons
United	10% off; $548 for 4 coupons	Varies by route
USAirways	10% off; $579 for 4 coupons	Limited to some routes

Source: *Consumer Reports Travel Letter*, June 1998, updated late 1999

Senior discount rates on most airlines also apply to companion of any age. Most airlines figure **compassionate rates** from walk-up coach/economy fares, often required to be round-trip; others waive advance-purchase restriction for 7-day excursion fare or make ad hoc adjustments.

AActive American Traveler Club. The club has zoned coach fares (but no premium-class option). Membership was closed temporarily but is now open. Membership costs $40 for an individual, $30 for each companion. Call 800 421-5600 or check *www.amrcorp.com*.

Senior discount. All the lines listed in the special fares table except Southwest (and many not listed) give a 10 percent senior discount on virtually any published fare for travel in North America, from the cheapest coach/economy excursions (including some short-term sale fares) up to first class. All except Midwest Express and Southwest give the same reduction to a

Child	Compassionate
Varies by route	50% off
—	50% off
Eligible for companion fares	7-day waived on most routes
—	35–50% off
Only to San Juan and Cancún	—
Reductions from full fare only	50% off
—	50% off
—	50% off
—	50% off
—	70% off
Varies by route	—
—	50% off or waiver
—	7-day waived on most routes
2–11 can use senior coupons with grandparents	Ad hoc

Child rates for children under two with a government-approved safety seat and accompanied by an adult are 50% of full adult fare.

companion of any age following the same itinerary as that of the qualified senior.

The 10 percent discount is a fall-back deal when you can't find anything better. On short-haul coach excursion tickets and sale-priced tickets, it doesn't amount to much. And coupons are usually a better deal for a long-haul trip.

Frequent-flier rules are generally the same as those for the any-age fare from which the senior discount is to be deducted.

Southwest publishes separate fares for seniors age 65 or over, usually with reductions based on the line's unrestricted coach fares. Seniors traveling on Southwest are often better off buying a 21-day advance-purchase ticket at the any-age fare and forgetting about the discount.

Fares to Europe. Seniors (minimum age 62) headed to Europe generally get the same 10 percent reduction they get within North America. Some airlines are more generous, but others offer no senior discounts at all—so shop around before booking. And although the reduction applies to most fares, it may not apply to all sale deals; check with individual airlines for particulars.

DEALS FOR JUNIORS

Infants. Those under age two may occupy a half-fare reserved seat on most airlines, if seated in a government-approved child safety seat provided by the adult traveling companion. Alternatively, an infant can travel free and can occupy an empty seat, if available. (On a full plane, an accompanying adult would be required to hold the child throughout the flight.) As a third option, an adult without a safety seat can reserve a seat for the infant, but only at an adult fare. (For safe flight information for your children, see Chapter 17.)

The half-price infant reduction applies to most published adult fares, including the cheapest 21-day advance-purchase excursions. However, the exclusions include senior-discount trips, military fares, and tour-package fares. Each traveling adult may purchase up to two half-price infant tickets, but seats are limited and may not be available on all flights.

On most international flights, children under age two without a reservation pay 10 percent of the accompanying adult's fare. Travelers who want a confirmed seat for an infant must buy a child's ticket, typically 50 to 75 percent of the adult fare.

Children and youths. Deals for children over the age of two are sparse. Some airlines publish children's fares on a few routes, though these fares are often based on reductions from full-fare coach or premium class and frequently cost more than an any-age coach excursion ticket. Otherwise, you're pretty much stuck with buying adult tickets for children ages two and older. Of course, they can take advantage of other deals— the 10 percent companion discount when accompanying a qualifying senior or the free-companion promotions that airlines often run. On most international flights, children ages two to 11 pay 50 to 75 percent of the adult fare (including economy excursion fares).

Youth/students. These deals are a sparse lot.

TWA youth coupons. These work almost the same as the airline's senior coupons—with the same conditions but without the companion option. They're a bargain whenever the cheapest alternative round-trip ticket is over $274.

American Internet program. Full-time college students of any age can enroll through American's web site *(www.aa.com/ college)*; the airline then sends them periodic e-mail bulletins about special fares and other deals.

Separate youth fares. Some U.S. and European airlines publish separate youth fares to Europe for travelers ages 12 to 24. Typically, travelers can make reservations only within 72 hours of departure; the return portion of the round-trip is left open, with the same 72-hour reservation limit, but with a maximum stay of up to a year. Seats are restricted and may be

AIRFARES & AIRLINES

blacked out on some dates. These fares may be no cheaper than discount (consolidator) tickets available to people of any age—compare before you buy.

COMPASSIONATE FARES

Air tickets booked at the last minute are normally very expensive. But most major airlines offer compassionate (or bereavement) fares. The most common formula is 50 percent off the lowest last-minute fare (usually that means unrestricted coach), which can still be quite a bit higher than the lowest restricted round-trip coach fare. A few airlines depart from that policy, and a few treat compassionate fares as individual cases. See the table earlier in the chapter.

On international routes, several overseas airlines, including Aer Lingus, Air France, Austrian, British Airways, Finnair, Lufthansa, Swissair, and Virgin Atlantic, waive the advance-purchase restriction on an economy excursion ticket.

Each airline has its own rules about the qualifying circumstances for compassionate fares. All airlines typically grant the fare for attendance at a relative's funeral. Only some allow it for severe illness or imminent death. Airlines differ in how distant a family connection can qualify. If the first airline you try turns you down, try another. All lines require proof of the relative's death—either a photocopy of a death certificate or the phone number of the funeral home.

PART FIVE

Smart Flying

CHAPTER 15

Guidelines for Frequent Fliers

If you fly just once or twice a year, joining an airline frequent-flier program can pay off. You can earn miles dozens of ways (some without even flying).

Frequent-flier programs—free to anyone who signs up—have taken off over the past 10 years as airlines sought to hold onto and reward loyal customers with free travel. Are programs worth it? Yes, but the true payoff depends on how you choose to earn your miles—and spend them.

WHAT YOU NEED TO KNOW

Complaints about the scarcity of awards—the biggest beef —are down 20 percent from 1997, according to the U.S. Department of Transportation. And for good reason: Airlines have been giving away more free seats. A mid-1999 analysis of DOT data by the CONSUMER REPORTS TRAVEL LETTER revealed that the seven major U.S. airlines booked a total of 6.5 million coach award spots on the most popular domestic and international routes in 1998. That's some 329,000, or 5 percent, *more* spots than they forked over in 1997.

How programs work. The basic premise is simple: You join the program, then every subsequent flight you take on that airline earns mileage—the actual mileage flown for coach/economy or sometimes bonus miles (usually 1.5 or 2 times the mileage flown) for business and first class. You can also earn miles in many other ways—from car rentals to hotel stays.

How much are miles worth? Figure that frequent-flier credit with the major airlines is worth somewhere between 1 and 2 cents per mile—perhaps a bit more if you use it well. But take note of the fine print regarding blackout dates.

SIGNING UP AND STRATEGIZING

Every airline's in-flight magazine has an application for its frequent-flier program. Strategize before you sign up.

Pick just one or two carriers. Enrolling in the programs of just one or two major carriers—depending on how much you travel—lets you rack up enough miles to cash in before some expire. (However, as of mid-1999, most U.S. airlines had greatly relaxed expiration rulings.) Pick the airlines based on your predicted travel plans: Determine where you're likely to travel for business—and where you might want to spend your vacations, then sign up with carriers that service those regions. You may also want to pick an airline with a mileage-accruing credit card (most now offer them in conjunction with major banks).

Study alliances. With the newly forged alliances among most domestic and international carriers, you can earn mileage on a flight by a carrier other than the one in whose program you're a member.

Check expiration policies. Most airlines' miles never expire—as long as you keep your account active. "Minding your miles" has specifics for major programs.

Keep boarding passes. If you don't belong to a program, keep your boarding passes anyway. You may be able to get credit later if you decide to sign up.

MAXIMIZING MILES

Once you're a member of an airline frequent-flier program, take steps to ensure correct mileage credits.

Give your number when reserving. Relay your account number to the agent when you book your flight; check-in can be so hectic, you might forget. If you use a travel agent, make sure all your numbers are coded into the computer when making reservations.

Check your statement. Your account should be credited for a flight in the next statement or two, although sometimes it takes longer. If you flew a partner airline, be extra vigilant: Keep your boarding passes and, if miles don't show up on your statement after two to three months, call customer service.

Keep a few miles on hand. You can sometimes use miles to "buy" things (such as confirmed seat upgrades) not available any other way.

Be flexible. When booking award travel, have several dates and times. You stand a better chance of getting the seat you want.

• Hotels are getting in on the action, with some chains offering three points for every $1 spent at their properties. These programs are some of the best mileage deals around. Among the players: Hilton (800 635-5955), Marriott (800 511-9113), and Sheraton (800 467-8462).

• Switching phone companies can earn you 5,000 to 10,000 miles plus as much as five miles for every long-distance dollar spent. Once you enroll in a frequent-flier program, you'll receive mailings with the various offers (mostly from MCI and Sprint.)

• Signing up for a bank credit card affiliated with a major airline (Delta, United, Northwest, and American all have them) can earn you one mile for every dollar spent. American Express also allows its card members to transfer "Membership Rewards" points to certain airline frequent-flier programs.

• Certain of these airline cards allow you to accrue 1.5 or 2 miles for every dollar spent on a ticket with that airline. For example, purchasing an $800 round-trip fare will earn you either 1,200 or 1,600 miles in addition to the actual mileage you fly.

• Dining programs such as American's AAdvantage Dining will earn you 10 miles for every dollar you spend at participating restaurants—up to 6,000 miles per qualified visit. (You can dine at the same restaurant just once a month.)

• Airlines also regularly offer "double miles" promotions on select routes. Flying just one long-haul round-trip, such as New York to Tokyo, can earn you a free domestic ticket.

Most domestic frequent-flier rewards require 25,000 miles, so it's relatively easy to earn free travel by accruing those extra miles. The 50,000 miles needed for European flights are a

MINDING YOUR MILES

New rules make it easier than ever to prevent frequent-flier miles from expiring. But you still have to be vigilant: Make sure you're keeping your account "fresh" with the right type of activity. Here's what counts with each airline.

Airline	When miles expire	What counts as "qualifying activity"
American *AAdvantage*	After 3 years if no activity in account.	Anything that adds miles to your account: card use, phone call, car rental, hotel stay, flight purchase.
Continental *OnePass*	Miles can expire after 18 months if no activity in account.	—
Delta *SkyMiles*	After 3 years if no activity in account.	Must fly Delta (not its partners) at least once every 3 years.
Northwest *WorldPerks*	Miles can expire after 3 years if no activity in account.	—
TWA *Aviators*	After 3 years if no activity in account.	Buy ticket, service, or merchandise from airline or one of its partners. Or, if using the credit card to keep the account active, must accumulate 10,000 miles on card in 3 years.
United *Mileage Plus*	After 3 years if no activity in account.	Anything that adds miles to your account: card use, phone call, car rental, hotel stay, flight purchase.
US Airways *Dividend Miles*	Miles issued after Jan. 1, 2000, expire after 3 years if no activity.	Must fly US Airways (not its partners) at least once every 3 years.

SMART
FLYING

111

bigger challenge, and the 60,000 to 70,000 required for trans-Pacific flights become even more difficult. But by taking just one or two long-haul round-trips (3,000 miles each way or more) a year and combining those miles with benefits from other promos, you can earn all levels of rewards. Your savings: $300 to $1,500, depending on the flight.

USING CREDIT WISELY

Cashing in those accumulated miles for a dream vacation isn't always easy: Consumers have racked up some 3 trillion unused miles—enough for 120 million award flights. (Restrictions on how the miles can be used is a major consumer complaint.)

Of course, you'll want as much value from your earned miles as possible. This means using it in ways that approach or even exceed the 2-cents-a-mile figure and avoiding flights that net you a value of 1 cent or less. These guidelines can help.

10 Tips for Earning Free Trips
How to rack up the miles

1. Be loyal. Concentrate your flying on one airline and you'll earn enough miles for a free trip sooner.

2. Watch for promotions. During slow periods (or when an airline wants to lure back customers) you can sometimes earn double miles on select routes.

3. Consider credit card tie-ins. Most airlines, in conjunction with banks, offer credit cards that earn miles for every dollar you spend. On occasion, some of these cards will offer "double miles" periods, where you earn two miles for every dollar spent. Miles can add up quickly if you are able to put a big-ticket purchase—new appliances, say—on the card during the promo. You can also allocate points earned in American Express's Membership Rewards program to certain frequent-flier programs.

4. Buy tickets with an airline credit card. Depending on the card, this may earn you 1.5 to 2 miles per dollar spent.

Domestic. A coast-to-coast flight costs the same number of miles as a short trip. So you're better off saving your credit for a long trip—one for which the cheapest ticket would cost up to $600.

If you live in the East or Midwest, save your miles for a trip to the West or Southwest. Use them for a short local trip only if the cheapest published fare is exorbitant—as is true in some monopoly markets. And don't spend them on a route where you can buy a ticket on a low-fare airline—between the Northeast or Chicago and the South, for example, on lines such as AirTran, Delta Express, or Southwest. Similarly, if you live in the West, save your miles for a trip to the East, Midwest, or Southeast. Don't waste them on a short trip for which you could snag a bargain ticket on Alaska, America West, Southwest, or United Shuttle.

Europe. The value you get for your miles depends on when

---

5. Dial for miles. If you don't mind switching phone companies, you can earn as much as 10,000 miles, plus 5 cents per dollar spent on long-distance calls.

6. Dine for miles. Certain frequent-flier programs also offer dining tie-ins: Pay with their credit card at affiliated restaurants and you'll earn 5 to 10 miles for every dollar spent.

7. Maximize miles with airline partners. Using certain hotels, rental cars, and code-share or traditional airline partners will net you miles. Opportunities are in the monthly statement newsletter.

8. Take advantage of alliances. The new alliances between carriers means you have more options for earning and cashing in miles.

9. Don't let miles expire. You may have to keep your account active or log one flight annually to prevent expiration.

10. Earn online. Most airlines give 1,000 or more bonus miles to passengers who book via their web sites.

SMART FLYING

you go. A frequent-flier ticket to Europe can be a poor deal in winter, when fare sales drop ticket prices to $400 round-trip—and your credit to as little as 0.6 cents a mile. But a frequent-flier ticket to Europe in the summer would be worth a lot more, since summer fares are at least twice as high as fares offered during winter sales. However, the airlines don't make many frequent-flier seats available for 50,000 miles in the peak summer season—and some lines offer none at all.

Hawaii. Depending on the departure point, a flight to Hawaii may or may not be a good use of frequent-flier credit. The big U.S. airlines ask an average of 35,000 miles for a round-trip seat in coach, not a good deal from the West Coast, where discount round-trip tickets to Hawaii regularly run less than $300. But if you're flying from the East, Midwest, or South, where regular fares run upward of $700, your frequent-flier ticket to Hawaii still costs the same 35,000 or so miles that West Coast travelers have to use—and so can be a very good deal. (Similar logic applies to West Coast residents going to the Caribbean.)

MOVING UP WITH UPGRADES

Hate to fly coach/economy? Then consider upgrades—a fine way to use frequent-flier miles. Positive-space (that is, space reserved at the time you book) premium seats are available at a reasonable price when you pay with frequent-flier currency. And frequent-flier miles are about the only currency most travelers can use to buy positive-space upgrades.

How many miles? Most big domestic lines require 20,000 miles to upgrade a round-trip domestic coach excursion ticket to the next class of service. In effect, you pay $400, a reasonable figure for a round-trip upgrade on a typical long-haul flight. Several airlines let you upgrade a full-fare coach ticket for even less mileage.

Upgrading economy excursions to Europe requires 40,000 miles, worth $800, on most airlines. Although that figure can more than double the cost of many trips, you'd still pay well under half the asking price for a business-class ticket. This ticket is an especially good deal for West Coast travelers.

PREMIUM-TRIP AWARDS

On all the big U.S. airlines, you can exchange frequent-flier miles for free business- or first-class tickets to most parts of the world. But before you cash in, look at what the big lines require for an off-peak, round-trip ticket on a premium class.

Domestic flights. For trips within the lower 48 states (usually also to nearby cities in Canada and the Caribbean), you typically trade in 35,000 to 45,000 miles. Figuring credit at 2 cents a mile, a premium domestic trip costs about $800, reasonable for most long-haul flights.

Hawaiian trips. For a trip to Hawaii, you usually surrender 50,000 to 60,000 miles. But 60,000 miles of credit is worth $1,200; using miles that way makes sense mainly for travelers from the East Coast, Midwest, or South. West Coast travelers can buy first-class seats for about the same money.

Europe, South America, and Asia. Going to Europe or South America, the typical bite is 75,000 to 85,000 miles; to Asia or the South Pacific, it's 80,000 to 90,000 miles. At about $1,600 in credit, a premium round-trip to Europe effectively costs many travelers over twice as much as a cheap economy excursion. Still, it's less than double the cost of a peak-season round-trip from many cities in the South and West, and less than half the big lines' business-class fares on most routes.

ELITE FREQUENT-FLIER CLASS

If you dream of escaping the misery of a coach seat, "elite" status may be just your ticket. And contrary to popular belief, you don't have to be a 100,000-miler to qualify for that very-frequent-flier class.

The major airlines have been quietly loosening restrictions on the kinds of miles that count toward membership in their

SMART
FLYING

115

top-tier programs. Flights on partner airlines and commuter carriers, as well as miles from one credit-card provider and bonus promotions, can speed your journey there.

But there's a catch. Although the airlines have made it easier to qualify for elite status, they've also made it harder to upgrade, particularly when flying on discounted coach tickets.

Even so, it's worth working toward entry-level elite status. Carriers generally offer a set of 15 or so core privileges to first-tier elite members. However, most travelers care about only two: front-cabin upgrades and preferred coach seating.

GETTING TO ELITE

Elite status is an easy target for strategy-minded leisure travelers. The key to success is concentrating all your flights on one airline. Just two trips to Europe plus one domestic flight per year may be all you need to break into the first tier.

In the past, there were only one or two levels of elite; today there may be as many as four. The net effect has been a downgrading of the first-level programs, once the only option for elite fliers. And as this "class" has devolved, so have the requirements for entry.

Elite perks kick in as soon as you earn them. Once you're a member, your status remains valid for a full calendar year or through February of the next year, depending on the airline.

Mileage thresholds. To qualify for elite status, you must log lots of miles—between 15,000 and 25,000 annually, which generally includes miles earned on short-haul trips of between 500 and 1,000 miles minimum. If you're a frequent shuttle flier, the biggest airlines will credit flight segments rather than miles. On Delta, for example, either 30 segments or 25,000 miles will earn elite status. So if you travel frequently to visit a nearby city, you may reach elite status faster than if you take several long-haul trips. The airlines are also bending a bit on another restriction—that only actual flown miles qualify toward elite status.

Code-shares and partners. Some airlines allow miles earned on code-share and partner airlines to count toward elite status. But beware: Code-share partners will often reduce credit for flights taken with members of an affiliated frequent-flier program. When making reservations, it pays to verify exactly how much credit you'll receive.

ELITE PERKS

For first-level elite members, the benefits outweigh those of standard-class frequent-flier status, but aren't as rich as those afforded the higher tiers.

Flight benefits. Members earn 25 to 50 percent more on each flight than the average frequent flier—in addition to bonuses earned for purchasing or upgrading to front-cabin seating or for limited-time promotions. Many airlines also offer bonus mileage for passing certain milestones. A handful give elite members the advantage on getting free seats. And some of those also allow their elite members to bypass blackout dates, a perk usually reserved for higher-level fliers.

Upgrades. Behold the brass ring. But for first-level elites with discounted coach tickets, this step up can be difficult, if not impossible. Timing is critical. That's because the farther up you go on the elite ladder, the earlier you can call in for an upgrade. Often, the highest elite programs allow fliers to confirm upgrades at the time of booking. For most elite fliers on cheap tickets, 24 hours before the flight is the closest they'll get. Call anyway: Reservation agents will sometimes confirm a low-level elite upgrade when the front cabin is empty.

Upgrade "currency" takes three forms: mile-based segments, one-way upgrades, and miles. When you qualify for an elite program, the airlines will generally send you a starter kit of upgrades that might get you through one or two trips, depending on how far you're traveling. The airline will reward your continued patronage with free coupons for every 10,000

SMART FLYING

117

miles you fly. Of course, you can always buy upgrade coupons before your flight (through city ticket offices, by mail, or online). But be careful. At anywhere from $25 to $40 per 500-mile coupon, those upgrades can sometimes cost more than the flight itself. Of course, you can also pay for upgrades with miles, like any other frequent flier.

Other benefits. Besides upgrades, most major carriers offer a host of benefits for their lowest-level elite members: Aisle and window seats toward the front of the coach cabin are typically blocked off for elite members of all levels; every carrier now lets you waitlist for sold-out flights as well as front-cabin upgrades; most airlines offer elite reservations phone numbers, plus a special check-in line at larger airports.

You'll also get online account access: Most major carriers have special password-protected areas on their web sites, where elite members can check their mileage balance, redeem miles for awards, and purchase upgrade coupons.

CHAPTER 16

Avoiding Flying's Biggest Hassles

Air travel is the fastest, most convenient way to get to most destinations around the world, but it's certainly not pain-free. These tips can help clear your flight path.

———————————————— ■ ————————————————

Are passengers more likely to face annoyances these days? Or just be fed up enough to report them? Whichever, overall passenger complaints against domestic airlines increased 30 percent in 1998 over 1997, according to the U.S. Department of Transportation.

WHAT PASSENGERS COMPLAIN ABOUT

Flight problems—delays, cancellations, and connection snafus—led the gripe list in 1998 with 2,552 complaints, up 35 percent over the previous year. Customer service, baggage problems, and ticketing and boarding bungles weren't far behind, with each of these categories chalking up at least a 23 percent increase in complaints over 1997. Passengers also groused about refund problems, bumping, fares, and frequent-flier awards.

The DOT adds up all complaints against airlines but doesn't determine if they're valid. Its year-end total doesn't include safety complaints, which are handled by the Federal Aviation Admin-istration (FAA). The DOT lists gripes by category against each airline, and calculates complaints per 100,000 passengers for the 10 largest carriers. In 1998, Northwest bottomed out with 2.21 beefs per 100,000 travelers, nearly nine times as high as the com-plaint rate against Southwest, which had the best record of the top carriers. The table below lists complaints by airline.

WHAT CONSUMER REPORTS FOUND

In mid-1999, CONSUMER REPORTS evaluated commercial air-lines using information derived from reader responses to the 1998 Annual Questionnaire. These survey findings were com-plemented with price data, which airlines are required to report to the DOT. More than 36,700 survey respondents detailed their experiences on more than 55,000 domestic flights taken between January 1997 and March 1998. Here's what they said:

They're increasingly unhappy. The proportion of passengers describing themselves as highly satisfied with their air-travel experiences has dropped from 52 percent to 39 percent since CONSUMER REPORTS 1994 survey. Air travelers have become *so* irate that their treatment by the airlines has become a political issue. Throughout 1999, Congress debated several bills that would strengthen passenger rights, although, as yet, the issues have not been resolved.

They see few differences among major airlines. Survey respon-dents scored the eight major airlines from a high of just 65 (out of a possible 100 points) for US Airways to a low of 60 for Northwest. All the majors except Continental rated lower with readers than in 1994. America West, Delta, Northwest, and TWA suffered the biggest declines in satisfaction.

They want a good price. Unfortunately, confusing pricing policies make it difficult for consumers to know if they've got-ten a truly low fare. Ticket prices fluctuate because airlines change the availability of low-fare seats in response to changes in demand—the better to extract the maximum revenue possible from each planeload of passengers.

Low-fare carriers are an option. Generally, the low-fare carriers give consumers a better deal than the majors. Low-fare pioneer Southwest, in particular, offered average fares at least 10 percent below those of its rivals on 72 percent of the routes it shared with competitors. Aloha and Midway also offered a superior combination of price and service.

ABOUT THAT AIRPORT

Does airport choice matter? Maybe. You can often get a better price if you use a secondary airport serving a major city, such as Newark International Airport across the Hudson from New York City, Oakland near San Francisco, or Midway in Chicago. Many of the low-fare airlines operate from these airports.

THE COMPLAINT FILE

Airline	Total complaints 1998	Complaints per 100,000 passengers 1998	1997
1. Southwest	147	0.25	0.28
2. Alaska	71	0.54	0.63
3. Delta	835	0.79	0.64
4. US Airways	490	0.84	0.78
5. Continental	424	1.02	0.77
6. American	929	1.14	1.06
7. United	1,111	1.28	0.95
8. TWA	309	1.29	0.83
9. America West	375	2.11	1.51
10. Northwest	1,117	2.21	1.39
SYSTEMWIDE	5,808	1.08	0.86

Ranking based on 1998 DOT statistics and includes carriers with at least 1% of total domestic scheduled-service revenues.

SMART FLYING

But convenience counts, too. Some airports are known for delays, the biggest complaint among airline passengers. In early 1999, the DOT released the findings (shown in "Airport report card," in this chapter.)

WHAT YOU CAN DO

Given increasing passenger complaints and decreasing competition in the domestic market, airline consumers may feel stuck. Still, you can improve your chances of a trip unmarred by delays and annoyances.

Arrive early. One of the cardinal rules of no-hassle flying is to arrive at least one hour before scheduled departure for domestic flights and two hours in advance for international trips. The airlines want you there for reasons of both efficiency and safety. If you don't show on time, they can assign your seat to someone else, even bump you from the flight.

But don't arrive too early. Most airlines won't let you check in earlier than three hours before your scheduled flight, especially if there's another flight to your destination departing before yours. Your luggage might be sent on the earlier flight, only to sit around unclaimed (and unguarded) at your destination.

The earlier the flight, the better. To avoid delays, choose a morning flight; even if it's delayed, it will still be the first one out. If you book an afternoon flight and there are delays, you could wait around for hours.

Fly nonstop. Nonstops will get you there faster than connecting flights, which typically add an hour, even two. And changing planes raises the risk of lost luggage. (On a direct flight, you and your luggage don't change planes, but only make a stop; but your bags could be mistakenly taken off the plane at that stop.) Of course, nonstop flights often cost more than those involving a stopover or connection.

Watch as your bags are tagged. At check-in, make sure the airport code of your final destination is on the tags; and be sure the agent staples your baggage claim stubs to your ticket. Depending on airport policy at your destination, you may need those stubs to exit the baggage claim area.

Attach a personal baggage tag. Use your business address, if possible, or just name and phone number: If your bags are lost or stolen, no one who handles them will know your home address —and know you're not there.

Get seat assignments when you book. Claiming your seat when you make your reservation affords the best shot at what you want. If you aren't happy with that seat assignment, ask the agent at check-in to see what else is available.

Don't schedule tight connections. If your connecting flight leaves anything less than an hour after your scheduled arrival, a delay of 20 to 30 minutes on the first flight can turn a connection into a heart-pounding race. The airline must get you on another flight—whenever that may be. If you miss the last flight of the night, you'll wait until morning.

Check on-time performance. Your travel agent or the airline can tell you the on-time performance of a specific flight. Some

AIRPORT REPORT CARD

The following 10 airports experienced the most delays (of 15 minutes or more) in 1998, according to the FAA:

Airport	City	# of delays	% of total flights
1. Newark International Airport	Newark, NJ	31,924	6.9
2. San Francisco International	San Francisco	29,409	6.8
3. O'Hare International Airport	Chicago	28,751	3.2
4. Hartsfield International Airport	Atlanta	27,764	3.2
5. La Guardia Airport	New York	24,689	6.8
6. Logan International Airport	Boston	16,400	3.0
7. Lambert Airport	St. Louis	15,925	3.2
8. John F. Kennedy International	New York	12,962	3.6
9. Sky Harbor Airport	Phoenix	11,757	2.2
10. Philadelphia International	Philadelphia	11,552	2.4

SMART
FLYING

123

web-based low-fare search engines provide this data. Avoid a flight with anything lower than a 50 percent on-time record.

Avoid code-share confusion. When you book, confirm that the flight is on your chosen airline. With all the airline alliances, your flight may be on Air France even though you may have

AIRLINE SERVICE-PLEDGE SCORES

At the end of 1999, 14 U.S. carriers vowed better treatment for airline passengers with new, voluntary "Customer Service Commitments." Just how much difference will these pledges make? To find out, the Consumer Reports Travel Letter evaluated airline promises in crucial areas. But remember, the scores rate only airline promises—and sometimes vaguely worded promises, at that—not whether they will be kept. And at present, no government enforcement exists, although the DOT will gauge compliance by tallying customer complaints.

Airline	Notice of delays, cancellations, diversions (a)	Baggage liability limit (b)	Meeting customer needs during long on-aircraft stays (c)	Ensuring good customer service from code-share partners (d)	Being more responsive to customer complaints (e)
American	Very good	Excellent	Fair	Poor	Good
Continental	Excellent	Fair	Good	Poor	Good
Delta	Very good	Fair	Fair	Good	Very good
Northwest	Very good	Fair	Very good	Good	Good
Southwest	Poor	Fair	Fair	Excellent	Good
TWA	Very good	Fair	Fair	Poor	Very good
United	Very good	Fair	Fair	Poor	Good
US Airways	Very good	Fair	Fair	Poor	Very good

(a) All promised prompt notification of flight variations. Continental will pay hotel costs if flight is diverted to another city. With no interline agreements, Southwest can't transfer tickets, meaning a possible additional fare in case of delays.

(b) Nearly all airlines requested a baggage liability limit raise (from the current $1,250) from the DOT. American voluntarily raised limit to $2,500.

(c) Most were "developing" plans. Northwest promised to move planes to a disembarkation point after holds of an hour. Continental affirmed better conditions in case of holds.

(d) Most promised "reasonable efforts." Delta and Northwest pledged to monitor code-share partners' performance. Southwest doesn't practice code-sharing.

(e) Delta, TWA, and US Airways vowed to respond sooner than the 60-day limit set by the Air Transport Association (ATA), the industry trade group.

Source: Consumer Reports Travel Letter, November 1999

booked through, say, Delta. Knowing the carrier helps you avert hassles at the terminal.

Book tickets in your exact name. By "exact," we mean the name on your driver's license or passport. This may pose a problem for recently married women who haven't yet changed documents, or for women who take their husband's name legally (and put it on documents) but do not use it professionally. To simplify, use one name on all travel-related documents.

Always carry a photo ID. For security you may be asked to show a driver's license, passport, or other photo ID at check-in.

Write down your ticket number. If your ticket is lost or stolen, you have a reference when calling the airline.

Keep a copy of your passport. Copy the first page, then keep it separate from the passport. International air travel demands a passport. If yours is lost or stolen, a copy will expedite the replacement process, lessening the chance that you'll miss your flight home.

Ask about "bad seats." Your travel agent or (sometimes) the airline ticket agent can help steer you away from uncomfortable seats.

Request a special meal. You don't have to be a vegetarian or on a diet to order one of the dozen or so special meals that airlines offer, often better quality than the typical fare.

Reconfirm all foreign flights. Airlines operating in foreign countries don't automatically assume your reservation is firm. Always confirm at least 72 hours in advance, especially in South America and Asia.

SMART FLYING

Ratings *Airlines*
& Recommendations

Behind the Ratings

We evaluated commercial airlines using information derived from responses by CONSUMER REPORTS readers to our 1998 Annual Questionnaire. We complemented survey findings with complaint data that airlines are required to report to the U.S. Department of Transportation (DOT). More than 36,700 survey respondents told us about their experiences on more than 55,000 domestic flights they had taken between January 1997 and March 1998. There were at least 200 responses for each of the 17 airlines rated here—nine regional or low-fare airlines and eight major carriers with extensive national routes. Survey respondents are not necessarily representative of the U.S. population as a whole.

The ratings are divided into two categories: regional or low-fare airlines (like Midway and Southwest), and major carriers (such as TWA and Delta). **Customer satisfaction** reflects readers' overall satisfaction with the flight they took. A score of 100 would indicate that the respondent was completely satisfied; a score of zero would indicate complete dissatisfaction. Differences of less than 4 points are not considered meaningful. Scores for **on time, baggage handling,** and flight-attendant **service** compare each carrier relative to the others. For the major airlines, we independently compared our readers' responses with available data on similar flight attributes gathered by the DOT and found that they tended to correlate.

Source: Consumer Reports June 1999

Overall Ratings

BETTER ◄———► WORSE

Within type, listed in order of customer satisfaction

Regional or low-fare airlines

Midwest Express
Customer satisfaction 88
On time ⊖ **Baggage handling** ⊖ **Service** ⊖
Rated tops in customer satisfaction, and the only airline to receive top scores with regard to service. And you pay more for the service. Also noted for its planes' generous seat width. Operates chiefly out of Milwaukee, Wis.

Aloha
Customer satisfaction 72
On time ⊖ **Baggage handling** ○ **Service** ○
Scored higher than the major airlines in overall satisfaction. Mostly connects Hawaii to the West Coast.

Horizon
Customer satisfaction 71
On time ⊖ **Baggage handling** ⊖ **Service** ⊖
A subsidy of Alaska Airlines, Horizon scored high in overall satisfaction, and received above-average scores in every category as regards service. Serves a limited network.

Hawaiian

Customer satisfaction 71
On time ⊖ **Baggage handling** ○ **Service** ○
Overall customer-satisfaction score has risen from among the lowest in the industry in our 1990 survey to be on par with other regional carriers.

Midway

Customer satisfaction 71
On time ⊖ **Baggage handling** ⊖ **Service** ○
This small carrier rated higher, overall, than the major airlines.

Alaska

Customer satisfaction 71
On time ○ **Baggage handling** ○ **Service** ○
Alaska's low complaint rate and convenient baggage claim contributed to a satisfaction score higher than the major airlines.

Southwest

Customer satisfaction 70
On time ⊖ **Baggage handling** ○ **Service** ⊖
Outscored the majors in customer satisfaction. Southwest's complaint rate, though higher than last year, was still among the lowest in the industry.

AirTran

Customer satisfaction 66
On time ○ **Baggage handling** ⊖ **Service** ○
Serving 31 cities from its hub in Atlanta, AirTran was about equal to Atlanta-based Delta in overall customer satisfaction, and offered better flight-attendant service.

American Trans Air

Customer satisfaction 61
On time ○ **Baggage handling** ⊖ **Service** ⊖
Serving 20 cities from its base in the Midwest, America Trans Air's complaint rate was among the worst.

Major carriers

US Airways

Customer satisfaction 65
On time ○ **Baggage handling** ○ **Service** ○
Rated slightly higher than other majors for flight-attendant service. Its frequent-flier program was below average.

Delta

Customer satisfaction 64
On time ○ **Baggage handling** ⊖ **Service** ⊖
Delta's overall satisfaction has fallen steeply since our last survey in 1994, and the complaint rate was up significantly. Offered fewer seats for frequent-flier awards than other big airlines.

Continental

Customer satisfaction 64
On time ○ **Baggage handling** ⊖ **Service** ⊖
The only big carrier that did not show a decline in overall satisfaction since our 1994 survey. In fact, the complaint rate has dropped by half since 1994.

United

Customer satisfaction 64
On time ○ **Baggage handling** ⊖ **Service** ⊖
Overall customer satisfaction has declined slightly since 1994. Ranked above-average in frequent-flier seat availability.

American

Customer satisfaction 63
On time ○ **Baggage handling** ⊖ **Service** ⊖
Ranked about average in satisfaction among the majors, and has dropped since our 1994 survey. Best among the majors for frequent-flier seat awards.

TWA

Customer satisfaction 63
On time ⊖ **Baggage handling** ⊖ **Service** ⊖
Steep decline in customer satisfaction since 1994. Frequent-flier seat availability better than average.

America West

Customer satisfaction 61
On time ○ **Baggage handling** ⊖ **Service** ⊖
Customer satisfaction has fallen since 1994. The customer complaint rate was among the highest in the industry and has increased in recent years.

Northwest

Customer satisfaction 60
On time ⊖ **Baggage handling** ⊖ **Service** ⊖
Complaint rate jumped dramatically last year and overall satisfaction has fallen.

SMART FLYING

127

Staying Safe and Sane

Some airline practices are annoying. Others are a potential

hazard to your health. Your best defense against either is

staying informed.

———————————————— ■ ————————————————

Airlines must follow governmental rules on practices from bumping to spraying for insects. Here's a guide to your rights:

BUMPING—A BUMMER OR A DEAL?

Bumping is what an airline does to you, or asks you to agree to do, when they've overbooked a flight. Here are U.S. Department of Transportation rules and tips on handling a potential bumping.

Voluntary bumping. When flights are overbooked, airlines always first ask for volunteers to give up their seats. A volunteer can exchange a ticket for a seat on the next available flight, plus additional compensation. But before you take the airline's offer, the DOT recommends a few precautions.

Determine the next flight on which the airline can confirm your seat. Do not allow yourself to simply be put on a standby list; you could end up stranded. Find out if the airline will provide free meals, phone calls, ground transportation, and a hotel room if you have a long wait until the next flight. Quiz airline reps about any restrictions on the free ticket the airline offers as compensation. When does it expire? Are there blackout dates? Is it good for international flights? Can you reserve the flight? "Free" may not be so free.

Airlines will try to get you to give up your seat as cheaply as possible. If you won't go for a rock-bottom deal, the staff will try to find someone who will. But if you happen to be the only volunteer, you've got bargaining clout.

Involuntary bumping. You've been caught in a traffic jam,

BUMPING BY THE NUMBERS

What are your odds of being bumped? The numbers below represent passengers holding confirmed reservations who were denied boarding on oversold domestic or international flight segments originating in the U.S.

| Airline | DENIED BOARDINGS | | INVOLUNTARY BUMPINGS PER 10,000 PASSENGERS | |
	Voluntary 1998 (a,b)	Involuntary 1998 (a,c)	1998 (a,c)	1997 (a,c)
Alaska	19,532	1,459	1.49	2.55
America West	36,790	1,536	1.12	2.10
American	163,872	2,312	0.42	0.72
Continental	54,513	375	0.13	0.11
Delta	189,886	9,639	1.24	1.69
Northwest	98,147	1,117	0.33	0.61
Southwest	60,802	8,136	1.84	2.36
TWA	26,041	2,987	1.69	1.34
United	110,274	3,542	0.59	0.50
US Airways	67,167	991	0.23	0.96

(a) For period January through September.

(b) Includes passengers who gave up seats in exchange for compensation.

(c) Includes both compensated passengers and passengers who did not qualify for compensation under oversale rules.

Source: DOT; January to September 1998

SMART FLYING

finally arriving at airport check-in with just 20 minutes to spare before departure. You hand over your ticket and the agent gives you the bad news: The flight was oversold and even though you had a confirmed reservation, you've been bumped. In other words, they gave your seat to someone else—someone who checked in earlier.

It can and *does* happen. Generally, travelers with the latest reservations or those who check in last are the first to be bumped. In the case of involuntary bumping, the DOT requires airlines to give passengers a written statement describing their rights and explaining who gets bumped—and who doesn't—when flights are overbooked. And there are more requirements:

• Frequently, the airline must fork over an on-the-spot cash payment, with the amount depending on a passenger's ticket price and the length of the delay. (There's no compensation if the airline can get you to your destination within one hour of your originally scheduled arrival time.)

• With certain exceptions, if the airline can get you to your destination only one to two hours later (for domestic travel), it must refund you the cost of your one-way fare, up to $200.

• If it takes more than two hours to get you to your destination (more than four hours for international travel), the airline generally must pay you twice the value of your one-way ticket, up to $400.

• You get to keep your original ticket—for a flight, not for a refund.

To be eligible for compensation, travelers must have a confirmed reservation on the flight from which they're bumped, must have purchased a ticket within the required number of days after making the reservation, and must have arrived at the boarding lounge by the check-in cutoff time. Most domestic carriers have a deadline of 10 minutes before a flight, but some deadlines can be an hour or more ahead. Check-in deadlines on some international flights can be as long as three hours.

The DOT requires no compensation for charter flights, flights between foreign cities, international flights inbound to the U.S., or flights on planes that hold 60 or fewer passengers, nor if the airline substitutes a smaller plane.

AVOIDING BAD SEATS

You settle in for the eight-hour transatlantic flight, then prepare to recline your seat. You press the button, but the seat reclines just an inch or so, then stops. "Excuse me," you say to a passing flight attendant, "but this seat must be broken." "Oh, no, it's not broken," comes the reply. "It's just a no-recline seat."

Airlines have names for their bad seats. American calls them "undesirable." Delta identifies them as "no-recline." Whatever the label, these seats are the airlines' inside secret. Reservation agents usually don't warn fliers about loser seats. Several airlines claim their computer reservations systems (CRS) don't even contain the data to make those disclosures.

Even the most diligent travel shoppers will find it frustrating—if not impossible—to keep track of the worst coach seats. That's because airlines constantly rejigger seat layouts, and "floor plans" also differ among airlines and aircraft. Nevertheless, seat location has become more important than ever now that airlines are cramming as many seats as possible into their planes and many planes are fully booked.

The no-recline trap. Although fliers don't generally ask if a seat reclines, they should—because when the person in front of you reclines his or her seat, you become a human sandwich. Why the immobile seats and where will you find them?

• Airlines try to pack as many seats as possible on an aircraft, since extra seats produce extra revenue—as much as tens of millions of dollars over the lifetime of the aircraft.

• Non-recliners exist for one of two reasons: The seat's back butts up against a bulkhead wall, giving it little or no space to

SMART FLYING

131

tilt. Or the seat is located in the row just forward of an emergency exit door.

• Seats can recline up to eight inches, but very few airlines ever reach that maximum.

• Boeing 747s have the most "stiffbacks;" 777s and L-1011s have the fewest.

• Nonrecliners can lose as much as five inches, or 20 percent, of horizontal space on a DC-10.

When reserving, always ask if your seat fully reclines. However, getting accurate seat-recline information from reservations agents can be difficult.

Suffering by the bathroom. Seats located near the lavatories are undesirable for obvious reasons—traffic and congestion tend to build up near the lavatory doors, particularly in the rear of the plane. The main problem is poor layout. (When airlines purchase planes from a manufacturer, they choose one of a variety of possible floor plans.) Some planes are worse than others.

Worst: Be careful choosing seats on Airbus A-300s, Boeing 767s, and MD-11s—they had the largest percentage of seats

SEAT ARRANGEMENT

COACH/ECONOMY		BUSINESS CLASS	
Plane	Configuration	Plane	Configuration
A300/310/330/340	2-4-2	A300/310/330/340	2-3-2, 2-2-2
A320	3-3	A320	2-2, 2-3
DC9/MD-80/MD-90	2-3	DC9	2-2
DC-10/MD-11	2-5-2, 2-4-3	DC-10/MD-11	2-3-2, 2-2-2
L-1011	2-5-2, 2-4-3	L-1011	2-3-2
737	3-3	737	2-2
747	3-4-3	747	2-2, 2-3-2
757	3-3	757	2-2
767	2-3-2	767	2-2-1, 2-2-2, 2-1-2
777	2-5-2	777	2-3-2, 2-2-2

Source: Consumer Reports Travel Letter

situated next to or across from a lavatory, with 12 to 13 percent of them located in restroom purgatory, fore and aft.

Better: The 747 and 777 families, the DC-10s, and the L-1011s were better, with only 8 to 9 percent of their seats located near the restrooms.

Stuck in the middle seat. Middle seats, cramped and imprisoning, are the easiest to identify. But middle seats are also hard to escape, because of their sheer number. Like near-to-the-lavatory seats, middles are a factor of layout.

• The 767 is your best bet if you want to avoid these seats. Its seven-abreast layout (2-3-2) means that only 14 percent of coach fliers are caught in between.

• The Airbus A300, with eight abreast (2-4-2), is your second choice.

• The 747, with 10 seats across (3-4-3) in the main cabin, is the worst. Some 35 to 39 percent of its seats are in the middle.

• The L-1011, MD-11, and DC-10 improve somewhat over the 747, with their 2-5-2 configuration.

Seat roulette: play and win. These strategies can help you get the most desirable seats on a flight.

Get seat assignments when you book. Never wait until you arrive at the airport.

Arrive early. Even if you already have a seat assignment, check in at the airport an hour or more before departure. If you get to the gate just minutes before takeoff, airlines may reclaim your comfy seat for more-favored customers, such as high-mileage frequent fliers. The later you check in, the greater your chances of landing a loser seat—or getting bumped.

Book away from high-traffic areas. Give yourself at least four rows' distance from both restrooms and galleys.

Probe reservation agents on non-recliners. Seat numbers change when airlines reconfigure the cabin—which they do quite frequently. Airline ticket agents should be able to determine if the recline status of your assigned seat has changed; if

THE MOST COMFORTABLE PLANES

The winners: The 767 family and the A300 series of planes had the lowest percentage of undesirable seats, averaging 30 and 37 percent, respectively.

The losers: The 747 family had the most undesirable seats—48 percent. And the MD-11 was a close second-to-last finisher, with an average of 46 percent of coach seats deemed undesirable.

not, speak to a supervisor. But remember, ticket agents don't always have this information in their systems. The best tactic is to avoid seats in any row forward of an emergency exit or in the last row of a section, against the bulkhead.

Request an exit row. If you are able-bodied, you may qualify for a coveted emergency row seat, which usually offers generous legroom by coach standards. Airlines cannot assign those seats over the phone; they must see you in person to assess your physical ability to assist in an evacuation.

Upgrade. Escape the misery of coach—and *all* its undesirable seats—by saving your mileage awards for upgrades, not free coach tickets.

If, despite all your efforts, you still get a miserable seat, complain and demand a better one. Should a packed plane prevent a seat change, demand compensation later. You might gain something like a free upgrade to first class for a future flight.

YOUR CHILD'S IN-FLIGHT SAFETY

Each day, thousands of babies and toddlers fly cradled on the lap of a parent or grandparent. But the safest place for a tot on a plane is in a firmly buckled child restraint seat fastened to the airline seat—which usually costs an extra fare.

The safety of young fliers is on the minds of aviation experts. Jim Hall, chairman of the National Transportation Safety Board (NTSB), declared 1999 the Year of Child Transportation Safety. Since 1979, the NTSB, which is charged with investigating air accidents and making safety recommendations, has urged the FAA to mandate that babies fly in a child-restraint seat. And for two decades, the FAA has refused to do so, despite clear evidence (including the FAA's own research) that child safety restraints provide youngsters with the most protection both in survivable crashes and dur-

Child Safety Aloft
Car seats aren't just for cars

Current rules. The FAA recommends—but does not require—that all children, regardless of age, be protected by an approved child-restraint seat appropriate to the child's size and weight. If you book a seat on a plane for your child and you have an approved seat, the airline must allow you to use it. It's prudent to check with the airline in advance.

Acceptable safety seats. Safety seats considered acceptable by the FAA are those with labels that read, "This restraint is certified for use in motor vehicles and aircraft." Somewhere on the shell, they will also carry a sticker with the letters "FMVSS," standing for Federal Motor Vehicle Safety Standard. (If the seat is not usable on a plane, the label will probably say so.)

Unacceptable seats. Neither booster seats (backless platforms with no internal harness to restrain the child) nor seatless vest or harness systems are allowed. Although approved for autos, both booster seats and harness systems don't work well in aircraft due to the fact that airline seats, unlike automobile seats, tend to fold forward in a crash.

Seat placement. A child safety seat must be placed in a window seat so it won't block an escape path in the event of an emergency. It may not be placed in an emergency exit row. Use the same care when buckling up the safety seat that you use in the family car. You should firmly push the seat into the airplane seat cushions while pulling all the slack out of the plane's seat belt. Make certain both the plane seat belt and the harness on the seat aren't twisted.

Who needs a safety seat? The FAA recommends that children weighing under 20 pounds be placed in a rear-facing child seat (facing the airplane's seat back) and that kids from 20 to 40 pounds use a forward-facing model. Children over 40 pounds should use the standard lap belt on all airline seats.

SMART FLYING

ing turbulence.

The effective weight of a 20-pound toddler, say FAA researchers, can soar to more than 100 pounds in milliseconds with the buffeting of turbulence: A parent's arms are not an adequate restraint. And federal weather researchers estimate that a commercial aircraft encounters significant turbulence somewhere in the U.S. every day.

After pressure from the NTSB and other groups, the FAA began actively promoting voluntary restraints of young children in 1996. But the FAA stopped short of mandating its recommendation and apparently has done little to clarify confusion about child safety on planes, among both adult passengers traveling with children and industry employees.

But change may be in the air. In July 1997, some airlines began offering as much as 50 percent off the full-price fare for young travelers. As of January 1999, each of the nine major airlines offered half fares for children under two (though none offered discounts for those two and older).

The discounts prompted the FAA to begin considering mandatory child restraints for small children traveling on U.S. airlines. It could take from "months to years" to develop a law, if one is deemed necessary.

Until the issue is sorted out, it's up to parents and grandparents to protect kids in the air. To avoid problems at check-in or on the plane, it's wise to bring a copy of the FAA regulations detailing your right to use a child-restraint seat on a plane. Call the FAA at 800 322-7873 to request a copy. Or print it from the FAA web site at *www.faa.gov*. Take particular care when flying on international carriers. Call ahead and request a written copy of the airline's policies.

PESTICIDES ALERT

In the not too distant past, many international flights would not allow disembarkation until flight attendants had sprayed the aircraft cabin—passengers and all—with insecticides from hand-held aerosol cans.

These days, you'll rarely find yourself in such a situation. Passenger outrage and pressure from the U.S. government prompted all but a handful of nations to stop spraying while passengers are onboard. In February 1998, the DOT, which led the battle against the practice, hailed the policy change as a "dramatic success."

But in reality, passengers are not necessarily safe from exposure to potentially toxic pesticides:

Countries That Require Spraying
Where you can expect pesticides

About a dozen nations still require some sort of pesticide treatment on all incoming aircraft.

Spraying with passengers aboard. Today, at least six nations—Grenada, India, Kiribati, Madagascar, Trinidad and Tobago, and Uruguay—still require the spraying of insecticides on all incoming aircraft while passengers are on board. Cabins are usually sprayed during the last minutes of the flight, as the plane makes its descent. Airport officials in India, for example, require the spraying of cabins while passengers are on board, even though India's government does not formally mandate spraying.

Spraying with no passengers aboard. American Samoa and Panama require an aerosol spray but let airlines treat their planes while cabins are unoccupied.

With or without passengers present. Five nations—Australia, Barbados, Fiji, Jamaica, and New Zealand—have granted airlines the option of spraying with or without passengers on board or treating cabins with residual insecticide that stays active for up to eight weeks.

Select "disinsection." Another half-dozen nations, including Switzerland and the United Kingdom, require disinsection of selected incoming flights—primarily from areas of "contagious diseases," "malarial countries," and "infected areas."

SMART
FLYING

137

• Many aircraft today are routinely treated with a variety of pesticides, some not even approved for use by the Environmental Protection Agency (EPA).

• Although the chemicals probably don't pose a risk to healthy people who fly occasionally, some health experts express concern about people with respiratory problems, pregnant women, and those subjected to repeat exposure, such as flight crews or very frequent fliers.

• Long-lasting pesticide treatments are now generally applied before passengers board the plane. (Usually unaware of the procedure, travelers don't question it.) Exposure now lasts for up to 10 or 12 hours rather than the old brief spray.

When did spraying start? The treatment of aircraft to kill insects, called "disinsection," became common in the 1940s as a way for many nations, including the U.S., to prevent the spread of diseases and crop-damaging pests. In 1979, the Centers for Disease Control and Prevention (CDC) amended its Foreign Quarantine Regulations so they no longer required insecticide spraying in airline cabins; many U.S. airlines, however, still treat cabins during layovers with domestically approved insecticides to discourage pests such as cockroaches.

The DOT campaign to persuade the rest of the world to stop spraying was only partly successful. At least a dozen foreign nations still require some kind of insecticide treatment of all incoming aircraft, including American carriers. Airlines that don't comply with the requirements could be subject to spraying by foreign officials using their chosen insecticide, which falls within the guidelines of the World Health Organization (WHO), an agency of the United Nations.

What's being sprayed? WHO has approved two different insecticides for use in aircraft cabins: d-phenothrin may be used for the spray disinsection of occupied aircraft; permethrin may be used for residual disinsection of passenger cabins. Both are nerve poisons (permethrin is classified by the EPA as a pos-

138

sible carcinogen). They are in the synthetic pyrethroids category, relatively nontoxic to mammals, and are common ingredients in most household insecticides, such as Raid. (Incidentally, the Raid can label says to use the insecticide only in areas with "adequate ventilation.")

Contrary to WHO approval, EPA policy does not allow the spray application of d-phenothrin in occupied passenger cabins or the residual application of permethrin in passenger cabins—occupied or unoccupied. That's because in 1994, the U.S. manufacturer of a popular d-phenothrin airline spray decided not to apply to register with the EPA for use in occupied cabins. Instead, the company requested that the insecticide be approved for application only in unoccupied aircraft. The EPA agreed to allow the spray to be applied in occupied cabins until inventories of the pesticide are exhausted; it will then be banned for this use.

The EPA likewise received no applications for the use of permethrin for disinfection of passenger cabins and thus does not

Dealing with Airline Pesticides
A defense strategy

There's little you can do to dodge pesticide spray on a plane when you're trapped onboard. You can try to avoid flights where pesticides are used, but that strategy is not always practical (and it's not always easy to identify those planes). These defense tactics can help:

• Consult your doctor if you have any concerns. There may be precautions you can take. If you're asthmatic, for example, you may have to stock up on extra medication for your flight.

• Get a note from your doctor if you're pregnant, asthmatic, or allergic to pesticides. Use it to try to get permission to disembark before the spraying begins.

• Don't bother with a pollen mask. The only gizmo that can totally block pesticide spray is a filtered breathing apparatus.

allow it to be used. The only EPA-permitted use of permethrin is in cargo holds in a very dilute—0.5 percent—solution. The foreign countries that spray with permethrin use a greater concentration—2 percent—in passenger cabins. To fulfill spraying requirements of foreign nations, U.S. airlines can apply the insecticide in cabins while planes are parked in other countries, far beyond the reach of EPA jurisdiction.

Who's at risk? Synthetic pyrethroids are considered among the "least worrisome" of the insecticides. Therefore, if you're healthy and you fly occasionally, most experts agree that you're not likely to suffer any significant health problems.

There may be cause for concern, however, among some groups: asthmatics, those with "multiple chemical sensitivity," pregnant women, small children, frequent fliers, and flight crews.

How do you know? No law requires airlines to tell passengers what chemicals are used on flights. Travelers intent on finding data may encounter contradictory answers, misinformation, and confusion about the subject among airline representatives.

The only information available to travelers today is a partial list of countries that require spraying (found at the DOT web site, *ostpxweb.dot.gov/policy/safety/disin.htm*). The bureaucracy and misinformation in some foreign nations have prevented the DOT from providing a complete list.

COPING WITH 'AIR RAGE'

You may have heard the term "air rage" used by newscasters reporting the apparently growing number of in-flight disturbances that threaten the safety of flight crews and passengers alike: A passenger attacks a flight attendant who won't serve her a drink; a plane must make an unscheduled stop to ditch a fan harassing members of a rock band.

The Air Transport Association, the trade association for the major U.S. airlines, estimates that among the 600 million passengers traveling globally on U.S. carriers in 1997, there were several thousand disruptive incidents. The FAA studied disruptive behavior and found that alcohol played a role in one- third of all the serious incidents it examined. Problems on American Airlines planes alone have more than tripled since 1994, to 921 incidents.

What's being done. Government officials and airlines are starting to crack down on disruptive passengers. American Airlines petitioned the U.S. Attorney General's office and the DOT in 1996 to prosecute unruly passengers. The carrier is now much more likely to deny boarding to belligerent or intoxicated passengers. The airline also presents a written notice to passengers onboard who are physically or verbally abusive, warning them that their behavior may be in violation of federal law and directing them to stop immediately.

After British Airways registered 266 incidents in 1997— most involving smoking, drunkenness, or abusive behavior— the carrier petitioned the British government to ensure that international law-enforcement personnel take action against disruptive passengers.

Responding to the rising number of disruptive incidents, the FAA instituted an experimental program in 1998 to accumulate evidence and work with the U.S. Department of Justice to prosecute offenders. Any passenger who interferes with a flight or crew member is violating federal law and faces possible civil and criminal fines and up to 20 years in prison.

What you can do. If you are disturbed by another traveler's abusive behavior, avoid confronting the individual. Instead, report the problem to a flight attendant, providing the passenger's seat number. Try to remain calm and communicate clearly. If you find yourself bubbling into a rage, take steps to calm yourself down: Breathe deeply, distract yourself with a stroll down the aisle, chat with a neighbor, or listen to music.

SMART
FLYING

CHAPTER 18

Strategies for Flying Overseas

Planning a smooth, efficient, and economical international travel itinerary is possible thanks to deals all over the globe.

————————————— ■ —————————————

Flying to Asia, South America, or the South Pacific? Once you get there, air travel is not only the fastest way to get around, it can also be surprisingly economical. And in Europe, you may want to use some flight segments along with car or train travel.

AIR PASSES ARE GREAT BARGAINS

Many countries and airlines offer tourist air passes. Visitors buy either an all-inclusive pass for air travel in a particular country for a set period, or coupons (usually sold in sets of two or four) for individual travel segments. Both options are priced far below prices charged to local travelers. Deals vary by region.

Europe. Several European airlines and airline partnerships offer special—and affordable—visitor fares.

The basics. The general formula is the same as most visitor airfares: You buy a specified number of flight coupons at a set price per coupon—typically $89 to $129 per coupon. Although coupon prices don't always beat the lowest economy excursion fares, they're usually significantly lower than unrestricted economy fares. And coupons carry far fewer of the restrictions that can make ordinary excursion impractical.

However, you must usually buy the visitor pass or coupons before you leave the U.S. Some fares also require that you buy an international air ticket from the U.S. to the area where the visitor program will be used (a "conjunction" ticket, in airlinese). Some conjunction tickets must be on the same line that sponsors the visitor airfare. And in most cases, free frequent-flier tickets do not qualify.

Most visitor fares do limit you to one stop in each destination city. You can usually travel through the sponsoring line's hub (or hubs) more than once, however, if just changing planes there. As their most serious limitation, most visitor airfares make you use a coupon for each flight segment. So a trip that entails a connecting flight requires two coupons, doubling the cost.

Most passes and coupons also require you to specify your full itinerary when you buy them; rerouting could be extra.

Which airlines offer them? Almost all European carriers have some sort of pass or coupon program. North American visitors will find the best bets among programs covering most or all of Europe. Several programs even include nearby points in North Africa and the Middle East. See "The all-Europe programs," later in this chapter, for a list of lines and passes.

National and regional tickets. About a half dozen single-country or regional air passes (mostly for Scandinavia) are on offer. Most people traveling within a single European country or a small multicountry region will probably do better with a rail pass or a rented car. But flying may still pay.

The low-fare option. Several low-fare carriers in Europe also offer unrestricted bargain fares between, say, Amsterdam and London or London and Dublin. Even if you travel mainly by car or train, you may want to include a flight segment to save time along the way or to get back quickly to your departure city.

SMART
FLYING

143

Australia/New Zealand. Expect to cover a lot of ground when visiting these two South Pacific nations—Australia is the size of the United States, New Zealand the size of California. Air travel is not only practical but economical.

Single-country passes. Qantas, Ansett, and Air New Zealand all have air pass/coupon programs that allow city-to-city travel in either country; coupons cost about $140 to $200 per segment, depending on distance. You must reserve and pay for these tickets before you leave the U.S., but you can schedule your flights once you've arrived. In most cases, you will need to have an international air ticket—but not necessarily with the airline that issues the coupons.

Both countries. Ansett and Qantas offer a two-country coupon program, which allows travel within both countries and between Australia and New Zealand (the flight from Sydney to Auckland takes about three hours).

Other South Pacific destinations. Air New Zealand has a very appealing South Pacific air pass allowing a predetermined number of stops not only in Australia and New Zealand, but in such South Pacific locales as Fiji, the Cook Islands, Tahiti, and Hawaii. You must fly round-trip from Los Angeles, schedule an itinerary before departure, and travel in one direction only, say, from Auckland to Sydney to Fiji to the Cook Islands to Tahiti, with no backtracking. Other airlines serving the region also offer air passes, so check with your travel agent.

South America. The major airlines serving South America, including Aerolineas Argentinas (Argentina), Varig (Brazil), and LanChile (Chile), offer several air pass options.

Mercosur Air Pass. An alliance of South American carriers provides this air pass, good for travel to Argentina, Brazil, Chile, Paraguay, and Uruguay.

LanChile South America Air Pass. Chile's carrier has a coupon-based air pass to most of the airline's destinations in South America.

One-country passes. Three South American airlines offer passes good only in their home countries: the Visit Argentina Air Pass from Aerolineas Argentinas; the Visit Chile Air Pass from LanChile; and the Varig Air Pass Brazil.

Asia. The recent economic downturn created airfare bargains for visitors. For example, in late 1998 and part of 1999, Hong Kong–based Cathay Pacific offered one of the best deals ever: a round-trip between the U.S. and Hong Kong and 30-day unlimited travel pass to more than a dozen Asian cities, all for $999. Singapore Airlines also has a Discover Asia Air Pass. Other carriers in the region offer similar passes; check with your travel agent for one that fits your itinerary.

ONE-WAY TICKET TACTICS

Buying from a consolidator overseas can save on a number of one-way tickets: a short-haul trip to close the gap in an open-jaw flight (a round-trip arriving and departing from different cities, say going to Athens and returning from Madrid); a local side trip; a one-way long-haul; or a one-way ticket back to the U.S. (though generally only when the dollar is strong).

When shopping for airfare discounts abroad, deal with a

AIR PASS PROGRAMS

Passes are an affordable way to see Europe.

Airline	Available passes
Air France	EuroFlyer Pass
Alitalia	Europlus Air Pass
Austrian	Visit Europe (in conjunction with Delta and Air Canada)
British Airways	Europe Air Pass
British Midland	Discover Europe Air Pass
Iberia	Europass
KLM	Passport to Europe (with Northwest)
Lufthansa	Discover Europe-Pass
Malev	Hungarian Pass to Europe
SAS	SAS Visit Europe Air Pass

consolidator that has an office in the country where you plan to buy. However, long term, you'll probably do better with a good local overseas travel agency, rather than working directly with consolidators. A retail travel agency can get discount tickets wholesale, then charge you about the same price you'd end up paying the consolidator.

Before you collect quotes from discounters, check the cheapest airline list prices. If the airlines are having one of their periodic price wars (and you can abide by the cheap ticket's restrictions), the airline's advertised price may be your best bet.

No matter what a consolidator's price list says, get a specific quote for an individual ticket. And be prepared to buy a full-fare ticket should the consolidator deal fall through.

HOW TO BOOK OVERSEAS FLIGHTS
Booking international tickets, either before you leave or while you're traveling, is fairly straightforward.

Booking before you leave. Practically all visitor air passes require you to reserve and buy in the U.S. Almost any travel agency will arrange them. Or call the sponsoring airline's North American office.

Using a foreign travel agent once you're there. Most foreign travel agents offer bargain package deals to nearby countries—for example, a three-night trip to Sydney from Auckland, New Zealand. And if the exchange rate is favorable to Americans, the deal is even sweeter.

REMEMBER TO RECONFIRM
When flying in a foreign country—especially in Asia and South America—a phone call to the airline 72 hours in advance of departure saves headaches. Some airlines simply do not consider you a "reserved" passenger unless you reconfirm. Neglect to call and they may give away your seat to another passenger who checks in earlier than you. Show up early for

any foreign flight, too, since language and customs problems could delay your arrival at the gate.

A FEW WORDS ABOUT SAFETY

How safe are foreign air carriers? Some, mainly those in Europe, Australia, and New Zealand, have safety records on a par with or better than those of U.S. airlines. Other carriers, in South America and some parts of Asia, are for the most part quite safe to fly. But Russian, Indian, and Chinese carriers have had some problematic safety records.

The FAA maintains a report on the adherence to international safety standards by different countries at *www.faa.gov*. The site provides a look at an individual country's ability to license and oversee air carriers in accordance with aviation safety standards; it does not rate individual airlines. For your protection, keep these factors in mind when flying overseas:

The reputation of the carrier. When booking a flight on a carrier you don't know, ask your travel agent about its safety record—any crashes or recent safety violations.

The equipment. Many of the world's airlines use modern jets from Boeing and Airbus; others fly older planes, including some with questionable safety records. In general, try to book flights on airlines with modern fleets of American or European-made jets.

The conditions. Consider local weather conditions and terrain. Navigation equipment is often not as sophisticated in some parts of the world as it is in the U.S. Radar may be old and wind-sheer detection nonexistent. So you may not want to fly into a mountainous region in fog, snow, or other perilous weather conditions.

SMART
FLYING

147

Hotel How-To

CHAPTER 19

Getting the Best Rates

Smart travelers rarely pay full price for a hotel room. Knowing your options can save you money both in the U.S. and overseas.

Hotel room rates vary widely—even for the same type of room in the same hotel on the exact same day. Borrowing a leaf from the airlines, profit-maximizing notebook, hotels now use a complex pricing system based on the predictions of room-occupancy rates for each date and location. Rates for empty rooms then drop as a given reservation day approaches.

Still, for most travelers, it's too risky to show up at a hotel hoping for a good price. And it's also unnecessary, since there are so many good sources for bargains.

SIX RATE-LOWERING TIPS

1. Check discount sources. There are a number of private sources of discounted hotel rooms—private in the sense that you need to be a member or know of their existence:

Half-price hotel programs. Hotels sell off excess room capacity through these programs, which often offer the best deals (see "Hotels at half price" later in this chapter). You may have to be flexible about locations or dates, especially during a peak-demand period.

Tour operators and consolidators. Tour operators book blocks of rooms at a special price—and may sell you just the lodging at a 20 to 40 percent discount, without the transportation or sightseeing that normally makes up a tour package. You can also get discounted rooms through some consolidators.

Local reservation services. In some cities, local services offer good deals. You can find them listed in tourist-board brochures from specific regions or cities, or on the web.

Alternative accommodations. If you're planning for a week or longer on an island, in the mountains, or in a distant major city, a vacation rental or home exchange may be cheaper, roomier, or more fun. (See Chapter 23.)

2. Call the hotel directly. Every type of hotel—from economy to full-service deluxe, and even resort properties—gives discounts off rack rate (list price). Simply call the hotel yourself to ask about the best rate; national reservations operators aren't always informed about local deals. Direct discounts come in several forms:

Sales and promotions. Rates at large hotel chains vary by location and time of year. The property you're considering could have special rates for the dates you want.

Weekend rates. Room rates at hotels that cater to business travelers during the work week drop dramatically on weekends. So do rates at resort hotels during the off-season.

Bargain destinations. Overbuilding in a region strongly affects hotel rates. Ask your travel agent which destinations offer the best deals. You can then either book through your agent (if you can get a good price) or call hotels yourself.

Corporate rates. Most hotels serving business travelers offer corporate rates—often available to any traveler who can produce even vague evidence of corporate or professional

HOTELS

employment at check-in (a business card will usually do). Regular corporate rates are available at thousands of hotels; they usually run no more than 20 percent off the rack rate and may be even stingier. And sometimes they're even a bit higher than the lowest rack rate, to cover some extra amenity, such as a "superior" room, an "executive" floor.

Advance-reservation deals. A number of chains reward you with lower rates if you book ahead—anywhere from seven to 29 days in advance. You pay for your first night's stay within a week of reserving. However, cancel without at least 15 days' notice and you lose your deposit. Prepayment requirements and cancellation penalties vary, so check before you book.

3. Surf the web. Many leading hotel chains allow you to room-shop right at your computer, where you can read detailed descriptions of properties, many accompanied by photos. Some chains offer special discounts for online booking; others post last-minute bargains—as much as 50 percent off—to web surfers looking for accommodations for the following weekend.

4. Investigate special rates. You will also encounter numerous ways to get discounts through individual affiliations:

Preferred rates. Such prices—a special kind of corporate rate specifically negotiated by a big travel agency, an independent booking service, or a travel club—may offer substantially better deals than corporate rates. Average discounts are around 20 percent, and some are as high as 40 percent. Preferred rates are typically available on a "last room" basis: You'll get the discount as long as the hotel has any rooms available, even if it's close to full. Some preferred-rate programs even have their own "blocked space" at certain hotels and may be able to confirm a room for you at the discount rate, even when the hotel is supposedly fully booked.

The only drawback to preferred rates is their limited availability—perhaps at just a fifth to a quarter of hotels that offer the corporate rates discussed on the previous page. And you'll only be able to get them through a travel agency, travel club, booking organization, or corporate travel office that has negotiated them. Furthermore, some preferred-rate breaks are only 10 percent or less. You can check into these discounts with a copy of your travel agency's current preferred-rate directory (or ask to see a display of available preferred rates on your agent's computer screen). The latest "Hotel and Travel Index," also at agencies, has information, too.

Prefer to arrange your own deals? The Travelgraphics preferred-rate program is available directly to consumers. Call 800 644-8785 for information. Buy a directory at the web site (*www.tgiweb.com*; $29; AE, Disc, MC, V), find a hotel that suits your needs, and call that hotel directly, mentioning the Travelgraphics booking code.

Membership discounts. Membership associations, such as the American Automobile Association (AAA) and the American Association of Retired Persons (AARP), line up special rates for members with select hotel chains.

Credit card rebates. Some banks offer lodging price breaks as benefits with their credit cards—usually rebates of 5 to 10 percent, often with a minimum hotel bill of $100 or more.

5. Use senior discounts. The good news is that senior perks save money. The bad news is that two expansions—economic and demographic—are gradually shrinking the bargains. The roaring economy of the late '90s fueled growth in both business and leisure travel and hiked demand for hotel space just about everywhere. Simultaneously, the baby-boom generation entered its 50s. So, many hotels won't be too generous.

Although dozens of chains and thousands of individual establishments still use price incentives to attract over-50 travelers, rates will probably continue to tighten up.

Senior programs are commonly set up in one of two ways: A relatively modest discount of 10 to 15 percent may be offered as long as the hotel has any vacancy at all. Or you

HOTELS

153

might get select reductions of up to 50 percent—competitive with the best bargains of a half-price program or hotel broker—but subject to availability and other restrictions. Such deals can be had through several means:

Deals for anyone. A majority of hotel chains offer a senior discount to anyone over a minimum age. (The AARP minimum is 50; many any-senior hotel programs apply the same minimum, but more than a quarter use 55, another quarter use 60, and a few require that you be 62 or 65.) All you need to qualify is a driver's license or other official ID.

Typical discounts are 10 to 15 percent. Although that's better than nothing, senior travelers choosing those chains would be wise to check for bigger discounts—through a half-price program, a travel agent's preferred-rate program, a hotel broker, or a chain's any-age promotion. Basically, the senior deal is the fallback at most chains if there's nothing better. Note, however, that budget hotels seldom give more than 10 to 15 percent off to *anyone*, so their senior deal is probably as good as you'll find.

AARP deals. AARP has arranged discount programs with about two dozen chains, listed in their Purchase Privilege Program directory. At least that many more chains unofficially honor membership for senior discounts. One big advantage is that membership lowers the discount-eligibility age to 50 (from 55 to 65). Many chains in both groups also recognize memberships in the Canadian Association of Retired Persons and other senior groups.

Hotel clubs. A number of chains (including Days Inn, Hilton, Marriott, Ramada, Best Western, Walt Disney World Resorts) run their own membership programs for senior travelers (minimum age, 50 to 60), but for the most part, members get only modest discounts. Some require AARP membership to qualify. Only at Days Inn, Marriott, and Hilton do the reductions (subject to restrictions) run as high as 50 percent. But their hotel-club deals can still be much better than their any-senior deals. If you're not already a hotel-club member, you can usually sign up on the spot as you register.

Beyond room discounts, the Days Inn, Hilton, and Disney clubs offer a variety of other benefits, including discounts at hotel restaurants and gift shops, reduced admissions, and promotional deals with airlines, cruise lines, and car-rental companies. The Hilton senior program is an extension of its frequent-stay program: Money spent at participating hotels earns credit toward hotel stays, airline tickets, and more.

Your own deal. Usually you can't combine a senior discount with any other reduction—half-price, corporate, group, or meeting. And even an advertised chain-wide senior discount may not be available at all times or all locations. So you'll probably have to call a chain's toll-free national reservation line to check. Many chains now also provide web sites of varying sophistication: Some merely furnish information, while others accept reservations.

Still, it's often a good idea to call each hotel's reservation office. You may discover other discount options and local promotional deals, as well as any local senior offers. Several notable chains that lack a uniform senior policy often have senior rates at individual locations. However, very upscale small chains and independent hotels may not offer anything. Smart strategy: If you're over 50, *always* ask about senior discounts when you reserve.

6. Investigate hotel brokers. These agencies provide a way for hotels to unload rooms they don't expect to sell at full price. Brokers won't always deliver the biggest discounts, but they are among the most reliable sources of decent ones, falling into two broad categories.

Wholesale brokers. Wholesalers generally contract with hotels on a yearly basis to sell rooms at a discounted price—many "own" a certain number of rooms. Some are tour

HOTELS

operators who sell rooms to independent travelers at the same rates they offer in package tours. (Tour operators not promoting themselves as brokers may do the same; you can sometimes find bargains by checking a range of tour brochures.)

Expect to prepay the wholesaler for your entire visit; you'll then receive a room voucher or, if the trip is on short notice, one will be waiting for you at the hotel. (But note that wholesalers often can't accommodate last-minute bookings at all.) Wholesaler rates typically include all tax and service charges—but beware, some quote prices on a per-person rather than per-room basis. Since most give commissions, your regular travel agent can deal with them for you.

Like preferred rates, wholesaler discounts are generally in the 10 to 40 percent range, although occasionally they're higher. When rooms are tight, however, the wholesale broker may sell the room with no discount to travelers who are happy to pay full price just to get accommodations.

The broker advantage. They provide the easiest route to a hotel deal—usually one phone call is all it takes. Simply tell the broker where you're going and when; the broker lists the current offerings and you choose the one you like. Unlike working with half-price programs, you don't have to call around from hotel to hotel to see which one is giving sizable discounts. A broker may also be able to get you a discount when half-price rates are blacked out. A few can even snag rooms when a hotel says it has nothing available.

The disadvantage. Most brokers offer a limited selection of hotels. Plus, broker deals are usually confined to fairly upscale properties, mid-priced and up. Some brokers handle hotels in only one or two cities (and seldom in small cities), mostly in downtown locations, and offer only a few choices in suburban or airport locations.

You must prepay. Many brokers require prepayment in full, which can be a hassle if you have to cancel or change your plans. In that event, you will probably forfeit one night's room charge—even brokers who don't ask you to prepay may impose a cancellation charge.

There are no guarantees. Although brokers are often valuable sources, they're not a sure thing. Sometimes they provide no more than a modest discount. Put in some phone time, and you may do better with a half-price program, a hotel's own promotion, or (if you're over 50) a senior deal. Before you accept a broker's rate—or a discount from any source, for that matter—know the hotel's own asking price.

HALF-PRICE HOTEL PROGRAMS

If you continually find your hotel bill is biting too deeply into your travel budget, a half-price hotel directory can be a worthwhile cost-cutter. Your savings from just a night or two at lower rates may more than offset the cost of joining one of the programs ($40 to $100 a year).

All the major half-price programs offer the same basic terms. The big differences are in geographic spread—the more hotels and locations in a program's directory, the better your chances of finding discounted rooms when and where you want them.

Program basics. From a hotel's perspective, joining a half-price program is a good way to try out yield management—the gambit pioneered by the airlines for selling essentially the same service for a variety of prices.

First, the hotel establishes an artificially high rack rate (list price), which it actually can only rarely get—during a big convention or sporting event, for example. That price then serves as a baseline for a variety of "discounts," some offered openly, others limited to certain guests. Typically, a half-price program yields the biggest discount at a given hotel.

To play the half-price game, you must enroll in a club (or buy a discount directory). You then receive a list of participating hotels and an identification card good for at least a year.

HOTELS

157

Before any trip, you check your directory for participating hotels along your route. The directories indicate each hotel's price range (usually with a symbol), address, phone number (and often fax number), and sometimes a brief list of services.

You contact hotels directly, name the half-price program you're using, and ask if the discount is available when you

Hotels at Half Price
Programs that can trim room rates

Entertainment Publications. (800 445-4137; $39.95 to $59.95; MC, V.) This program offers a catalog of directories for U.S. and foreign hotels, plus local discount books. The "Hotels & Travel Ultimate Savings Directory" covers prime destinations and includes discounts on airfares, car rentals, and cruises. ID cards valid for 12 to 18 months.

ITC-50. (800 987-6216, $52; AE, DC, Disc, MC, V.) You'll find U.S. listings, plus extensive coverage of Canadian and overseas locations. ITC also offers cruise and airline discounts, and car-rental breaks.

Encore. (800 444-9800; $69.95; AE, Disc, MC, V.) Besides hotel listings, this one also features a separate section of small inns and bed-and-breakfasts. Expect discounts on airfares, car rentals, cruises, and admission to visitor attractions.

Great American Traveler. (800 548-2812; Total Portfolio Package, $99.95, $49.95 to renew; Great American Traveler hotel program, $49.95, $29.95 to renew; AE, Disc, MC, V.) You'll find only meager hotel discounts, but the parent company, Access, offers reductions on condo rentals, percent-off greens fees at many golf courses, and amusement park discounts.

Quest. (800 742-3543; $99; quarterly hotel updates, $8 a year; AE, Disc, MC, V.) Expect only small discounts on hotels, airfares, and cruises, some deals on condo and car rentals. (Quest is often discounted via associations and credit cards.)

GetAway Travel Club. (800 218-5862; $49.95; MC, V.) This one offers almost entirely first-class or better hotels, many not available from other programs. GetAway rebates 5 percent on all airfares and cruises booked with them.

want it, then make your reservation (guaranteed by credit card, if necessary). No half-price rate on your dates? Then the hotel may offer you a lesser discount. Alternatively, you can try for a different date or check with another hotel. You must usually call at least a few hours ahead for a reservation—not just show up at the desk.

On checking in, you show your program's ID card. You pay when you leave, by either cash or charge card. Note that the half-price ID covers only one room per night. While some clerks may bend the rules, if your party requires two or more rooms, assume you must have a separate membership for each.

Room discounts. Large programs offer a broad mix of independent and chain hotels at a range of prices in downtown, suburban, airport, and highway locations. However, the offerings are usually thin at either price extreme. Some budget rates are already so low that discounting isn't feasible, and deluxe properties often don't participate.

The half-price rates are generally available on any day of the year—subject to availability. That means no discount when a hotel expects to be more than about 80 percent full; and seasonal blackouts often apply. Peak-season discounts are often available only on weekdays in resort areas and on weekends in cities. A few hotels impose a minimum or maximum stay. Restrictions are usually noted in the program directories.

Extras. Directories generally include a laundry list of additional discounts and deals. Probably the most useful offers are dollars-off airline coupons, which let you knock as much as $175 off the regular price of a coach-excursion ticket—usually with only a few restrictions.

How to join. All the programs listed in "Hotels at half price" accept enrollment (or sell directories and coupon books) by phone, with payment by a charge card. Some also have web sites. Except as noted, all directories and memberships are valid for one year from the date of purchase.

HOTELS

Membership in a half-price plan may also be included as a benefit of some other program or organization you've joined. Some are also occasionally offered as premiums in promotions and charity drives or as an extra employee benefit through corporate personnel offices.

Buyer beware. Despite their apparent advantages, half-price programs aren't the answer to a traveler's every prayer. You may encounter some of the most common glitches:

Nonavailability. Hotels really mean their "subject to availability" limitations. You won't get a discount when a hotel expects to be busy. So don't join a program thinking you'll pay half price for all your stays.

More meager discounts. The real deal may be less than a full 50 percent off the price other travelers pay. Travelers have sometimes found that their "half-price" rate was only a few dollars less than they'd have paid if they had just walked up to the desk and asked for a room.

Hotel dropout. Don't be surprised if the reservation clerk at a listed hotel tells you that it no longer honors a program's card. There's extensive turnover in participants.

No card, no deal. You won't get a half-price deal just by mentioning the name of a big program. Hotel clerks generally ask you to produce a valid card.

Noncombination. There's no combining a half-price discount with any other reduction—a corporate, senior, or weekend rate, say—for which you might otherwise be eligible.

You must do it yourself. Half-price rates aren't commissionable, so your travel agency won't arrange them for you.

FREQUENT-STAY PROGRAMS

Hotel frequent-stay programs can deliver a decent return in free stays and other payoffs even if you spend only as few as eight to 10 nights a year in hotels. The basic principle is the same as that of frequent-flier programs: You get a reward in proportion to your use of the sponsor's service. Membership in most hotel programs is free. You may have unlimited time to earn an award—or only a year.

Some big chains offer only a "customer recognition" program—no free stays, just membership benefits, such as late checkout and room upgrades.

Point-based programs. Most give points or some other credit based on what you spend at the hotel, in many cases for food, room service, merchandise, and other on-site purchases in addition to your room charge. Some also allow credit for rooms occupied at a preferred, senior, half-price, or other discounted or promotional rate (though they may not give credit for the deepest discounts).

The others typically limit credit to travelers who pay rack (list) rate or the hotel's published corporate rate. If program literature specifies that earnings are confined to "qualifying" rates, check whether your rate qualifies when you reserve.

Some programs give points for using car-rental or airline partners, usually during the time of a hotel stay. And some allow you to "double dip"—to earn both hotel and airline credit for the same stay.

Several offer one or more levels of very-frequent-stay (VFS) status, similar to an airline's very-frequent-flier status. VFS provides faster earning and/or more generous benefits.

Point-based benefits. All these programs provide free hotel stays as awards. Most also let you redeem points for a wide range of other travel services as well as merchandise.

The typical minimum award is simply one free night: at any time in some programs, during a weekend (or an off-peak night at some resort locations) in others. Usually, higher-credit awards are simply multiples of a basic award: If 10 paid nights earn a specified award, then 20 paid nights earn a premium twice as big or valuable.

Night-based programs. The formula is fairly straightforward.

HOTELS

After staying the required number of nights—generally 8 to 12—you get a free night's stay. And many programs offer at least some worthwhile benefits even if you never earn enough credit for a free stay: room discounts, free breakfast, late checkout, free local calls, and priority reservations or a special reservation phone line.

Choosing a program. Consider the participating hotels. If your travels take you to a wide range of destinations, you'll want a program that allows credit wherever you go. But if you visit just a few places, a small chain with convenient locations may fit your needs.

The more earning opportunities, the better. Programs that give credit for all money spent, not just the room cost, have an advantage. Payoff counts too. The mid-priced and budget chains generally run the most generous programs, giving one free night for every eight to 12 paid nights. And a program that provides benefits you can use right away may be preferable to one that requires a minimum number of stays to qualify.

BUDGET HOTELS

Looking for decent lodgings at a very affordable price? Budget hotels can meet your needs with a good-size room and a well-equipped bathroom, plus only the facilities and extras you absolutely need.

Most budget hotels/motels—called "economy/limited-service lodgings" in hotelese—are part of large chains. The biggest now offer more than 100,000 rooms in over 1,500 locations. Some chains are independent, others are subgroups of giant organizations. No matter, because $50 or less a night (once you're outside the big cities) usually buys all you need for comfort in overnight lodgings. And intense competition demands that even the cheapest chains renovate, redecorate, and update facilities and services on a regular basis.

What you get. If your pocketbook demands a stay in budget accommodations, know what to expect:

Car-convenient locations. Budget hotels are generally situated outside city centers—along major highways, in suburban areas, and near airports.

Basic rooms and services. Typically, chains provide modern bathrooms and clean, comfortable 250-to-300-square-foot rooms. You'll also get 24-hour front-desk service, choice of a smoking or nonsmoking room, individually controlled heat and air conditioning, and ice and vending machines.

Room for kids. All but a handful of chains allow one or two kids—usually with an age limit in the teens—to stay "free."

Reasonable prices. There's no precise definition of the "budget" price range. Rate classes really depend on location; what passes for a budget price in a city center would be mid- or high-priced along the highway. Similarly, a highway budget rate would barely buy a flophouse bed in central Boston, Chicago, or New York. That said, an average room runs about $50. Rates start at about $30—the current average for Motel 6, which promotes itself as the lowest-priced national chain.

Some discounts. Most budget chains offer at least a modest reduction to seniors—typically 10 percent, but you may have to be a member of AARP—as well as discounts to members of the AAA or other auto clubs.

What you give up. Budget hotels might not offer all the convenience and amenities you want or need. For instance, it's rare to find new, comfortable budget hotels in central business districts of major cities—and when you do, they're often in marginal areas.

Large rooms, luxury features (such as a health club), hotel services, and on-site restaurants will probably be lacking. But budget chains may offer a few perks you haven't even considered. Quite a few let you make local and toll-free calls without a charge. Swimming pools are more common than ever. (If this

HOTELS

feature is important to you, check when you reserve.) Many chains provide a complimentary morning meal, though it may be no more than rolls and coffee or tea.

Chains are also responding to economy-minded business travelers with more and more business features: such as incoming fax services and modems. Hotels near airports may provide free airport shuttles, too.

Basic cable has become so common these days that it's not really an extra. However, some hotels include free access to such premium channels as HBO and Showtime. Some also offer in-room VCRs—free or at a daily charge—with an on-site library of rental tapes.

CHAPTER 20

Hotel Ratings Explained

Is the cost difference between a "Superior Deluxe" and "Deluxe" hotel worth it? What defines "First Class" and "Tourist"? Industry ratings will help you differentiate.

In the U.S. at least, the most widely used hotel grades are those published in the "Official Hotel Guide" (OHG)—which is published for the travel industry, not consumers. When a tour, brochure, or newspaper ad promises a certain grade of hotel, the claim is probably based on OHG classifications.

OHG ratings combine two elements: quality of lodgings, which refers to room size and standard of furnishings, and extent of facilities, covering the number and size of public and meeting rooms, restaurants, and shops. Handbooks geared primarily to consumers also rank hotels—some more candidly than the OHG. And around the world, some government agencies also assign ratings.

DECODING THE OHG RATINGS
The OHG divides hotels into three main categories—Deluxe, First Class, and Tourist—with subcategories under each. Here's

what each of the rating terms really means (reprinted with the permission of the OHG).

Deluxe. These establishments range from ultra luxurious to less opulent, but still quite plush.

Superior Deluxe. Exclusive and expensive, often palatial, these hotels offer the highest standards of service, accommodations, and facilities, along with elegant and luxurious public rooms and a prestigious address.

Deluxe. Outstanding and with many of the same features as Superior Deluxe, this type may be less grand—and more reasonable—than those above yet just as satisfactory.

Moderate Deluxe. Accommodations or public areas may be less luxurious than fully Deluxe properties. In others, the hotel may be a well-established famous name, depending heavily on past reputation. The more contemporary hotels may be heavily marketed to business clients, with fine accommodations and public rooms offering Deluxe standards in comfort, yet with less emphasis on atmosphere and/or personal service.

First class. This category runs the gamut from very high-quality accommodations to those that are much less luxurious (but more reasonably priced).

Superior First Class. Expect an above-average hotel, perhaps an exceptionally well-maintained older hotel, but more often a superior modern hotel specifically designed for the First Class market, with some outstanding features. Accommodations and public areas will be tastefully furnished and very comfortable. These can be good values, especially the commercial hotels.

First Class. The rating indicates a dependable, comfortable hotel with standardized rooms, amenities, and public areas—and maybe a superior executive level or wing. Don't look for luxurious facilities or special services.

Limited-Service First Class. Although the property offers full first-class accommodations, you'll have limited public areas, food service, and facilities. Usually moderate in size, these hotels often utilize a residential scale and architecture, and many offer complimentary breakfast and evening cocktails in the lobby or in a small, informal restaurant. This bracket is geared to the individual business or pleasure traveler.

Moderate First Class. These are essentially First Class establishments with comfortable if somewhat simpler accommodations and public areas, these may lack desirable features such as a restaurant. While adequate, some rooms or public areas may tend toward basic and functional. But rates are also reasonable.

Tourist. Such a rating encompasses everything from budget hotels to strictly "port-in-a-storm" properties.

Superior Tourist Class. The top subcategory denotes a budget property with mostly well-kept, functional accommodations (some up to First Class standards). Public rooms may be limited or nonexistent. Although often just a place to sleep, the hotel may have some charming or intimate features, and is usually a good value. The amenity/low-rate ratio may balance for individuals or groups on a budget.

Tourist Class. Expect a purely budget operation with some facilities or features of Superior Tourist Class, but usually no First Class accommodations. Use these places with caution.

Moderate Tourist Class. These low-budget operations, often quite old and sometimes not well kept, are feasible only if no other accommodations are available.

About the ratings. When you use OHG ratings—or any other hotel classification system—be sensitive to the nuances of the report. The travel industry is reluctant to say flatly that any establishment is out-and-out bad, so the OHG and other sources often resort to code words and euphemisms. When the

---

RATINGS BY THE BOOK

Three solid guidebook series that include ratings of lodgings are AAA TourBooks, Michelin's Red Guides, and Mobil Travel Guides. Each series uses a rating scale of 1 to 5, with 5 the highest.

HOTELS

description says "may not be well kept" or "should be used only in a pinch," read it as "this hotel is a dog."

OVERSEAS RATINGS

Once you clear customs, a whole new world of hotel accommodations and ratings systems awaits you. Many travelers rely on the ratings in their preferred guidebooks, but you can also mine other sources.

What's available. Government agencies assign hotel ratings in Australia, Austria, Belgium, France, Greece, Indonesia, Italy, Mexico, the Netherlands, New Zealand, Switzerland, and the United Kingdom. These ratings may be noted in hotel and tour brochures in place of, or in addition to, OHG ratings. Government systems tend to rely on statistical measures, such as dimensions of guest rooms or percentage of rooms with bath.

What's not. The governments of any important tourist countries (including Denmark, Finland, Germany, Japan, Norway, Sweden, and the U.S.) don't rate hotels. Travelers to those countries, as well as tour operators and travel agencies, have to rely on nongovernmental sources.

Ratings aren't everything. In many parts of the world, hotels more basic than those that the OHG rates can be quite adequate. In fact, OHG doesn't even list many low-end hotels. Budget travelers in Paris, for instance, may be perfectly happy in hotels with a government rating of only one or two stars— if they know what to expect. Similarly, travelers in the U.S. often find budget hostelries a great buy even at list price.

CHAPTER 21

Extended-Stay and All-Suites

These roomy, well-equipped—and generally affordable —lodgings provide a comfortable home away from home when you plan to stay for more than just a few days.

———————————————— ■ ————————————————

Staying out of town for two or three weeks because of a family crisis? Need a place to crash while your house is being renovated? On assignment for a few weeks and want more than a hotel room to call home?

If you face that kind of situation, you'll appreciate an extended-stay or all-suite hotel. Two elements distinguish these facilities: Long-term rates, which can provide a substantial savings over nightly rates for stays of a week of more, and special features, such as full kitchen facilities.

Most extended-stay hotels also accept transient guests (provided space is available) and will offer one-night rates. Ultimately, the differences are in perception and promotion— a hotel chain is "extended stay" when it says it is.

The extended-stay segment of the hotel business somewhat overlaps the all-suite group. Many all-suite features—notably the food-preparation area—appeal to touring families as well as extended-stay visitors. However, not all extended-stay chains are all-suite, and not every all-suite chain offers long-term rates.

Most chains are national. Sites are generally in the suburbs, with many in or near office and industrial parks or close to shopping malls or airports. But quite a few are downtown.

RATES AND DISCOUNTS

The rates at extended-stay hotels vary widely—from $150 or so a week at budget-oriented properties to nearly $2,000 a week for a two-bedroom suite at one of the upscale chains. Some chains don't quote weekly and monthly rates; instead, they negotiate extended stays individually. As with most chains, rates vary by location and often by season.

Most extended-stay hotels usually offer a discount when you contact them, in advance, about staying more than a week. But only about half of the chains offer either weekend reductions or senior discounts of any kind.

Individual travelers should call the hotel directly. Tell the reservations agent or sales manager how long you plan to stay, and ask what sort of deal is available.

Business travelers need to check with their corporate travel office or agent about negotiated rates—especially in the case of ongoing training programs or off-site assignments.

LAYOUTS AND FEATURES

Extended-stay hotels range from basic to luxurious, but some generalizations can be made.

Unit configurations. Whether you wind up with a studio or a separate bedroom—or bedrooms—depends on both price and what an individual location offers.

Studios. Most chains provide some studio rooms. About one-quarter offer nothing but studios—one room for both sleeping and daytime living with, at best, some sort of furniture as a divider.

One-bedroom units. Many offer at least some one-bedroom suites, with sleeping and living area in two rooms separated by walls and doors. Distinct sleep and work/relaxation areas are the ideal, but true suites are confined mainly to the upper-end establishments.

Two-bedroom suites. About half the chains feature these, fine for larger families on vacation or two-person business teams who want separate bedrooms but a common living area.

Room/suite size. Roominess varies with layout and price—from just over 200 square feet at some budget chains to 1,000 square feet for a multi-room unit (with a price to match).

Kitchen. A food-preparation area marks the primary difference between extended-stay hotels and typical all-suite properties. A large majority of the extended-stay chains provide a full kitchen with full-size appliances; many all-suites provide only mini-kitchens (possibly just counter areas with a microwave and mini-refrigerator).

Extended-stay extras. The special features in each chain reflect the two markets that extended-stay establishments target: families on vacation and long-term business travelers. The business orientation of many chains is obvious. Some have two phone lines per room or a single line with extra data ports, and some offer a central business center with fax, copier, and such. Several chains furnish CD players and VCRs. The hotel may also have a small tape or CD library; if not, you'll probably find a rental outlet nearby. And parking is usually free.

Some sacrifices. You probably won't find all the traditional services and facilities of a full-service hotel. Extended-stay hotels tend to have relatively few service employees. At a few, even check-in is automated. Towels and bedding may be changed only once or twice a week (or when a new guest arrives), rather than every day.

An on-premises restaurant or coffee shop is fairly rare, though you can probably locate one nearby. You won't have

HOTELS

HOW SUITE IS THAT SUITE?

A quick look at what you'll get in some suites.

Hotel chain	Reservations	Web site (http://www.)	Online booking
AmeriSuite	800 833-1516	amerisuites.com	✔
Aston Hotels	800 922-7866	aston-hotels.com	✔
Best Suites	800 237-8466	bestinn.com	—
Best Western Intl	800 528-1234	bestwestern.com	✔
Candlewood Suites	800 226-3539	candlewoodsuites.com	✔
ClubHouse Inn & Suites	800 258-2466	clubhouseinn.com	✔
Comfort Suites	800 228-5150	comfortinn.com	✔
Country Inns & Suites	800 322-9992	countrysuites.com	✔
Country Inns & Suites By Carlson	800 456-4000	countryinns.com	✔
Crossland Economy Studios	877 276-7752	exstay.com	—
Doubletree Guest Suites	800 222-8733	doubletreehotels.com	✔
Embassy Suites	800 362-2779	embassy-suites.com	✔
Extended Stay America Efficiency Studios	800 398-7829	exstay.com	—
Hampton Inn & Suites	800 426-7866	hamptoinn-suites.com	✔
Hawthorn Suites	800 527-1133	hawthorn.com	✔
Hawthorn Suites Ltd	800 527-1133	hawthorn.com	✔
Hilton Suites	800 445-8667	hilton.com	✔
Homestead Village	888 782-9473	stayhsd.com	—
Homewood Suites	800 225-5466	homewood-suites.com	✔
InnSuites Hotels	800 842-4242	innsuites.com	✔
La Quinta Inn & Suites	800 687-6667	laquinta.com	✔
MainStay Suites	800 660-6246	mainstaysuites.com	✔
Manhattan East Suite Hotels	800 637-8483	mesuite.com	—
Marc Resorts	800 535-0085	marcresorts.com	✔
Marriott Suites	800 228-9290	marriotthotels.com	✔
Outrigger Hotels & Resorts	800 688-7444	outrigger.com	✔
Quality Suites	800 228-5151	qualityinn.com	✔
Residence Inn by Marriott	800 331-3131	residenceinn.com	✔
Sheraton Suites	800 325-3535	sheraton.com	✔
Sierra Suites	800 287-9728	—	—
Sierra Suites Hotel	800 474-3772	sierrasuites.com	✔ (i)
SpringHill Suites by Marriott	888 287-9400	springhillsuites.com	✔
StudioPLUS Deluxe Studios	888 788-3467	exstay.com	—
Summerfield Suites Hotel	800 833-4353	summerfieldsuites.com	✔
TownePlace Suites by Marriott	800 257-3000	towneplacesuites.com	✔
Woodfin Suite Hotels	800 237-8811	woodfinsuitehotels.com	✔

Note: Rates may vary by season or market.

(a) No charge for additional persons using suite.
(b) Rates per week.
(c) Average price.

Source: *Consumer Reports Travel Letter*

1-Bedroom rack rates (per night)	Children free up to age	Weekend discount rates	Average square feet	Kitchens
$89-129	18	✔	380 sq. ft.	mini
$125-505	18	—	560-1,196	varies
$70-100	18	—	400	mini
$65-399	varies	varies	varies	varies
$99-195	18(a)	✔	425	full
$108-149	18	✔	600	mini
$50-70	18	—	380	—
$178-298	12	✔	680-800	mini
$75-125	18	varies	420	mini
$159-1999(b)	—	—	227	full
$126(d)	18	✔	475	mini
$119-229	18	✔	550-600	mini
$199-299(b)	—	—	300	full
$75-129	18	—	499	full
$89-229	—	00	400	full or mini
$69-199	—	—	500	full or mini
(d)	18	✔	500	mini
$39-69(e)	18	—	260-400	full
$85-120	18	varies	493-833	full
$59-149	17	✔	410	full or mini
$89(c)	18	varies	525	mini
$55-65	18	—	400	full
$268-383	— (a)	✔	450-650	varies
$119-450	18	—	300-1,600	varies
$110-255	(a)	✔(f)	465	—
$1i65-400	17	—	600-1,300	full
$75-90	18	—	400	—
$85-110	(a)	✔(d)	453	full
$87-339	17	✔	456	mini
$64-109	—	—	1,000	full
$49-159(b)	—	varies	335(h)	full
$75-95	(a)	✔(d)	343	mini
$299-399(b)	—	—	300-425	full
$89-199(i)	varies	✔	500	full
$55-65	(a)	✔	520	full
$129-159	6	✔(d)	576	full

(d) Check with hotel.
(e) Studio; rate based on weekly stay.
(f) Up to 20% with Friday-night stay.

(g) Minimum square footage.
(h) Studio.
(i) Weekday rate.

HOTELS

24-hour room service, but there's a good chance the hotel will permit (or even encourage) delivery from nearby restaurants. The spacious lounges, lobbies, or meeting rooms are missing, as are the hotel-type attendees in public spaces and elevators. And with most extended-stay properties, you'll give up proximity to major tourist attractions.

At the budget end of the spectrum, these hotels may have outside- rather than inside-corridor entrances—undesirable from a security standpoint, especially in hotels with limited full-time personnel.

SUITE—OR NOT?

Be warned. You won't always find separate rooms in "all-suite" hotels; even hotels in the same chain can vary dramatically. So determine the hotel's definition of a "suite" when you reserve. It may mean a separate room with a door—or simply separated sleeping and living areas. If you need food-prep space, get the kitchen details, too.

"How suite is that suite?" offers a comparison of facilities in 36 chains. Of course, you should confirm exactly what you're getting when you book.

ALTERNATIVES

Other urban accommodations. In big U.S. cities, you'll find independent apartment buildings that have been converted to weekly or monthly rentals. Check your target city's classified ads and the phone book under "apartment rentals" for individual buildings and apartment brokers.

In resort locations. At a popular tourist destination, a vacation rental may be a better bet. Chapter 23 has specifics.

CHAPTER 22

Hotel Discounts Abroad

Overseas accommodations can be pretty pricey these days. Here's how to find bargains.

———————————— ■ ————————————

You've snagged a true bargain airfare to Paris or London. But when you look for a hotel room, will you chalk up an equally appealing deal? Maybe—or maybe not. A night in a First Class or Deluxe hotel in London or Paris at rack (list) rate can easily set you back $300 to $400 these days. To save, you need to know all your options.

FOREIGN HOTELS AT HALF PRICE

The major half-price programs concentrate on North American and Caribbean hotels. Properties in Europe, Asia, and other popular destinations, if covered at all, are rather an afterthought. Still, a few top programs offer overseas listings.

Because a night in a First Class or Deluxe property in a major European city can run more than $300, you'll offset the membership cost of even the stiffest half-price programs in just one night. (And, of course, your membership fee entitles you to discounts at participating U.S. hotels, too.)

How they operate. Half-price hotel programs work the same overseas as at home. When you sign up, you get a directory of participating hotels and an ID card. About a month or two before you want accommodations, you call or fax hotels directly, mention your specific program, and ask for a room at the half-price rate. The hotel will (supposedly) provide one if it doesn't expect to be more than 80 percent full.

FINDING A DEAL IN EUROPE

Affordable accommodations in Europe? Yes, it's possible. Although lodging costs in the major cities can be notoriously high, travelers can find some bargains with a little advance

French-Accented Accommodations
Cheap lodgings? Mais oui!

Rural France. The French countryside is full of small inns where you can often find accommodations in the same price range offered by sub-budget chains. However, very few of these inns are listed in guidebooks published in the U.S. The easiest way to find them, almost anywhere in France, is to study the current edition of the Red Michelin Guide:

Cottages. In addition, many city tourist offices maintain lists of gîtes (cottages) available for rent in the nearby countryside. Although rentals are usually by the week, you can sometimes negotiate a deal for a shorter stay.

In the cities. Hotel booking offices, run by the local community or its tourist office, are located in most French cities (as well as in cities throughout the rest of Europe), usually in or near the main rail station. Stop to check room availability and make a reservation for one of the many inexpensive hotels using this system.

Hotels. Those listed with the guide's "quite comfortable" or "modest comfort" symbols (small cottage icons) often have rates as low as the sub-budgets.

Restaurants. Countryside restaurants that are noted as "avec chambres" can sometimes offer better room deals, although the main business of these establishments is food service.

planning. You simply need to consult the right resources and, if true savings are important to you, alter your definition of an acceptable room. In general, affordable rooms are smaller, with fewer of the amenities, such as mini bar, room service, and hair dryers, that American travelers have come to expect from even mid-priced U.S. hotels. You can sort through your options via several channels.

The Internet. The web is a virtual treasure trove of travel bargains. Lodging options are particularly diverse online, ranging from sites operated by international and country-specific hotel chains to those run by country or city tourist boards to the individual sites of small pensions, bed-and-breakfasts, and inns. You'll also find information on hostels—by far the cheapest places to stay. (See Part Three)

Wholesalers and tour companies. Both types of travel providers buy up discounted blocks of hotel rooms in anticipation of filling them. Wholesalers, who advertise in Sunday newspaper travel sections, frequently work with both travel agents and independent travelers to book these rooms. Discounts typically range from 20 to 40 percent. Tour companies expect to fill the rooms with travelers buying complete packages, but if they have excess capacity, they may sell you just the lodging at a full or partial discount.

A travel agent. Travel agencies often negotiate special deals directly with hotel chains or wholesalers. If your agency has nothing especially appealing, check around with some others. Depending on your travel dates and length of stay, someone may be able to turn up preferred rates (deeply discounted corporate rates) on select properties.

Promotions. The leading international hotel and resort chains will often offer weekend, holiday, and off-season sales, so you can stay at top properties for sometimes 50 percent off.

Senior discounts. As in the U.S., hotels in Europe may offer discounts to over-50 travelers. Ask before you book.

HOTELS

Think small. Europe is full of small inns, many of which are family run, providing excellent value and a different type of travel experience. There's more information on these lodgings later in this chapter.

FINDING A DEAL IN ASIA

Locating lodgings in Asian cities can be tougher than finding rooms in Europe for obvious reasons: Language and time zone barriers are more extreme, and currency conversions can be trickier. Several travel tools can assist you.

Half-price programs. Can you go the half-price route? Perhaps. But although the Asian offerings of half-price programs have greatly improved in recent years, they still remain pretty thin for some areas.

Wholesalers. Depending on your destination, you might instead want to try a wholesale agency, basically a tour operator that guarantees suppliers a certain volume of bookings in exchange for price cuts.

When arranging your room, tell the agency where you're going, when, and indicate any preference for location or specific facilities. If you already have one or two favorite hotels, ask what deals the agency might have there. Otherwise, determine what's available in your price range.

You reserve in advance and prepay by check. The wholesale agency sends you a voucher that you present on arrival. (In some cases, the vouchers are sent directly to the hotel.) Cancel well before departure and you get a full refund, less a modest fee; cancel closer to departure and you forfeit the cost of one night's lodging. If you prefer to have a travel agent make the arrangements, some wholesaler listings are commissionable.

Be forewarned. As with any prepaid lodging, once you get past the cancellation deadline, you're locked into the deal. Book through a wholesale agency only if your travel plans are firm and you know the hotel where you'll be staying.

SMALL INNS AND BUDGET MOTELS

Two types of money-saving accommodations are plentiful overseas—and they could not differ more from one another.

Small inns. These individually run establishments—variously referred to as inns, guest houses, pensions, or bed-and-breakfasts —can provide a comfortable stay for budget travelers. You typically stay in an interesting, even historically important, building or home. Breakfast, eaten communally with other guests, is included. Rooms may be small but are usually nicely decorated and quite clean.

But there are minuses. Not all rooms have a private bathroom. To get the cheapest prices, you may have to share a bathroom with several other guests. You will also forsake hotel services, and rooms are not likely to be air-conditioned.

Remember that some small inns are more exclusive than others; prices at these well-appointed establishments can rival those of First Class hotels.

Tight Squeeze
Assessing quaint accommodations

Small, atmospheric inns and pensions in Europe and other parts of the world can be challenging for travelers with some physical limitations. Charming and picturesque could also mean:

• Steep steps or an incline leading to the front door.

• Steep staircases (sometimes spiral) leading to upper-floor rooms. Such stairs are especially difficult to negotiate when you carry your own luggage.

• Extremely small in-room bathrooms (the larger facilities are usually shared).

• Tubs rather than showers. And the tubs often have very high sides, making getting in and out somewhat perilous.

When you book a small inn or pension, ask whether room access involves steep or narrow stairways. And get a clear description of the bathroom, including tub or shower.

HOTELS

179

Budget motels. Will you take efficiency over charm? Then budget motels, especially in Europe, are a great bargain.

For example, the U.K. has the Granada Inns chain, located next to Granada gas stations and restaurants along the motorways. Even cheaper are the Little Chef Lodges, affiliated with a U.K. fast-food chain.

You'll find the most budget-motel chains in France, in several classifications: sub-budget and another category a notch or two above. There's no real U.S. counterpart to the French subbudget hotel. At somewhere near 100 square feet, the rooms are less than half the size of those you find at even bottom-end U.S. chains, and all lack air conditioning. They're furnished with one standard double bed (with, perhaps, an overhead bunk or a foldout minisingle as well). Bathrooms are tiny, with a shower down the hall. Check-in counters may be open for only a few hours in the morning and again in the evening. (At other times, guests can check themselves in automatically with a credit card.) But rooms are clean and serviceable.

In France, you must go upmarket two levels to find an establishment resembling a U.S. budget motel. Chains such as Climat de France and Campanile approximate what you'd find at Motel 6. Even so, the rooms are smaller than those found in the U.S. chains—and cost more. The bath is similar to U.S. models, but air conditioning is relatively rare.

YOUR OTHER OPTIONS

Even dedicated discount shoppers are sometimes forced to reserve a room at rack rate. In those cases, you can still save yourself some money by comparing rates among different hotels in the same location. There are generally three ways to determine room availability and cost in overseas hotels with no U.S. reservation numbers.

Reserve by computer. Many hotels abroad are listed in the computer-reservation systems used by travel agents. Rooms at these hotels can be booked in the same manner as a domestic hotel. For most agencies, the commission on a hotel booking for a few nights would never cover the costs of extensive comparison shopping. But once you've identified your preferred properties, a travel agent will probably agree to check the prices in a reservation computer—especially if you then book the accommodations through that agent.

Contact the hotel directly. International phone calls can be expensive and cumbersome—especially with time zone and language barriers—but they may be your best bet. Although fax messages are convenient, they may be ignored by personnel at larger hotels when received from an unknown individual traveler. When you call, have specific dates and requirements ready to minimize costly phone charges.

Check hotel reps. Many overseas hotels are represented in the U.S. by one or more hotel agents, independent booking services that will sell you a room at specific properties. Unfortunately, a representative is actually the least attractive option because you often are charged more than rack rate. But when the convenience is worth the extra cost, go ahead. Many reps list their rates in travel industry computer reservation systems and will also book overseas hotels through those systems. (A hotel is often listed more than once in a reservation system at different rates—in the hotel's own listing and through one or more representatives.)

Reps can usually issue immediate space and rate confirmations by phone. Most require a deposit (the cost of one to three nights) or a credit-card number to confirm reservations; others ask for full prepayment. Also, some charge extra for last-minute reservations (booking one day ahead, say). Most impose cancellation limits—usually one night's charge for a no-show, but sometimes up to a three-night penalty. The resort-accommodations cancellation policy may be more stringent during the high season.

HOTELS

Payment procedures also vary. Some reps accept payment directly, either for one to three nights as a deposit or for the entire stay. In most cases, cash or credit cards are the currency, although a few reps accept personal checks. The advantage of paying a rep is that in case you cancel, your deposit is refundable from a U.S. organization. Also, a few reps accept the U.S. dollar payment at the booking-time exchange rate, then honor that rate regardless of any subsequent currency fluctuations.

Other hotel reps obtain credit-card guarantee information and forward it to the hotel. Your rate is computed and paid in foreign currency at the time you check out; any refunds due must come from the hotel.

CHAPTER 23

Villas, Condos, Home Swaps

If you plan to stay in one place for a week, a month, or perhaps even longer, a vacation rental can deliver more space for less money.

For extended stays (or even for shorter ones) a vacation rental can be an economical and relaxing alternative to a standard hotel room. Vacation units range from rustic one-room cottages to estates that can accommodate a dozen or more people. Some are used exclusively as vacation rentals; others are owner-occupied and rented or exchanged only occasionally.

Rentals are listed with agencies, on web sites, and in travel ads. You may book through an agent or from the owner. Although some web sites merely augment standard rental catalogs available from agencies, others let you "view" properties and even arrange rentals or home swaps directly with owners.

RENTAL PLUSES
If you're in the mood for a relaxing vacation, a house or condo setting has some advantages.

Less money. You can often save a bundle. For example, many one-bedroom rentals include two double beds in the bedroom and a convertible sofa in the living area. That one rental could accommodate six people—a group that would require two or three hotel rooms—for a lower cost. Such an arrangement is ideal for ski or other destination-oriented trips where you'll be out most of the day.

More space. A house or larger condo rental provides a lot of extra space at about the same cost per person as a hotel—with completely separate living and sleeping quarters.

Lower living costs. A rental with a kitchen helps you cut food expenditures, always a plus for families or anyone on a budget. These properties often have a washer and dryer too.

Added convenience. Rentals frequently include access to private yards, pools, and other recreational facilities. In resort areas, they may be handier to beaches or ski slopes than hotels, and will usually have free on-site parking. You can also live as casually as you do at home and dress as you like.

Local color. When you rent, you can live like a local—shopping for food and other necessities and just exploring. In an overseas unit, with no English-speaking person behind the reception desk to make arrangements, you'll be able to hone your language skills as you cope with village or city life.

RENTAL MINUSES

Vacation rentals can have a downside, too, which can prove both disappointing and expensive.

Minimum service. For some travelers, a resort hotel's cushy amenities—daily maid service, fresh towels, on-site restaurants, room service—are what make a vacation enjoyable. Even if your rental provides access to some of those services, you usually pay extra. More than you'd think have no TV or, if they do, they don't have cable. Many rentals aren't air conditioned, even in warmer climates.

Housework. Spending your time cooking, making beds, doing laundry, and cleaning isn't everyone's idea of a vacation.

Uncertainty. You can't always be sure of what you're getting for your money. The only protection is whatever screening the rental agency may have done.

Inflexibility. You typically have to reserve and prepay the full price far in advance—rather than the single-night deposit required by a hotel. If the property is unsatisfactory, you can't spend just one night, check out, and move elsewhere.

Still, there are ways around most problems. If you want housekeeping services, on-site restaurants, or another amenity, look for a rental that provides these as part of a package or an option. To avoid getting stuck with a lemon, check on the property conditions with someone who has rented there before. And look for a large complex catering to short-term renters, with an on-site manager.

RENTAL MECCAS

Most of the action in the vacation-rental market centers around a few popular areas.

Resorts. U.S. vacation rentals seem to be concentrated in Florida, especially near Walt Disney World, in California, Colorado, Utah, and New England ski areas; and in Hawaii. You'll also find quite a few along the East Coast, near beach and golf centers.

Beaches. Outside the U.S., rentals concentrate in most highly developed, warm-water beach areas, especially in the Caribbean, Mexico, and along the coasts of Spain.

Big cities. Rental apartments are becoming increasingly popular as hotel alternatives in the world's major tourist cities, like London, New York, Paris, and San Francisco.

Rural Europe. The largest numbers are in France (particularly in Provence and the Dordogne), Italy (especially in Tuscany, Umbria, and the Northern lake region), and in England.

HOTELS

TIPS FOR HASSLE-FREE RENTING

Considering a vacation rental? These suggestions can make your stay less expensive and more fun.

Consider the season. Just like resort-hotel rates, vacation-rental costs go up and down seasonally. ("Travel seasons," in Chapter 5, gives a basic picture of peak- and off-season times around the world.)

Time your stay. Many vacation rentals require a week's stay minimum. You may also have to rent on a fixed weekly schedule—usually Saturday to Saturday—and perhaps bend your itinerary. However, during low season, rental properties may be glad to have your business on your terms. Also consider extending your stay. Some accommodations offer reduced rates for long-term rentals (a month or more) or for large groups.

Book ahead. A vacation-rental booking usually requires a long lead time—as much as six months in advance for popular destinations at peak season. If space is still available, most agencies will work with shorter notice, but you may have to pay extra for phone calls or delivery of paperwork.

Negotiate. Feel free to haggle: List prices often aren't firm. Many vacation-rental brokers demand an up-front payment (as much as $50) as a "registration" fee or as a charge for brochures. You'll want to apply that fee to the rental cost.

Be prepared to pay. Beyond having to prepay the full rent in advance, even on fairly long rentals, you may also have to prepay for bedding or maid service. The agent may also ask for an additional cleaning or security deposit. Be aware that many brokers don't accept credit cards; you may have to write a check. Cancellation penalties can be stiff, especially if you cancel close to the occupancy date. Consider trip-cancellation insurance for any vacation rental (see Chapter 34).

Get move-in and property information. You may have to make an appointment with the property manager, local agent, or neighbor to obtain the keys, turn on the utilities, and arrange phone service. Note that rentals are not necessarily equipped with linens—find out when you rent.

Or wait until you get there. In an unfamiliar destination—but not during peak season—you may want to wait until after you arrive to arrange a vacation rental. Stay in a hotel for the first day or two, giving yourself enough time to scout out the rental options; then make a deal through a local realtor or the manager of a large rental complex.

Evaluate your options. For a last-minute choice or shorter-

The Reality of Rentals
Quirky homes away from home

CONSUMER REPORTS TRAVEL LETTER staffers have sampled a variety of rentals around the globe—from Cape Cod to Florida to Scotland to Waikiki—and learned from experience.

Assembly-line condos such as you'll find in Hawaii present few surprises or challenges. You get more space than in a hotel, but fewer services. Housekeeping is available if you want it.

One-of-a-kind cottages or private apartments, on the other hand, can be quirky. At their best, they're superior to any but the most elaborate hotel suites for privacy, peace, and living space. At their worst, they're weird—a Paris apartment, for example, where most of the beds were on "mezzanines" reached by climbing steep, spindly ladders.

Be prepared to cope like a homeowner if something does go wrong. Someone in your group should be handy with basic tools. And never head out to a rental without at least a screwdriver and pliers. Also, you may have to figure out how to use appliances whose manuals have long since disappeared.

Bring your own utensils. In all of our vacation rentals, we've yet to find a sharp kitchen knife or a frying pan with a flat bottom.

You'll probably need a car. But remember that renting one can be very expensive in France or Italy.

Rural rentals often have no phones. If a communications cutoff is a problem, take a cellular phone or rent one for the duration of the trip.

HOTELS

term stay, an apartment-style or all-suite hotel can provide many of the same advantages as a rental.

RENTAL AGENCIES

It's highly likely that you'll arrange your rental through one of the two main agency types specializing in vacation real estate:

Wholesale booking agencies. Such agencies focus primarily on developing extensive rental listings. Some large wholesalers publish elaborate, full-color brochures. Typically, wholesalers provide commissions to retail travel agencies that book their rentals, and some also act as retail bookers.

Retail booking agencies. These agencies will sometimes arrange airline tickets and rental cars. Some retailers develop a portion of their listings; others simply sell from a wholesale catalog. For European rentals, quite a few U.S. retail booking agencies use wholesalers based in Europe.

Any good rental broker should be able to provide professional advice about destination areas and individual rentals.

OTHER OPTIONS

Check other rental sources as well.

Travel clubs. They may offer vacation rentals exclusively or as part of their larger mix of accommodations.

Half-price hotel programs. Some of these programs may claim to offer "discounts" on vacation rentals. But since many rental properties have no official published rate, you can't really tell whether a quoted rate is discounted or not. Both travel clubs and half-price programs charge annual membership dues or charge for directories.

Tour operators. A number of companies sell package tours that include vacation-rental accommodations.

Realtors. In popular vacation areas, realtors often handle local rentals as a sideline.

The web. More and more vacation-rental agencies are listing properties on web sites. And some owners offer individual rentals on their own web sites. You can track down both by searching for a specific area plus the word "rental."

DO-IT-YOURSELF RENTALS

You can also make your own arrangements, which can save money, since rentals typically involve several markups: The owner, wholesaler, and retailer all get cuts. Rental information is available through a range of sources.

Classified ads. Newspapers and magazines run ads for apartments, cottages, and houses in all price ranges. English weekend newspapers, found at newsstands stocking foreign publications, typically contain classified ads for a wide variety of vacation rentals—extensive listings for the United Kingdom

Should You Swap Homes?
Ensuring a safe home exchange

Switching houses with another family is an option some vacationers find appealing budgetwise: You essentially get cost-free lodging. But a home-swap is not without its risks, mainly of damage to your property.

The organizations that list houses for exchange—International Home Exchange *(www.homeexchange.com)* is one of the largest—will bear no responsibility for the behavior of temporary tenants. You do your own screening and take your own precautions. Follow these prudent steps.

You may prefer to exchange only with families you already know or with those who belong to a group promising a close match in interests.

Be sure your homeowner's insurance covers you for any damage a house-exchange visitor might do, as well as for liability if a visitor is injured while staying in your house.

Securely store anything you don't want a visitor to use. At a minimum, that means a securely locked closet or storeroom. But it's safer to cart your things to a separate storage facility.

Word your exchange contract so tenants must pay the replacement value of anything damaged or missing.

HOTELS

BUYER, BE WARY

Be wary of telephone or mail solicitations telling you "you've won a vacation." Law enforcement agencies are cracking down on unscrupulous brokers promising "free" vacations in return for listening to time-share pitches. People can end up paying more for their "free" trips than if they'd used a travel agency.

and France, and scattered listings for many other countries.

Tourist offices. In some locations, tourist offices maintain lists of nearby vacation rentals. You can write ahead for those lists or get them when you arrive. In Europe, it's possible to find on-the-spot countryside vacation rentals available at very low prices (except during July and August).

CRACKING THE CODE

No matter how you rent, a primary source of information about individual properties is likely to be a brochure. Whether it's a simple photocopied tear sheet or an elaborate, full-color catalog, the brochure normally lists, at minimum, the location, number of rooms, and number and type of beds, and describes kitchen facilities. Many also include photographs, drawings, or floor plans.

But many brochures overaccentuate the positive. Look more closely to separate truth and exaggeration.

Photos. Compare the descriptions to the photos, and scrutinize both closely to get the hard facts. Clever wording can disguise a shack as a quaint cabin, and a wide-angle lens can make a broom closet look like a ballroom.

Sleeping specifics. The specified number of people a rental "sleeps" is often more appropriate to an army barracks than a comfortable vacation property. Unless you're willing to stack your travel party like cordwood, judge your space needs by the number of rooms and types of beds—not the number of people the brochure says you can shoehorn into the place.

Never assume. Don't expect anything that isn't specifically promised, especially in Europe. If a brochure doesn't actually say "shower," you're apt to have nothing more than a tub.

THE TIME-SHARE TRAP

Many of those "free-trip" come-ons you get in the mail (or by phone, fax, and even e-mail) are from time-share promoters willing to foot the bill for your weekend just for the chance at a hard sell. Here's the pitch: For a modest price, you can "own" a luxury condo in some fabulous beach or ski area for a week every year (or even every other year). You may even be able to trade your time-share for a week in some other equally fabulous area, even overseas.

But watch out. Time-share ownership may become a trap.

How do time-shares work? Time-shares carry the concept of a condo one step further. In a condo, a building is carved up into individually owned units; in a time-share, the ownership of those units is then subdivided into weekly time slots. As with a condo, you pay the purchase price. Then you add a pro-rated share of the maintenance costs of the individual apartment and the building grounds.

However, time-shares are not all alike. With some, you buy a specified week each year; others allot a floating time slot. You may get an actual deed to a specific occupancy right. Or you may simply join a "vacation club" that promises to have space available every year.

Why they're often a headache. With your time-share, you usually get a chance to join (and pay a fee to) one of two big international time-share exchange networks: RCI or Interval International. Through either organization, you can trade time with other exchange members throughout the world—your week in a ski area, say, for a week in the Caribbean or Europe. The deal may sound okay, but there are definite drawbacks.

High cost. Owning a week in your own vacation condo may not be any cheaper than simply renting. With maintenance and cleaning fees, membership in RCI or Interval International, and other charges, your week can easily cost $500 to $600.

Tough resale. Worse, it's almost impossible to sell. When

HOTELS

you try, you're apt to be competing with the developer, who is often selling units in your program. Owners who try to walk away lose their investment—while maintenance fees continue to mount. And a foreclosure may put a blot on an owner's credit record.

Difficult timing. As an owner, you're in another kind of competition with the developer: When you try to claim a floating time slot, you may find that the developer aims to rent the most desirable weeks to nonowners instead. Some developers actually oversell a time-share, figuring that a certain percentage of owners won't find a suitable time to visit.

No renting. Try to rent out your time slot on your own and the developer may again block you—with obstacles as broad as a flat ban on rentals by individual owners or as small as refusing to have someone to give keys to your tenant.

Are you still interested? Despite these problems, the time-share concept may still appeal to you. If so, buy a resale unit from an individual owner. There are more sellers than buyers, so you should be able to drive a hard bargain. In some cases, you might even be able to assume ownership merely by taking on the current owner's long-term maintenance obligation.

To find a motivated private seller, check the ads in newsletters and local papers in resort areas. You might also nose around some of the more attractive time-share complexes: Talk to current owners and check bulletin boards. A few real estate brokers also specialize in time-shares. Triwest time-share brokerage in Los Angeles runs periodic time-share auctions (*www.triwest-timeshare.com*, 800 423-6377).

PART SEVEN

Traveling by Car

CHAPTER 24

Renting and Driving in the U.S.

You want to get the best rental car deal—and then drive off in the right direction. Comparison shopping gets you the deal; new high-tech tools guide your route.

Rental prices vary from one rental company to another and from place to place. And add-ons can add plenty. But a knowledge of rates (and rental company tactics) helps keep costs down.

Whether you rent or drive your own car, new computer programs and web sites will not only provide you with maps but also plot a route, determine drive times, and list suggestions for hotels, restaurants, and sights along the way. High-tech devices that you plug into a laptop computer (or that are built into the dashboard of some luxury sedans and rental cars) then link you to global positioning satellites (GPS) to navigate your route. (For map program details and GPS device Ratings, see the end of this chapter.)

SMART RENTAL SHOPPING
Ask for what's advertised. Rental-car company promotional ads regularly appear in the Sunday newspaper travel sections and

in monthly travel magazines, most trumpeting deals on rentals for the coming months or specials limited to certain states or regions.

But if you call the company to reserve a car for the dates and locations specified, will you be quoted the advertised rates? Probably not. Without mentioning the ads or asking for discounts, you may find that only a handful of agents volunteer them. The rest will need quizzing, sometimes nudging, to offer the advertised rates. Many may hold fast to the originally quoted price, even when pressed to check further.

To ensure the best deal—typically the one that's been advertised—remember the following tactics: Compare advertised rates and hold onto the ads until you make calls. When you speak to a reservation agent, quote directly from the ad, referring to the promotion's discount code—usually found in small print below the boldly displayed rate or in the description of the terms and conditions of the rental.

Use coupons (but read the fine print). Members of airline frequent-flier programs or subscribers to discount travel or dining programs may find rental-car discount coupons included in the offerings. Coupons typically offer a percentage or dollar amount off weekly rentals or a free weekend day. However, scan the small print carefully and you'll encounter a variety of stipulations—such as the class of car (usually mid-size or above) or specific rental locations. The free-weekend-day rates almost always require a three-day rental—the third day is the freebie. Even if you meet the coupon's requirements, you often can find better deals in advertised rates or simply by paying the regular rate for a smaller car.

Surf the web. The Internet offers the most comprehensive comparison shopping for rental cars. The travel supersites—Expedia and Travelocity—each offer rental-car features that search and compare rates for most travel destinations. In addition, all the major rental companies are online with their own

CARS & TRAINS

195

sites. In the past, most have offered online bookers a discount—typically 20 percent.

WEEKLY AND WEEKEND RATES

These offer excellent savings over daily rates.

Weekly rates. Rental-car companies consider a "weekly" rental anything from five to seven days. So that $109 weekly rate advertised for a compact car is a very good deal for five days ($21.80 a day) and an excellent deal for seven days ($15.57 per day). By comparison, a four-day rental at a compact-car rate of $33 per day would total $132.

Remember the five-day "weekly" rule—but also remember to return the car on time (usually a week to the exact hour or anytime before). Otherwise, you may get stuck with a surcharge—extra hours, even a full day.

Weekend rates. If your schedule permits renting a car over a weekend, you can often snag a bargain rate. Companies also offer the "Saturday night keep," a low price that depends on your using the car over a Saturday night.

Weekend rates are usually in effect from noon Thursday through noon the following Monday, and often include unlimited mileage. But you must shop carefully. Even on a simple weekend rental, you face a crazy patchwork of options. The lowest costs vary considerably in different cities—and even among companies in the same city. Prices are based on a uniform daily rate, usually with a two- or three-day minimum. Or you may see flat rates pegged to the length of the rental—generally, the longer the rental, the lower the daily toll. Some locations don't offer weekend rates. Also watch for additional costs:

• Extra-driver charges are often high enough to make a difference in your weekend rental bill.

• In some locations, renting a car at an airport and returning it downtown (or vice versa) runs far more than the advertised weekend price.

• With some companies, missing the return deadline makes the entire weekend rental revert to the more expensive weekday rate. If you think you may keep the car beyond the usual weekend period, ask about extra-day pricing when you make the reservation, and try to rent from a company that doesn't cancel the weekend rate if you miss the return deadline. When you can't find such a deal, return the car by the deadline and re-rent it for the extra day or two at weekday rates.

AIRPORT RENTALS MAY COST MORE

Picking up a rental car at a major airport upon arrival rarely offers the best deal. (Renting downtown is often cheaper.) And these days, airport rentals usually don't offer much extra convenience anyway. Most on-airport rental companies now have only a counter inside the terminal. To get your car, you must board a van or bus and ride to some outlying location.

But you might consider renting from an airport-area hotel, where one or more large rental companies may have a desk—and better rates, although you'll need to check first. Simply take the hotel's courtesy van from the baggage claim area. (You may have to call for one.) If you plan to arrive late at night, you can book a room in the hotel and get your car the following morning—saving a day's rental and the stress of dealing with a strange car in a strange city after a long plane trip.

Rental companies also often have downtown rental locations in major cities. When reserving, ask the agent if there's a different rate for rentals from airport and downtown locations. If the difference is major, it might be worth the inconvenience to get to the downtown location—via public transport or a shuttle from a nearby hotel.

LOOK FOR DISCOUNTS

Some rental-car companies extend discounts to seniors—typically 5 to 10 percent off and often tied into membership in a

CARS & TRAINS

senior organization such as the American Association of Retired Persons (AARP). But discounts usually don't apply to certain sale rates and are not available in all locations, so seniors will generally get a cheaper rate by comparison shopping short-term promotions.

Members of the Automobile Association of America (AAA) are entitled to discounts of 5 to 20 percent (dependent on vehicle class) off standard rates at Hertz. Again, shopping around for short-term promotional rates may offer more savings.

AVOID HIDDEN EXTRAS

Rental-car companies typically promote low basic rates—then heap extra charges on top of them. So when you get to the rental counter, you face a hard-sell combo of extras, threats, and fine print. The National Association of Attorneys General estimates that surcharges, taxes, and fees can increase the cost of your rental by as much as 75 percent—which can wipe out any savings earned from hours of searching for low hotel rates and airfares. Beware of these ploys.

Additional drivers. Rental companies may add $3 to $15 a day or a flat $20 or $25 per rental for each additional driver in your travel party. Most allow a spouse to drive at no extra cost, but some may not.

Don't try to save money by not listing additional drivers. If there's an accident when another person is driving, the company could claim you violated your contract and thus withhold any insurance or service benefits. If you plan to share driving chores, shop around for a company that provides a competitive rate without that extra-driver gouge.

Young drivers. Most rental companies won't rent to drivers younger than age 21. And some will not rent to anyone younger than 25. Those with the younger cutoff usually require an additional charge for drivers aged 21 to 24.

Upgrade switches. Those low rates you see in newspaper ads usually apply to a subcompact car. At the rental desk, you may be pressured to upgrade to a vehicle that's larger, more powerful, or more comfortable. Some agents will try scare tactics to convince you that local driving conditions make the subcompact (many of which have manual rather then automatic transmissions, especially outside the U.S.) inadequate for the job. That switch can balloon your bill, so decide exactly what kind of car you want before you reserve.

Collision insurance. Beware of the collision-damage waiver or loss-damage waiver (CDW/LDW)—the quasi-insurance that nets car-rental companies fat daily fees of $7 to $15 or more for waiving their right to hold you liable if the rental car is damaged or stolen.

Do you need it? Probably not, since you'll likely be able to cover your risk of damage or theft with a combination of your regular auto insurance policy plus coverage from the credit card to which you charge your rental. For the overall picture, see "Collision-Damage Waiver" in this chapter.

Fees and taxes. Yes, even airport projects and local taxes can boost your rental-car bill. In fact, the AAA predicted early in 1998 that travelers would pay 5 percent more in 1999 to cover rental-car firms' rising insurance costs and airport operating fees.

Airport surcharges. Some companies will charge what they term a "concession recoup fee" to cover the additional cost of operating an office at an airport. The fees vary from city to city. Agents are generally required to disclose such fees at the time of booking, including any charges specific to a certain rental location.

Frequent-flier-miles tax. In response to a government-imposed tax on the purchase price of frequent-flier miles that rental car companies buy from airlines, Hertz and Avis have both been charging a nominal "tax" to renters who earn frequent-flier miles with their car rental. It doesn't amount to much—only about 40 to 50 cents on a $200 weekly rental—but the charge can be annoying to consumers.

CARS &
TRAINS

Construction costs. In certain cities, you'll pay a flat fee to fund either airport or urban construction projects. In Boston, renters in 1999 paid $10 on top of nearly 20 percent in local taxes and fees to finance a new convention center.

Drop-off charges. In rental-car lingo, "rent it here, return it there" refers to pickup and drop-off in different cities and may be limited to certain models, seasons, and dates. Some companies allow you to pick up a car from one office and return it at another within the same metropolitan area for no extra charge. Many travelers use that provision to rent a car downtown and drop it off at the airport. However, local one-way drop-off policies vary by rental company and location, so be sure to ask before you reserve.

Drop-off charges on one-way rentals between two cities are

Rental Checklist
Inspect before you drive away

Most rental cars are relatively new—in fact, some are brand new. (A quick glance at the odometer indicates how long the car's been on the road.) However, an older or ill-maintained rental car exposes you to potential hazards that are both physical and financial.

And when you sign a rental-car agreement, you may be agreeing that the car is in good condition—and that agreement may limit your recourse if you spot a defect later. So take a close look.

• Check the tires (including the spare) for bulges, cuts, and excessive wear. Be sure there's a jack.

• Walk completely around the car (some rental companies now require this). Have any obvious body or mechanical damage noted on the contract, so you won't be charged for it later.

• Test the windshield wipers, seat belts, seat adjustments, and all lights, including the brake lights.

• Make sure there's an owner's manual (usually in the glove compartment). If not, have the agent demonstrate the use of important controls and convenience features, from locks to cruise control.

more common. All the major rental companies reserve the right to charge a fee of some sort when you rent in one city and return in another. Franchised offices are often especially reluctant to feature attractive one-way rates. (Second-tier companies have a greater proportion of franchised locations than the Big Four—Avis, Budget, Hertz, and National.) You may find a low one-way rate at a franchise location if you're traveling between two cities with a pattern of heavy one-way rentals (or if the franchise operates in both cities).

If you are interested in a one-way rental, ask the reservations agent about drop-off fees or charges for additional mileage, as well as specific locations where one-way rentals are available.

Fuel charges. A number of companies rent cars with a "full" gas tank. They then require that cars be returned full—or charge a premium price to refill the tank upon the car's return. (Always note at the time you rent if the tank is indeed full. If not, alert an agent.)

When you rent, you'll be asked which option you prefer: To fill the tank yourself before returning the car or to prepay at a per-gallon rate set by the company and be allowed to bring the car back empty. Filling the tank yourself is usually the most economical option. Very rarely are you able to return the car near or at empty, so since the advance-pay option covers a full tank, you may pay for gas you don't need.

PITFALLS AND POTHOLES

In addition to the assorted hidden fees and charges that raise costs at the rental counter, a variety of restrictions can add an "annoyance tariff."

Documentation. If you plan to rent a car at an airport but aren't arriving or departing on a flight, make sure the quoted rate doesn't require you to show a ticket.

Geographic limits. Some companies that offer cheap rentals impose limits on where you can drive. For example, if you rent

CARS &
TRAINS

in California, the company may prohibit you from driving into any other state (except for short side trips to Las Vegas or Reno). And don't assume that the rental company will never know whether you drive outside the permitted areas. Run into trouble (a breakdown or accident) and it will be obvious you've violated the contract. When arranging your rental, tell the agent where you plan to drive, then make sure the quoted rate covers your itinerary.

Mileage limits. Currently, the industry has adopted unlimited mileage as a standard for noncorporate rentals. But it may not always be your best deal. If you use a rental car mainly for local trips in your destination area—visiting relatives or nearby attactions—a low daily or weekly rate with 100 or 150 free miles a day may save. When planning any trip, estimate how far you plan to drive and compare alternative deals.

Redlining. You many also run into redlining—the marking of certain areas where *residents* who rent cars locally must pay higher rates or pass extra screening. If renting near your home, ask about surcharges when you reserve.

Record checks. Rental-car companies in certain states are increasingly checking driving records before renting. You probably won't know it's happening—the process takes just a few seconds. But if the check turns up a record the company deems risky, the agent can refuse to rent you a car.

So be sure you know what's on your driving record. If you have a clean record, rent from whichever company offers the best deal. Ditto if you have only a few problems or live in a state that doesn't disclose driving records. But those with problem records who live in states that permit screening may have to rent from a company that doesn't check records. You can ask for company policies when you call around for comparison rates.

Don't know the status of your driving record? Check with your local motor vehicle department. To see exactly what car-rental companies' computers will display, you can contact

TML Information Services, one of the companies operating online data services (800 388-9099). For $9.95 plus tax ($7.95 plus tax for AAA members—with a membership number) TML will screen your driving records against the criteria used by the rental companies and fax or mail you the resulting report. (The service is available for about 35 states, but is prohibited for California or Pennsylvania drivers.)

COLLISION-DAMAGE WAIVER

When confronted by sales pressure at the car rental counter, remember that the Collision-Damage Waiver/Loss-Damage Waiver (CDW/LDW) is optional. For most people it's added protection—at a high added cost. By signing the CDW/LDW, you pass responsibility for all damage to the car back to the rental company. And you accept the stiff fees the rental company charges for the privilege. (*Note:* Both New York and Illinois have outlawed the sale of the CDW/LDW and have capped the amount of damage for which you can be held liable. Other states, including California and Nevada, have capped the price of the CDW/LDW.)

Before deciding whether to pay $7 to perhaps more than $20 a day for CDW/LDW, consider these factors.

Your personal auto insurance may cover you. Most renters can take care of their risk of damage or loss without the CDW/LDW. Those risks are often included in your regular auto policy for most rentals in the U.S. However, a few big auto insurers have backed away from providing complete, automatic coverage for rental cars as part of personal policies.

Your personal insurance may not extend to business travel or international rentals, so be sure to check your policy.

Credit-card insurance varies. Many credit cards provide CDW/LDW coverage. However, most—though not all—offer only *secondary coverage*. So you must submit a claim to your own insurance carrier first.

CARS & TRAINS

Sales pressure can be intense. Some rental agencies instruct their agents to aggressively push the CDW/LDW. First, it's immensely profitable. Second, the company can headline low-ball prices and still profit from the markup on insurance. Articles in the trade press indicate some rental offices and employees are rated, in part, on their success in selling CDW/LDW. Thus some agents will use scare tactics:

• "Our company doesn't have an arrangement with your credit-card issuer." This is irrelevant—the card issuer's deal is with you.

• "Without the CDW/LDW, you won't be allowed to leave the state until an accident claim is settled." Not true. A car-rental company cannot restrict your freedom of movement because you (or your insurance company) owe money for repairs.

Look for loopholes. Even if you buy CDW/LDW, the fine print may still slant the contract in the rental company's favor. So read it carefully.

Be sure you have liability coverage. Liability insurance covers damage someone in a rented car might do to other persons or property. Neither the CDW/LDW offered by rental-car companies nor the protection offered by major credit cards covers liability.

Your own auto insurance. If you own a car, you probably carry liability insurance that would cover you while driving a rental. Should there be a claim that exceeds your own coverage, the car-rental company's policy would make up the difference, up to its limit. However, taking a primary hit on your own insurance would probably increase your rates.

Extra liability coverage. If you don't own a car and therefore don't have automobile insurance, the rental company's secondary insurance becomes de facto primary. (In California, however, you could be uninsured.) The liability insurance that satisfies most states' requirements is probably enough to cover repair of someone else's car or to fix minor damages to a building. But it's apt to be woefully inadequate in protecting your personal assets from a big personal-injury claim. You'd be wise to buy extra liability insurance, no matter where you rent.

If you frequently rent cars but don't own one (or if you often drive cars borrowed from others), you should consider a year-round, non-owner policy—several auto insurers sell them. If you rent infrequently, you can buy $1 million in additional liability coverage from most rental-car companies for about $7 or $8 a day.

MAPPING AND NAVIGATION PROGRAMS

For everyone who's ever been fed up with trying to refold a paper map, you could consider generating an electronic version. Or for up-to-the minute directions, we've provided

LOCAL MAPPING

These CD-ROM programs map streets in the United States.

Program	Helpful features
RAND MCNALLY STREETFINDER 1999/ STREETFINDER DELUXE 1999 Rand McNally, $29.95/$49.95 For Windows 95/98 (www.randmcnally.com) Street-locator programs with planning tools and detailed travel info.	Includes a database of a million businesses searchable by name, address, or location. Provides maps of 47 U.S. airports, city overview maps with attraction info, and Mobile Travel Guide.
DELORME STREET ATLAS U.S.A. DeLorme, $54.95 6.0 for Windows 95/98, 4.0 for Mac (www.delorme.com) Offers a complete U.S. street atlas (down to dirt roads) on one CD-ROM.	Will search by city name, ZIP code, area code/prefix (can search larger cities by numbered streets). Connects to online database for road/weather stats.
PRECISION MAPPING STREETS 4.0 Chicago Map Corp., $29.95 For Windows 95/98 (www.chicagomap.com) Displays street-level views of virtually every U.S. street segment, park, waterway, rail line, airport, landmark, and political boundary.	Can search by city, county, state, crossroads, street name, ZIP code, landmarks, area code/prefix, address, and latitude/ longitude coordinates. "Street hints" displays street name/block with cursor point on any segment. Image underlay feature

CARS & TRAINS

Ratings *GPS navigation tools*
& Recommendations

Recommendations

Those traveling by car can now use the same technology the military and mariners have long had at their disposal. Satellite-based global positioning system (GPS) technology is available for as little as $350 for a portable GPS receiver to more than $2,000 for installed models. It's also available as a rental-car option in some locales.

The use of GPS for road navigation is still evolving, and most people will want to wait before buying such a GPS device—if they ever do. Installed models are clearly superior to portable units. The best of the ones we tested were the Alpine NVA-751AS and the VDO Carin 522. Among the portables, we'd choose the Garmin StreetPilot ColorMap. Within type, models are listed in order of performance.

Source: Consumer Reports October 1999

Details on the models

Portable models

Typically the size of a large video remote control. Easy to move from one vehicle to another. Will place your location on a map, but won't select a route. Unless you purchase an optional antenna, the unit must be placed where it can "see" the sky.

Garmin StreetPilot ColorMap $700

Best of the tested portables, but requires programming for route guidance.
NAVIGATION: ○ Won't choose a route, though you can create one by clicking on turns with a cursor before you start driving. • Next turn shown on screen by large arrow and name of next road. • Uses preprogrammed MetroGuide cartridges, $100 to $200 each. The cartridges let you locate street addresses and zoom in on streets in their metropolitan area (we tested New York City only). *DISPLAY:* ○ 13½x1¾ in.; color much easier to read than monochrome display on other tested portables. *EASE OF USE:* ○ • Intricate routes take a long time to program—though programming can be completed before you get in the car, without satellite access. • Doesn't replot the route if you deviate. • Dashboard mount is difficult to switch from one car to another; an extra mount is $15.

Garmin GPS III Plus $350
Magellan Map 410 $350

Basic models that tell you where you are, but little about how to get where you're going. For road navigation, a map is better.
NAVIGATION: ◒. • Won't choose a route, though you can create one by clicking on turns with a cursor before you start driving. Magellan requires tedious extra steps of naming turns and selecting them a second time. • With Garmin, arrow on screen map points to next waypoint; with Magellan, you must switch to another screen for the arrow. *DISPLAY:* Garmin: ◒ Magellan: ●. • Monochrome display (Garmin, 2¼x1⅜ in.; Magellan, 1⅜x2⅝ in.), not as easy to use as color. • Major (and some minor) roads and towns shown, but Garmin doesn't show programmed route, and Magellan's road labeling is sparse. • Unless you erase them, trails left by previous trips can clutter the screen. *EASE OF USE:* Garmin: ◒ Magellan: ●. • On Magellan, GPS signal was lost more frequently than on other units. When panning with cursor, display vanishes and takes about 30 seconds to fully reappear • Garmin attaches to dashboard with Velcro strip. • Magellan must be mounted on bulky bracket, about $15 extra.

Laptop models

These have of an antenna-receiver that you put on the dashboard and connect to your laptop, and software you install in the laptop's CD-ROM drive—one disc to install the program, and one that contains map data, which you leave in the laptop. The tested models work only with PC laptops with Windows 95 or 98 (not Macs). Controls are your laptop's keyboard and touchpad/trackball, so laptop models work better if you've got a copilot; voice commands are also possible for some models.

TravRoute CoPilot 2000 $350
DeLorme Earthmate GPS Receiver
$200 including Street Atlas 6.0 map software

Navigation is fine, but using a laptop in a car is inconvenient. And all-but-essential extras—power adapter, $100; screen hood, $30—drive up the cost.
NAVIGATION: ☻ • Provides trip routing; you spell out your destination—and for DeLorme, your start point—and the software chooses a route. • TravRoute also replots the route if you deviate or ask for a new route. • Screen display and a computer-generated voice alert you to upcoming turns. • Software offers very thorough street detail. *DISPLAY:* ☻ • Large screen of typical laptop makes details easy to see, but daytime ambient light can easily wash out the screen image. *EASE OF USE:* ☹ • Very inconvenient and unsafe to look at laptop screen or use keyboard while driving solo. • Antenna-receiver powered by laptop or cigarette lighter; DeLorme also runs on four AAA batteries.

Installed models

These are similar to systems that are available with some expensive cars. Hardware includes antenna, processor, monitor, and, for some, remote control. CD-ROMs, $150 to $170 each, supply the data; you need seven to nine to cover the whole country. Some models also have voice-recognition technology. As you approach a major intersection, you'll typically get instructions even if all you're doing is continuing straight ahead—helpful in unfamiliar territory.

Alpine NVA-751AS $2,250 including TME-M006SA monitor, $500; other monitors available
VDO Carin 522 $2,300

The best performers, but very expensive. Best for people who often travel to unfamiliar places and who don't like paper maps.
NAVIGATION: ☻ • Provide trip routing; you spell out your destination or click on it with a cursor, and the software chooses a route. • Can display the road you're on at the bottom of the screen, the next road on the top; alternate screen shows large, clear arrow in direction of next turn. • Provide advance warning of turns, then another message when you're at the intersection. • Replot the route if you deviate or if you ask for a new route. • CDs for all regions could cost more than $1,000 extra. *DISPLAY:* Alpine: ☻ VDO: ☺ • Easy to see, and large enough (Alpine 4½x3¼ in.; VDO, 5x2¾ in.) to provide ample map detail. • Roads clearly drawn; interchanges shown in detail. • Alpine's contrast on maps is a bit better than VDO's. *EASE OF USE:* ☻ • Controls and remote are easy to use. • Computer voice is reasonably understandable. • Helpful instructions.

Clarion AutoPC P310C $2,100

Versatile; it's also a radio, CD player, voice-memo machine, and e-mail receiver (with additional hardware).
NAVIGATION: ☻ • Score (and price) is with optional Odyssey software; without that, navigation is very limited. • Provides trip routing; you spell out your destination, and the software chooses a route. • Provides visual and audible advice for upcoming turns, including street name, distance, and direction to turn. *DISPLAY:* ○ • Small (3⅜x⅞ in.) color screen much harder to see than larger screens of other installed models. • Map details are well drawn, but it can be hard to tell which road a label applies to. *EASE OF USE:* ☻ • Control unit replaces the vehicle's original radio in the dashboard. • Without optional CD changer, you can't use the CD player while using the GPS. • Tedious to shuttle between radio and GPS to change stations.

CONSUMER REPORTS Ratings of global positioning satellite (GPS) navigation systems.

Surfing for maps. Internet maps are yours for the clicking Freebie maps from Internet sites can be viewed, printed, e-mailed to others, or embedded in web pages. You may also be able to plot trips and create itineraries. But mapmaking online is noticeably slower than with CD-ROM programs, and a site may be down when you need it. Two places are still worth a look.

MapBlast! *(www.mapblast.com).* Locate places by address, intersection, city or state, then create overview and thumbnail maps.

MapQuest *(www.mapquest.com).* Browse and zoom to cities and towns worldwide.

CHAPTER 25

Renting Around the World

If you rent a car overseas, you'll have to consider currency conversions, and language barriers, as well as foreign road signs and rules.

———————————— ■ ————————————

Independent travelers often calculate that renting a car is the most cost-effective and convenient way to visit a foreign country. But you don't want to cut too many corners. Your rental vehicle ought to be not only priced right, but well maintained and reliable.

RULES OF THE RENTAL ROAD

Here are suggestions that can smooth your ride.

Choose a U.S. or large multinational company. At gateway airports worldwide, you'll see many of the familiar logos of multinational rental companies or their affiliates: Alamo, Avis, Budget, Dollar, Hertz, National, and Thrifty are all represented. Renting from a known company confers two big advantages.

Agents probably speak English. While there's no guarantee, it's a good bet that employees of a U.S.-based company will have at least a basic knowledge of English. If you do have difficulty understanding an employee at a rental desk, ask to talk to a supervisor. If there's still a problem, request the company's customer-service number.

You'll resolve disputes more easily when home. Should you have a billing or damage liability dispute, you (or your insurance and/or credit-card company) will probably resolve it more quickly with a U.S. company than with a foreign one.

Consider local rental companies carefully. Local rental-car company rates may be lower than those of a large multinational company, but vehicles, service, and maintenance may not measure up to what you're used to in the U.S. Guidebooks or travel agents can generally steer you toward reputable local rental companies in the city or country you plan to visit.

Book before you leave. Researching (and booking) your rental before departure can save money. Comparing costs on your own via the phone or the Internet, or through a travel agent, can uncover special promotions or upgrade deals. And reserving now guarantees you a car upon arrival, so you won't have to scramble from counter to counter, looking for both a car and a deal.

Read the contract thoroughly. Make sure the specific rate you were quoted when you reserved matches the rate on the contract you sign. Do a quick calculation (rates will be in local currency). And question any extra charges, such as taxes or fees.

Learn local driving rules. Even when driving in an English-speaking country, you'll find the rules of the road to be quite different from home. Before you get behind the wheel, familiarize yourself with the terrain.

Right or left? Your comfort level with "reverse driving" may influence your decision to rent at all. (See "Driving on the left" in this chapter.)

Speed limits. In many countries, the speed limit is higher than we're accustomed to in the U.S. In Germany, France, and Italy, for example, cars in the fast lane often zip along at over 100 mph. Maximum speed limits also vary greatly from open highways to urban areas.

Mph or kph? Depending on the country, speed limits and distances will be indicated in either miles or kilometers. Determine which it is before setting out.

Seat belts. Wearing one is compulsory in an increasing number of countries around the world.

Child-safety seats. Are they required, and for children up to what age? Some countries also prohibit young children from sitting in the front seat of vehicles.

Traffic conditions. In some foreign countries, roads are extremely congested; in others, they are notoriously dangerous—as a result of reckless drivers, poor conditions, or a combination of both. Guidebooks usually indicate if driving is even a viable option.

Weigh the language barrier. An international driver's permit allows you to rent a car in a country where you don't speak the language. Whether doing so is advisable is another matter. Many Americans safely rent cars in non-English-speaking countries in Europe, getting by with rudimentary language skills and good maps. Navigating in a country with a language based on unfamiliar characters or symbols, such as Japan, Korea, China, Russia, or most of the Middle East, can be decidedly more difficult. Again, guidebooks can tell you whether it's feasible to rent a car. (In some countries, you can "rent" both a car *and* a driver, often your best bet, although it costs more.)

THE CDW/LDW OVERSEAS

You may find it especially tough to avoid CDW/LDW when you rent from a local agency overseas. Many foreign rental companies apparently continue to rely on CDW/LDW for

CARS & TRAINS

profits; some may threaten to put a hold on your card to cover possible damage if you decline their coverage. (If you carry more than one credit card, you could charge your rental on one card and put day-to-day expenses on the other.)

Your best defense is to prearrange the rental through a U.S. office or agency. Specify when you reserve and rent that you intend to use your credit card for collision protection and won't buy the CDW/LDW. If you wait to rent until you arrive at your destination, choose a major multinational company, which should be used to dealing with Americans who rely on credit cards. And if you somehow find yourself about to be denied a car unless you buy CDW/LDW, accept the terms but note on the contract that you agreed under duress, then demand a full refund as soon as you return home.

However, double-check your card's overseas rental coverage before you depart. Credit-card companies are quietly shaving insurance benefits, especially on foreign rentals. American Express, for instance, has withdrawn CDW coverage in several countries, citing rising costs; it no longer covers rentals in Australia, Ireland, Israel, Italy, Jamaica, and New Zealand. If you are renting in one of those countries, and are not covered by either another card or your personal auto insurance, you may have no choice but the rental company's CDW/LDW.

RENTING AND DRIVING IN CANADA

Driving up north is almost like driving from your home to a nearby state. However, you must meet certain requirements, whether you're renting or visiting with your own car

Documents. To drive, you need only a valid U.S. driver's license, proof of liability insurance, and the vehicle's registration. But to return to this country you must show proof of U.S. citizenship or legal residence. Your driver's license won't do—you need a passport, green card, or certified copy of your birth certificate.

Liability insurance. To drive in any Canadian province, whether in your own car or in a rental, you must carry coverage against damage you might do to someone else's property or person. The legal minimum is C$200,000 (U.S., about $140, 000) everywhere but Quebec, where it's C$50,000 (U.S., about $35,000). If you're involved in an accident, you'll have to show proof of insurance.

Liability coverage for driving in Canada is probably included in your regular automobile insurance, whether you're in your own car or a rental. But before you leave, check with your insurance representative—if you aren't covered, you'll need to buy a separate add-on policy. If you are covered, ask your company to send you a Canadian nonresident inter-province motor vehicle liability insurance card, which certifies that you carry the statutory minimum liability coverage to drive in Canada.

Rental-car company procedures concerning liability insurance vary. For example, Dollar requires renters who plan to visit Canada to buy supplementary liability insurance whether they need it or not.

Driving a borrowed car. If you drive a car registered to someone not in your travel party, you'll need a letter from the owner granting you permission to take the car into Canada.

Driving a U.S. rental car. The rental contract serves as the rental-car company's official permission to drive a car into Canada. But many local rental offices establish additional limits of their own. For example, Seattle car-rental offices may limit Canadian driving to British Columbia only. And some U.S. renters impose mileage caps on Canadian driving.

Of course, rental companies have no way to enforce their geographical limits—provided nothing goes wrong. But the limits are an enforceable part of the rental contract: If you have an accident or a mechanical problem outside the allowable driving area, you're liable for towing and repair.

CARS & TRAINS

Renting in Canada. As with any foreign rental, you'll need a driver's license, a charge card, and an insurance card. The rental company is supposed to give you a card that discloses its provided liability coverage for the vehicle you're renting. But that coverage may be below the Canadian requirements, so get the nonresident interprovincial card from your own insurance company as well.

Collision insurance, covering damage to the car when you're driving, isn't legally required. But unless the rental is an old wreck, it's a wise precaution. Your own policy's collision coverage probably applies in Canada, but be sure to check before you leave.

Credit-card collision coverage works in Canada in the same way it does in the U.S. If your own auto insurance includes Canada, the card provides additional, secondary coverage. (It may also pick up any liability not covered by your car insurance, up to a stated limit.) And should your personal auto insurance exclude Canada, your card's collision coverage becomes primary.

RENTING AND DRIVING IN MEXICO

Like bureaucracy? You'll love driving in Mexico. Be prepared whether you go in your own car or rent once you arrive.

Documents. Crossing the border in either direction requires proof of U.S. citizenship or residence. To drive, you need a valid U.S. driver's license and a Spanish translation of it. (Get an international driving permit, available through AAA offices. Details are given later in this chapter.)

When you travel beyond the immediate border areas (Tijuana, Tecate, Mexicali, or Baja California) or you stay in Mexico more than 72 hours, you'll also need a Mexican tourist card (tarjeta de turista), free at Mexican consulates and tourist offices, border offices, and auto-club offices. The tourist card is valid for stays of up to 180 days and must be used within 90 days of its issuance. Visitors must carry it at all times while in Mexico or risk incurring a fine.

Insurance. U.S. insurance rarely covers liability in Mexico. Whether you drive your own car or a rental, you'll almost certainly need to buy separate Mexican liability insurance, widely available from independent agencies in border-crossing areas, through border-area AAA offices, or, if you rent, through a rental agency. Some liability coverage is included in Mexican car rentals; it varies by location and company. If the amount isn't close to what you carry in the U.S., buy extra.

Your U.S. insurance probably won't cover you for collision, either. If you don't want to buy the collision-damage waiver from the rental company, use credit-card coverage. Should your own insurance exclude Mexico (as it most likely does), the card's coverage will be primary. (Check with your credit-card company before you rent for any exclusions and conditions.)

Driving a private car. No special procedures are required if you confine your driving to a "free zone," typically within 15 miles of the border but including most of Baja California. Just arrange your insurance and go.

You'll need a temporary car importation permit to drive beyond the free zone, however. To obtain the permit, you must present both the original and a copy of your vehicle's title certificate and registration at a border station, about 12 to 16 miles below the border.

When driving a car registered in a name other than your own (another individual, a bank or credit union, a corporation, or a leasing company), you must also have a notarized letter or affidavit from the legal owner authorizing you to drive the car into Mexico.

The permit fee (about $11) is payable only by a credit card issued in your name by a bank outside Mexico; cash or traveler's checks aren't accepted. (That hassle is designed to ensure that you won't sell the car in Mexico.) A hologram is then applied

CARS &
TRAINS

215

to the inside of the vehicle's windshield and must be removed by Mexican border officials when you return to the U.S.

Driving a U.S. rental car. Company policies vary, so confirm when you rent. Some offices near the border may prohibit any driving in Mexico; others may limit how far below the border you can go or cap the distance you can drive in Mexico before you start paying per-mile charges.

Mexico puts you through the same car-permit rigmarole with a rental car as with your own car. However, the rental company provides the necessary proof of ownership. Be sure to let the rental agent know you intend to drive into Mexico.

Renting in Mexico. Renting a car from a Mexican rental office lets you avoid the border-crossing paperwork. All you need is a valid driver's license, a credit card, and Mexican insurance sold by the rental company. But be aware that Mexican rental costs can be substantially higher than they are in the U.S.

Bottom line: You're much better off with a U.S. rental, despite the red tape, as long as the geographic restrictions don't interfere with your plans.

RENTING AND DRIVING IN EUROPE

Driving in Europe affords flexibility and can allow you to roam beyond the big cities, enjoying smaller towns and stunning countryside. But you, like many other people, might not relish coping with unfamiliar roads and traffic rules. European travelers often use cost as a tiebreaker to choose between renting a car and traveling by rail.

For two people touring Europe, a car rental beats train travel in all countries but Italy, where car-rental rates are high, and France, where both modes of travel cost about the same. A solo traveler, however, would do better traveling by train in all cases except on a short trip in the Europass area (France, Germany, Italy, Spain, and Switzerland) and in the U.K., where car and train costs are about even. If you choose to travel Europe by rental car, know in advance what to expect.

Documents. At the rental counter in Europe, you'll need a reservation confirmation or voucher (reserving in advance reduces hassles), a valid U.S. driver's license, a credit card, and your passport. An international driving permit isn't required in any country but Italy, but it is recommended for travel in Austria, Germany, Spain, Eastern Europe, and the Middle East.

Rental company choices in Europe. Arriving at one of Europe's gateway airports is almost like landing at a major U.S. airport. After clearing customs, you'll see signs and kiosks for a host of familiar rental-car names. The major multinational companies are all represented, including Alamo, Avis, Budget, Hertz, National, Payless, and Thrifty. In addition, you'll find Europcar, an affiliate of U.S.-based Dollar, as well as three European-based renters—Kenning, Town & Country, and Woods—all of which have U.S. representatives.

The wholesale tour operator option. You can also rent a car from several U.S.-based wholesale tour operators: Auto Europe, AutoNet, DER Car, Europe by Car, European car Reservations (ECR), International Travel Services (ITS), and Kemwel Holiday Autos. All arrange rentals through various Europe-based renters, multinational as well as local.

Payment alternatives. Typically, tour operators require full payment up-front, while multinationals have you pay when you return the car. Some multinationals, however, offer a choice between prepayment at a rate guaranteed in U.S. dollars and payment in local currency when the car is returned. (Unless the prepaid price is significantly lower, the pay-at-return option is less hassle if your plans change.)

Car decisions. Rental car prices are keyed to a car's letter code—but with little consistency. One country's B-class car may be another country's C-class car. In fact, a single company may class the same model as an A in one country and a B in

CARS & TRAINS

another. For that reason, it's smart to shop by car model—when reserving, ask for cars by specific model, not letter code.

Here's what's generally available by size.

Standard subcompacts. These are the smallest cars comfortable for two touring adults. Typically, these cars are two- or three-door models, which can accommodate two people and their baggage—but have rear-seat room for only one or two infants or small children.

Specific models include: Alfa Romeo 145/146, Citroen Saxo/Xsara, Fiat Brava/Bravo/Punto/Uno, Ford Fiesta, Hyundai Accent/Elantra, Lancia Delta, Mazda 323/Lantis, Mitsubishi L Sedan/Lancer, Nissan Micra/Sunny, Opel (Vauxhall in the U.K.) Astra/Corsa, Peugeot 306, Renault 5/Clio/Megane, Seat Cordoba/Ibiza/Marbella, Skoda Favorit/Felicia, Subaru Justy, Suzuki Swift, Toyota Corolla/Starlet, and Volkswagen Golf/Polo.

Standard midsized cars. Mid-sized models are the smallest cars that will comfortably accommodate parties of three or four adults or two adults with larger children. They're usually four-door sedans, two classifications up from standard sub-

---

When Is Renting a Good Deal?
Some countries are very expensive

Rental car prices in Europe vary greatly from one country and company to another. When deciding between car and train travel, you'll want to compare prices. (See Chapter 26 for rail guidelines.) To help, we've listed which countries generally offer good-value rental-car rates and which are notably expensive.

Good value: Austria, Belgium, France, Germany, Luxembourg, the Netherlands, Portugal, Spain, Switzerland.

Expensive: Bulgaria, Czech Republic, Denmark, Finland, Hungary, Iceland, Ireland, Italy, Norway, Poland, Romania, Slovenia, Sweden, the United Kingdom.

compacts, with adequate rear seat room for two adults.

Specific models include: Alfa 155/156, Alfa Romeo 164, Audi A4, Citroen Xantia, Fiat Croma/Marea/Regatta/Tempra, Ford Mondeo/Sierra/Tempo, Hyundai Sonata, Lancia Dedra/Thema, Mazda 626/636, Mitsubishi Galant, Nissan Bluebird/Primera, Opel (Vauxhall in the U.K.) Cavalier/Omega/Vectra, Peugeot 405/406/505/506, Renault Laguna/Safrane, Rover 414/620, Seat Toledo, Toyota Camry/Carina, Volkswagen Jetta/Passat/Vento, and Volvo 440/S40.

Rental companies (and tour packagers that offer rental cars) often push four-door models of some of the roomier subcompacts (Citroen Xsara and Renault Megane, for instance) or cars that bridge the gap between subcompact and mid-sized (Ford Escort) as adequate for four travelers. But you'll probably find those cars are too tight for rear-seat passengers.

Cheap come-ons. Some rental companies feature cramped, severely underpowered subcompacts at lowball prices. While these models, such as the Fiat Cinquecentro/Panda, Ford Ka, and Renault Twingo, may be fine for tooling around town, they're unsuitable for the open highway.

Economical automatics. Now fairly common in many European countries, automatics are no longer the extravagance they once were. Often an automatic is just one category up from the standard subcompact group—fine for two, but skimpy for four. In some countries, however, you'll find an automatic shift only in large, luxury cars.

Air conditioning. Air conditioning has become more common —and less expensive—in the past few years, especially in warmer countries. If this feature is important to you, check availability when you reserve your car.

Recreational vehicles. Minivans and campers have also become popular in Europe, but rental rates are high, too, especially in summer.

The best deal. No single company is consistently either the

**CARS &
TRAINS**

219

cheapest or the most expensive from country to country—or for all models within the same country. But some rates are better than others.

Weekly touring rates. These are usually the top bargains you can book in the U.S. for summer driving in Europe. (Longer rentals are usually prorated at a per-day rate of one-seventh the weekly price.) Typically, you must keep your car five days to qualify. Return the car early and the company may recalculate at the local daily rate, which can often run up your bill.

Basic prices are usually uniform throughout each country. But you can expect to pay a surcharge at many large airports; rates in Greece and Spain may vary at island locations.

You'll generally be able to find deals in Europe that include unlimited mileage. In a few countries, costs are higher in July and August. However, rates are always subject to change, with some company's charges more volatile than others—check exact rates for exact dates before you depart.

Can't set your itinerary in advance? If you decide to rent after you arrive in Europe, a local rental office will probably quote you a much higher price than had you reserved in advance—maybe with a mileage cap, too. Unless you are renting for just a day or two, don't pay that extra amount. You can probably get the weekly touring rate by calling a multinational rental company's North American reservation office or your travel agent back home.

An alternative. Kemwel sells a CarPass good for three consecutive rental days in any of seven countries. You must return the car in the same country, but not necessarily in the same city, in which you rented it. Per-diem rates are higher than the weekly rate allows but lower than you'd pay on the spot.

One-way rentals. Most companies don't charge extra for a rent-it-here, leave-it-there rental within a single country. However, to rent in one country and return in another, check first with the multinationals—some provide one-way rentals between a few adjoining countries at no extra cost. (You pay the originating country's rate and tax.)

Change gateway? Most tourists pick up their rental car in the country in which they arrive. So you may find it worthwhile to choose your gateway country for its low car-rental rates. In past surveys of rental rates, both Belgium and Germany offered low rates. And airfares to these destinations from the U.S. and Canada were generally at least as good as to neighboring countries. Other low-rate countries were the Netherlands, Portugal, Spain, and Switzerland. For a long-term rental, the availability of French leases makes Paris an inviting gateway.

Extras and limitations. European rentals have add-ons and restrictions. Some you can't avoid—but a few you can.

VAT. European auto rentals are subject to value-added tax (VAT), which can boost your rental cost by as much as 25 percent. Note that rental-brochure rates usually exclude VAT, so always ask how much it will add when reserving. Services such as car rentals are "consumed" locally, so in most European

A GALLON OF GAS COSTS HOW MUCH?

In mid-1999, seven of the nine highest gas prices worldwide were in Europe, according to Runzheimer International, a Wisconsin-based consulting firm. The cheapest prices were, not surprisingly, oil-producing countries.

MOST EXPENSIVE CITIES Prices per gallon		LEAST EXPENSIVE CITIES Prices per gallon	
Hong Kong	$5.04	Caracas	$0.48
Oslo	4.57	Lagos	0.49
Paris	4.47	Kuwait City	0.51
Amsterdam	4.35	Jakarta	0.61
London	4.27	Riyadh	0.62
Milan	4.21	Manama	0.82
Brussels	4.05	Abu Dhabi	0.85
Buenos Aires	3.97	Cairo	1.03
Stockholm	3.97	Manila	1.05

CARS & TRAINS

countries, travelers can't claim the VAT refunds available on goods bought locally but "exported" outside Europe. While most rental companies list identical VAT rates, a few tour operators apparently manage to get a partial VAT refund —which they then pass along to customers—because they're "exporting" car rentals to travelers who live in North America.

Airport expenses. Quite a few European airports impose fees that rental companies pass along to renters. Most are trivial—in total, they might add up to less than the cost of a taxi from the airport to a downtown rental office. But in Austria, Belgium, Italy, Luxembourg, Switzerland, and the U.K., renting from an airport location can add as much as 10 to 14 percent to the total cost—enough to make you consider dealing with an off-airport office. (The fees don't apply to cars that you simply return at an airport.)

Highway charges. Any car driven in Austria or Switzerland must have a sticker indicating payment of that country's highway fee. Local rental cars normally have that sticker. But if you rent in an adjacent country, you (not the rental company) must buy the sticker or pay a stiff fine. Rental cars in such border-area cities as Milan and Munich often have a sticker already— ask for one if you plan to drive in Austria or Switzerland.

Geographic limits. At some locations, car-rental companies restrict your driving destinations. The most common ban is on driving Western European rentals into Eastern Europe, with some exceptions (cars rented in Austria and Germany can often be driven into the Czech Republic, Hungary, and Slovakia). Whenever you reserve a rental car in Europe, ask if your entire itinerary is acceptable. When it's not, check with other rental companies.

Age restrictions. Minimum and, occasionally, maximum age limits vary by country and company. Should your party include an under-25 or over-70 driver, be sure to check age restrictions when you reserve.

DRIVING ON THE LEFT

When visiting countries that are currently or were at one time under the rule of Great Britain, you'll get to experience one of the greatest challenges for American tourists—driving on the left. Among these countries, islands, or territories are the United Kingdom (England, Scotland, Wales), Ireland, Malta, Gibraltar, Australia, New Zealand, South Africa, India, the British Virgin Islands, Grenada, Jamaica, Hong Kong, Fiji, the Cook Islands, and Tonga.

Before arranging to rent a car in a foreign country, check guidebooks to establish whether traffic circulates on the left or the right. In countries adhering to the British system, be ready for this very different driving experience.

Know the basics. Cars built to drive on the left are the mirror opposite of those driven on the right. The driver's seat is on the right side of the car, so you'll look to the left to view the rearview mirror. The turn signal and window-wiper controls are also reversed. If the car has a manual transmission, you will shift gears with your left hand rather than your right.

An International Driver's Permit
You may need it abroad

Some countries, predominantly those where English is spoken, will allow you to rent a car using a valid U.S. driver's license. Many others require that you have what is known as an International Driver's Permit (IDP). Valid in over 150 countries, the IDP contains your name, photo, and driver information, translated into 10 languages.

If you travel a lot and enjoy the flexibility allowed by renting a car, the IDP is a worthwhile investment. And you can easily obtain one through any AAA office. Bring your valid U.S. driver's license, two original passport-size photos, and $10. You can also print out an application at the AAA Web site *(www. aaa.com)* and apply by mail using a photocopy of your U.S. driver's license.)

CARS & TRAINS

When driving, you always keep to the left. This means left-hand turns are an easy 90-degree maneuver, while right-hand turns require you to wait in the intersection for oncoming traffic to clear. Many left-side-driving countries favor roundabouts, which you enter to the left; just remember you must stay to the left as you exit as well.

Avoid renting in a downtown location. An airport pickup is preferable to starting out in the heart of a traffic-congested city such as London, Sydney, Bombay, or Capetown. When renting from an airport location, you're likely to first experience local roads or highways rather than crowded, narrow (and often one-way) city streets. So you will have a chance to get used to the new sensation of sitting on the right side of the car, keeping to the left, and looking to the left to see in the rearview mirror *before* you encounter heavy traffic challenges.

Give yourself time to adjust. Before venturing onto roads that require attentive driving skills—busy city streets, curving mountain or coastal roads—drive around in less-crowded areas. Back roads and residential neighborhoods are good places to allow yourself to get acclimated to "thinking left."

Avoid manual-shift cars on your first rental. Whereas a rental car with a manual transmission will save you money (quite a bit in some countries), it can greatly increase the frustration factor for novice left-hand drivers. Having to shift gears—with your left hand, no less—while still adjusting to the disorientation of driving on the left and navigating unfamiliar streets and highways, is difficult at best. At worst, it could lead to an accident. If you've never driven on the left, reserve an automatic transmission—even if you favor a stick and drive one at home. If you adjust well and feel comfortable driving on the left, next time your visit a country with the British road system, try a manual shift and see how you fare.

PART EIGHT

Taking the Train

CHAPTER 26

When Rail Travel Makes Sense

Sometimes a train is the most practical or economical way to travel, expecially if you're country-hopping in Europe. Often, it's more scenic.

━━━━━━━━━━━━━━━━━ ■ ━━━━━━━━━━━━━━━━━

Worldwide, the rail industry is a study in contrasts: In some highly developed countries—Germany, France, and Japan—high-speed trains (called ICE, TGV, and bullet trains, respectively) whisk passengers through the countryside at speeds of 150 to 200 miles per hour. In Western Europe and the U.S., the trains are mostly modern (there are a few exceptions), but schedules may be limited in some areas. Amtrak, for example, serves only 44 states. And in lesser developed areas like China, Russia, Eastern Europe, and parts of South America, rail travel hasn't advanced much in the past 30 or 40 years.

RAIL TRAVEL FACTS

Many Americans may ride commuter trains or light-rail trains to work every day, but as a vacation travel option—either in the U.S. or overseas—flying or renting a car both come first.

Rail service varies greatly by country. Japan's modern, efficient rail system serves 20 million people a day; 3.8 million people a year ride VIA Rail Canada; and Amtrak had 21 million passengers in all of 1998. In some developing countries, train service is a throwback to a bygone era—and only the hardiest of travelers will find the conditions bearable. Before you put a rail journey on your itinerary, check your guidebook or consult your travel agent about the status of rail service where you plan to visit.

Europeans rely on train travel for a large portion of their city-to-city travel, and trains are generally modern and comfortable. An extensive rail network covering over 100,000 miles links the countries of Western and Eastern Europe. Because most European countries are relatively small, the usual travel times are conveniently quick; three or four hours on a train covers a lot of track. But since rail travel is such a favorite, you may need reservations at peak times.

TRAIN TRAVEL IN NORTH AMERICA

Amtrak, the company that has controlled intercity domestic rail travel since it was created by the government in 1971, can get you to most places (500 cities in 44 states) on trips ranging from under an hour to three full days.

Most Amtrak trains offer comfortable seating and plenty of leg room. Many overnight trains have a full-service dining room and a two-level sightseeing lounge car open to all passengers. Sleeping berths are also available on longer trips.

You must make reservations well in advance for peak summer travel. By May, you may discover it's too late to book your preferred route.

In Canada, intercity rail travel is controlled by VIA Rail Canada. The company, founded in 1978, services the majority of Canada's provinces with routes to 450 cities—although 85 percent of its ridership is concentrated in the Quebec/Windsor corridor, which includes the cities of Montreal and Quebec.

CARS &
Trains

227

Rail travel takes time. Taking the train in the U.S. cannot compete with flying for time—except on some short, intercity trips like New York to Washington, D.C., or Portland to Seattle, when travel to and from airports tags on almost the same amount of time as the train trip itself.

On longer trips, you can expect to spend eight to 10 times as many hours on the rails as in the air. For example, a flight from New York to Miami takes about three hours, while the trip by train takes 24 to 28 hours. Trains can be time-competitive with auto travel, however, since you needn't factor in traffic and rest stops.

It's not always cost-competitive. Train travel is not cheap. And costs rise when the trip covers several days—say, New York to Los Angeles—and requires sleeping accommodations. On journeys of 12 to 20 hours, many people opt to simply sit in standard cars rather than book a sleeper berth, thereby cutting costs. If you've ever sat on a plane for 10 to 12 hours, imagine sitting on a train for twice that time.) And the cost of

RAIL PASSES & DISCOUNTS

Bargain fares in the U.S. and Canada, as of late 1999 (in U.S. dollars)

Pass name	Discount	Special deals
Amtrak Explore America fare: a three-segment trip, to be completed within 45 days, between June 16 and August 20, $419.	50 percent for children ages 2 to 15 when accompanied by paying adult; 15 for full-time students, seniors over 62, and the disabled.	Discounts as high as 60 percent; select routes only at certain times; listed under "Rail sale" on the web site.
VIA Rail Canrailpass Canada allows 12 days of unlimited travel in a 30-day period to any stop; $416 high season and $256 low season	50 percent for children ages 2 to 11; 40 percent for ages 12 to17 and full-time students over 18; 10 percent for seniors over 60.	Super Saver fares in low season: limited number of seats at 25 to 35 percent off, with advance purchase. (U.S. dollars).

Joint North America Rail Pass, offered by Amtrak in conjunction with VIA Rail Canada, allows 30 consecutive days of travel to 900 destinations in U.S. and Canada; peak season (June 1 to October 15), $645; off-peak (October 16 to May), $450.

the ticket is about the same as some low-fare airline prices.

Train travel is almost always more costly per person than auto travel, even when rental-car costs are figured in. And if two people travel together, they split the cost of the car.

But the train can be convenient. Most people who regularly travel by train appreciate the fact that stations are located in the heart of the city, cutting out painstaking (and costly) trips to and from the airport. So the three-and-a-half hour trip from New York to Washington, D.C. is almost time competitive with a flight. (The trip is soon to be faster with Amtrak's new higher-speed Acela trains.) And in contrast to auto travel, you simply get on the train and get off.

EUROPEAN TRAIN TRAVEL

Though a rental car is often an American's first choice when traveling through Western Europe—mainly because we're so used to driving—trains often make more sense. They are generally faster and eliminate traffic or parking worries. Fares are also quite affordable—much more so within Europe than plane tickets, which can be very expensive.

Train travel in Europe is especially smart if you're traveling alone, are staying mainly in big city centers where parking can be a nightmare, or will be racking up a lot of mileage—say on a multiweek, multicountry trip. Plus you won't have to decipher foreign-language road signs.

But the advantages go beyond economics and ease. New tracks permit very high-speed (186 mph) service, for example, from Paris to Brussels. And new tilt trains travel at somewhat lower (but still high) speeds on conventional tracks. Trains can also take you just about anywhere on the continent. On main routes, they run often and are convenient and comfortable.

However, driving does deliver more flexibility. Taking the train, you must adhere to preset schedules and routes.

CAR OR
TRAIN

229

EUROPEAN TRAIN PASSES

Pass	Duration/cost
EURAILPASS Unlimited first-class travel in all 17 Eurailpass countries.	15 days: $554 21 days: $718 1 month: $890 2 months: $1,260 3 months: $1,558
EURAIL SAVERPASS Unlimited first-class travel in all Eurailpass countries for 2 to 5 people traveling together for duration of pass; prices per person; 15 percent less than standard Eurailpass.	15 days: $470 21 days: $610 1 month: $756 2 months: $1,072 3 months: $1,324
EURAIL YOUTHPASS Unlimited second-class travel in all Eurailpass countries for anyone under 26; 30 percent less than standard Eurailpass.	15 days: $388 21 days: $499 1 month: $623 2 months: $882 3 months: $1,089
EURAIL FLEXIPASS First-class travel for set number of consecutive days over 2-month period.	10 days: $654 15 days: $862
EURAIL SAVER FLEXIPASS First-class travel on Flexipass terms for 2 to 5 people traveling together for duration of pass; prices per person; 15 percent less than standard Flexipass.	10 days: $556 15 days: $732
EURAIL YOUTH FLEXIPASS Second-class travel on Flexipass terms for anyone under 26; 30 percent less than standard Flexipass.	10 days: $458 15 days: $599
EUROPASS First-class travel for set number of nonconsecutive days over 2-month period in France, Germany, Italy, Spain, and Switzerland; choose 2 more countries from Austria/Hungary, Belgium, the Netherlands, Luxembourg, Greece, and Portugal for additional fees.	5 days: $348 15 days: $728 (More options are available.)
EUROPASS SAVERPASS First-class travel on Europass terms, in Europass areas, for 2 to 5 people traveling together for duration of pass; prices per person; 15 percent less than standard Europass.	5 days: $296 15 days: $620 (More options are available.)
EURO YOUTHPASS Second-class travel on Europass terms, in Europass areas, for anyone under 26; 30 percent less than standard Europass.	5 days: $233 15 days: $513

Prices as of late 1999

TICKETS AND PASSES IN EUROPE

Rail travelers in Europe have many choices, from simple one-way tickets to multi-week passes. Students and those over 65 may also qualify for discounts.

One-way and round-trip tickets. If you plan to take a train from one major European city to another, then a single one-way ticket is your best bet. You can choose either a first- or second-class ticket as well as the type of train—classified in each country by such standards as speed or number of stops. A first-class ticket generally costs about one-third more than a second-class ticket. While second-class cars in most European countries are perfectly comfortable, they are more crowded.

Multinational passes. There are currently about a dozen multinational pass options available to overseas travelers in Europe, the most well known being the Eurailpass. Note, however, that all multinational passes must be purchased in the U.S. prior to departure. If you have questions about what is covered by a Eurailpass, check first with Rail Europe, the official Eurailpass representative in the U.S., at 800 438-7245 or on the web at *www.raileurope.com.*

The Eurailpass. The classic Eurailpass allows unlimited first-class travel plus free or reduced fares on many suburban trains, long-distance buses, and boat and ferry lines in the following 17 countries: Austria, Belgium, Denmark, Finland, France, Germany, Greece, Holland, Hungary, Ireland, Italy, Luxembourg, Norway, Portugal, Spain, Sweden, and Switzerland. It is the most expensive but least restrictive option available. ("European train passes" has details and prices.)

Limited multinational passes. Groups of countries also offer regional passes, with travel limited to the participating countries. And second-class passes are available to everyone—not just those 26 and under—resulting in a 20 to 40 percent "discount" for those who choose to travel second class. Two

CARS & TRAINS

examples in Western Europe are the Benelux Pass (Belgium, the Netherlands, and Luxembourg) and the Scanrail Pass (Denmark, Finland, Norway, and Sweden). In Eastern Europe, two regional passes are the European East Pass, which covers Austria, the Czech Republic, Hungary, Poland, and Slovakia, and the Balkan Flexipass, covering Bulgaria, Greece, Macedonia, Romania, Serbia, Montenegro, and Turkey.

National passes. Most or all of the countries that participate in the Eurailpass also offer their own national passes, practical if you confine your travels largely to one country; a national pass will almost always be cheaper than a multinational pass of the same length. And unlike Eurailpass, many national passes are available in second class. National passes are especially good deals in France, Italy, Switzerland, and the Netherlands.

Great Britain does not participate in the Eurailpass program but offers its own BritRail pass. In 1998, BritRail introduced the BritRail Party Pass, which offers reduced-price packages for three or four adults traveling together. Up to two children travel free with each party of three or four adults (or seniors)— so bring along grandma, grandpa, or aunts and uncles.

Go First Class?
It costs one-third more

Should you pay one-third more to travel the rails first class? If you get a Eurailpass—and you're over age 26—you don't need to make that decision. All "adult" Eurailpasses are good for first-class travel. But if you are taking only a few train trips during your stay and so are buying individual tickets, you'll be asked "Which class?" at time of purchase.

Going first class generally means the train cars are a bit more comfortable and also less crowded—the first-class compartments seat six passengers, for example, while those in second class seat eight. (Cars are clearly marked on the outside with either a 1 or a 2.) You may want to consider first class on longer journeys, but if you're on a tight budget, most second-class cars are perfectly adequate.

Although a national pass may not have all the extras of a multinational pass, some offer perks or features of their own. The Swiss pass, for example, provides free or discounted travel on important private railroads that Eurailpass excludes.

Discounts for seniors. Since most European railroads give reductions to senior travelers, those over 65 may do better with individual tickets (usually discounted 30 to 50 percent) than with travel-all-you-want rail passes. Here are a few deals:

• Seniors who show ID (typically a passport) can get discounts on tickets in Denmark, Finland, Norway, and Portugal, but travel may be blacked out on peak days or at peak times.

• In Austria, France, Greece, and Sweden, seniors who buy an official ID from the railroad, good for a year, get discounts, too. You can have an ID card issued on the spot at a main rail station booking office. In most cases, you'll need a passport-sized photo—but many stations have photo machines. Austrian cards are also available in advance by mail.

Still, a Eurailpass may prove more convenient for multi-country rail trips, since it cuts out time-consuming waits in ticket lines for each leg of a trip.

TRAIN TRAVEL AROUND THE WORLD

In general, most comprehensive guidebooks—especially those geared to budget travel—will give you an overview of the state of a country's rail system. For example, you will learn that you can take a comfortable, super-speed rail journey in Japan but that in Turkey the bus system is much more modern and reliable. Or you'll discover that a rail trip in New Zealand delivers superb sightseeing and pleasant surroundings, but one in India will combine vistas with delays and uncomfortable conditions. As you've surmised, trains aren't always the best option for long-distance travel.

Decide if you want to go the distance. It might sound romantic to take a rail journey across the Australian outback from

CARS & TRAINS

Sydney to Perth. The reality, however, is 65 hours of hot, rolling landscape. And with a series of affordable air pass coupons from either of Australia's domestic airlines, you could make the trip in about six hours—like a transcontinental U.S.

Do You Have Reservations?
You may need one to sit down

Many Americans may find the need for reservations on European trains confusing. Both a ticket and a pass entitle you to board a train, but neither will guarantee you a seat. To be certain you have a seat on many popular trains, you need a reservation—which "assigns" you a specific seat in a specific car on the train for which you hold a ticket.

Reservations, which generally cost from $5 to $8 depending on the country and the train (sleeper car reservations are more expensive), are made at a separate counter. So once you've purchased a ticket, you must then wait in another line to reserve a seat. If you have a Eurailpass, you need only wait in the reservation line—but since reservations are not included in the price of a Eurailpass, you'll pay the same reservation fee as non pass-holders.

You can also make reservations in the U.S. through Rail Europe before departure. But the service costs $11 per standard reservation, so it's no bargain—although you will avoid waiting in line at assorted stations. Advance reservations may be wise, however, for certain highly popular routes during peak travel season.

Do you really need reservations? The answer is yes and no. On certain high-speed day trains—such as the TGV, ICE, AVE, X2000, and Eurostar—and on all overnight trains, you are required to reserve a seat, couchette, or sleeper. And on certain InterCity and EuroCity trains (which are popular because they are faster and make fewer stops), reservations are also a must. Reservations are not available in Belgium, Holland, Luxembourg, or Sweden, unless the train is going to another country. On most other trains, seat reservations are generally not required. You simply sit wherever you find an unreserved seat in a car designated by the class of your ticket—either first-class or second. For a reservation strategy, see Chapter 27.

flight. If you've always wanted to take a leisurely, scenic journey across a country, do it. But research the setting first and, on a long trip, be prepared to pay a premium for sleeper accommodations.

Try a mix of transport types. A particularly scenic region of a country is a prime candidate for train travel. But you might consider pairing train trips with flights to save time. Or, if you arrive by ship in a port city, a day or overnight trip by train could be an ideal way to see the countryside.

CARS & TRAINS

CHAPTER 27

More Rail Miles For Your Money

You can stretch that rail pass to create an even better deal. What it takes: careful planning, some rail "smarts," and knowledge of the extras many pass-holders overlook.

———————————————■———————————————

The following strategies will help you squeeze every penny from your pass without wasting time or sacrificing convenience. You may need to forgo some spontaneity. But an organized plan will save time and money.

MAP OUT YOUR ROUTE

Whether you're traveling in the U.S. or abroad, research and planning save both time and money.

European plan. A Eurailpass can go farther than you think. For example, it's possible to stretch a one-month Eurailpass into a six-week journey. Follow these tips:

Have a firm itinerary. On longer trips (a month or more) preplot your course. You can save about 20 to 25 percent by purchasing a two-month Eurail Flexipass. It allows either 10 or 15 days of travel during that time rather than the unlimited travel allowed by the more expensive Eurailpass.

Don't backtrack. Plan your route so you progress from country to country without doubling back. It's often desirable to start in either a northern city (such as Amsterdam) or a southern one (such as Rome) and work your way in the opposite direction. This course will take you the farthest distance in the least amount of time.

Validate wisely. Choose as your rail departure point a city that you want to visit for three to five days. Then don't have your pass validated until the exact day you actually leave that city—even if you make your seat reservation a day or so earlier.

Perfect your endgame. If you plan to visit Great Britain, which does not participate in Eurailpass, end your train travels in a city with affordable access to London by plane or ferry.

Travel with a companion. Traveling with another person will allow you to purchase a Eurail Saverpass, which is 15-percent cheaper than a standard Eurailpass.

North American design. In the U.S. and Canada, longer distances between cities mean even more careful planning to get the most miles with an Amtrak or VIA Rail Canada North American Rail Pass.

Choose your spots. With the 30-day North American pass, don't try to see too much or you'll spend more time in transit than enjoying the places you visit. Concentrate your travels in a particular region of the U.S. and/or Canada.

Divide the trip. Shape your itinerary so you take eight to 10 short- to medium-distance (300 to 800 mile) segments. Following this plan, you'll sit no more than 12 hours on the train at a time and avoid the cost of sleeper accommodations. Plus, you'll spend only one-half to one full day on the train every three to five days, a reasonable pace.

VALIDATING A EURAILPASS

After you purchase a Eurailpass in the U.S. (they must be bought prior to your departure for Europe), the pass will not

CARS & TRAINS

be usable until it has been "validated" by a Eurail representative at your first departure station. (Look for the Eurail office or window at the station.) Validation is simply a stamp on the pass that records the first day of usage—and thus also indicates the day it expires.

Because station lines during peak travel periods can be long—sometimes requiring up to an hour of waiting—you may want to have your pass validated prior to the first day of train travel. After you get settled at your hotel, visit the train station and find the Eurail office. But make sure you tell the representative to validate your pass for *the date you first plan to use it,* not today's date. Don't assume all agents will speak English, although a good number do. It's always smart to have your request written in whatever language is spoken locally. At the very minimum, write out the date for which you want your pass valid. If that's June 1, 2000, write it like a European—1/6/2000—the day first, then the month.

Once you have a validated pass, familiarize yourself with the station. Notice the lines? European train stations are notorious for them, so don't wait till the last minute to make a reservation, should one be required.

WHEN YOU DON'T HAVE RESERVATIONS

The matter of reservations is one of the trickier questions facing anyone with a Eurailpass. Yes, you already have your ticket, but a ticket doesn't guarantee a seat. Certain trains require reservations, which cost an extra fee. These guidelines can help you get a seat without reserving.

Pack light. The fewer pieces of luggage you have to haul onto and through the train, the easier it is to spot an unreserved seat and settle in.

Arrive early. You'll have plenty of time to find the platform and the appropriate first- or second-class cars.

Find the train configuration chart. Most stations in Europe have charts either at the head of each track or along the platform that show where the first- and second-class cars will be located. The cars correspond with letters (A, B, C) along the platform. You can then situate yourself next to the appropriate car and be one of the first to board.

Look for reservation markers. Reserved seats will have a slip of paper either on or above the seat. Avoid them and look for unmarked ones. If no one shows up to claim a seat right away, don't be tempted—even if the seat is better than the one you have. The reserving party will probably get on at a future stop.

LEARN 'INSIDER' TIPS

After a few weeks of riding the rails in the Europe, you'll be an old pro. Until then, a few tips can avert hassles:

Plan ahead. For example, upon arriving at your destination, make plans for your departure. Consult train schedules, decide on a train and time, decide if you'll need a reservation, then make it, so you won't have to wait in lines later.

Mark your territory. When visiting the lavatory or the dining car, leave a newspaper or magazine to alert other passengers that the seat is taken. Take precautions and you won't have to call the conductor to oust an interloper.

Watch for smoking and nonsmoking cars. Unlike the U.S., many Europeans can pretty much smoke wherever and whenever they want. But trains feature both smoking and nonsmoking cars. If smoke bothers you, make sure you're not in a smoking car when you grab that unreserved window seat.

Keep your ticket. Never discard your ticket until you've left your arrival station. Eurailpass-holders needn't worry—you'll keep your pass for the duration of your trip. But those riding with one-way or round-trip tickets must hold onto them, since you may be asked to show your ticket as you exit the station platform. If you've thrown it away, you might be asked to buy a new one.

CARS & TRAINS

239

COMBINE NATIONAL PASSES

The Eurailpass generally proves cost effective on trips to multiple countries over a period of a few weeks. For shorter trips, or for those that include only two countries, a combination of rail passes may be more economical, especially since you'll have the option of choosing a cheaper second-class pass. For example, if you were to visit Italy for a week, then Switzerland for a week, two eight-day, second-class passes ($182 for Italy and $238 for Switzerland) would total $420. Since a 15-day Eurailpass costs $554, you'd save $134.

Before deciding which pass or passes to buy, go over your route and compare costs. In some instances—if you'll take three or four long trips between major cities over the course of two weeks, for example—buying separate tickets may save money, especially if you're entitled to a senior citizen discount, given by most countries to single-ticket purchasers but not to Eurailpass holders.

TAKE ADVANTAGE OF 'EXTRAS'

Many Eurailpass holders don't realize their pass provides extras, including free trips or reduced fares on a number of boats, buses, and private railways. For example, in Austria the Eurailpass covers a free cruise on the Danube between Vienna and Passau. In Belgium, Denmark, Finland, and Sweden, numerous ferry and boat trips are free or 50 percent off. In Switzerland, there's a fare reduction on several scenic cable car lines. And in Germany, a pass entitles you to a free sightseeing cruise on the Rhine between Cologne and Mainz.

Not all these bonuses are detailed in the Eurailpass brochure you'll receive with your pass. To get every freebie or reduction available, show your Eurailpass whenever you purchase a bus, boat, ferry, train, or cable-car ticket during your trip.

PART NINE

Tours and Cruises

CHAPTER 28

Tours and Package Deals

Tours—prepackaged vacations lasting from a few days to several weeks—can be an economical way to see a lot of faraway places in a short amount of time.

───────────────── ■ ─────────────────

One of the main appeals of a tour is the all-in-one price, plus ease, security, and structure. But tours are notoriously regimented, and may seem stifling to travelers used to setting their own pace and sightseeing independently. Careful research and planning are the best way to ensure a pleasant trip.

THE ABCS OF PACKAGE TOURS

Package deals or tours, put together by organizations known as wholesalers or tour operators, give you two or more travel elements, such as air transportation, lodgings, meals, ground transportation, entertainment, car rental, airport transfers, and sightseeing. The tour menu has steadily become richer and more varied, now ranging from golfing jaunts in Scotland to trekking journeys in Nepal to bicycling trips through Italy.

Interested? Your travel agent has plenty of information, including the "Official Tour Directory." Also check newspaper travel section ads, travel magazines, and web sites. Friends who've taken such trips are another useful source.

You'll find several tour types, each with pros and cons.

Basic package deals. If you're off to a city (London, Paris, Hong Kong) or sun-and-surf locale (Florida, Hawaii, the Caribbean, or Mexico), these are often good deals. Your price break comes from the packager's ability to buy airfare, hotel, ground transfers, and sightseeing in bulk.

Such packages, widely available from tour operators and from major airlines and hotel chains, typically provide airfare, hotel, airport transfers, and/or a rental car, as well as limited sightseeing options or discounts. You'll reap discounts without having to travel as part of a group, as you would with an escorted tour. But you must also tote your own luggage, navigate sightseeing, and arrange your own meals, except for breakfast, often included in the hotel portion.

Escorted tours. On these jaunts, virtually everything is handled for you, including what you see, eat, and do once you reach your destination. Most local touring is done by bus, with either a local guide or an escort who accompanies you throughout the entire trip.

On the plus side, an escorted tour means traveling with minimal effort and fuss (unless you get a bad tour), and provides camaraderie (unless you have little in common with other travelers). You pay lower prices—especially at hotels—and may also get special access, since a tour is often the only way to take part in certain activities or go places otherwise off-limits to tourists. And generally the facilities and itinerary have been carefully selected and prescreened.

But escorted tours also have certain disadvantages. The tour's "flavor" and success very much depend on the quality of the tour guide and on the personalities of your fellow travelers—both out of your control. The regimented schedules may prove annoying. And the pace is generally only as fast as the

TOURS & CRUISES

slowest person on the tour. Your whole trip is also prepaid—so you're locked in even if things turn out to be unsatisfactory.

À la carte options. Since many people don't need—or even like—handholding when they travel, many tour operators provide à la carte options that let you travel independently once you reach your destination, but still save on airfare and accommodations. You can always have a travel agent or tour operator tailor a trip to your specifications, though that's the most expensive way to travel.

BROCHURES: READ THE FINE PRINT

Once you've gathered brochures about a few potential tours, make sure you read that tiny, boring type. The fine print spells out the specifics of what's included and what's not, as well as important requirements and restrictions. Since some tour operators aren't completely frank about what they're offering, what you don't know can hurt you.

The brochure's teeny-type sections normally apply to all tours listed. As a result, some copy covers official corporate names and tour numbers as well as purchase conditions, such as required paperwork and cancellation provisions. Beyond those basics, provisions seem designed mainly to protect the operator in case things go wrong, although some tour operators also try to inform the traveler of potential problems. (You can tell a lot about a tour operator's concern for its customers by whether these sections are even legible.) So get out your magnifying glass and look for some very important "details."

Changing prices. The fine print will almost always note that brochure prices are subject to change—reasonable enough, since prices are set far in advance. But ascertain the actual price and conditions before buying the tour. The terms may also protect the operator's right to increase the price or modify what a tour provides *after* a traveler has paid a deposit or even paid in full (with some changes specifically ruled out as grounds for a full refund). Avoid such tours if possible. Some operators will, however, guarantee the price in the brochure.

The airfare. Although airfare affects price, most brochures never list an airfare. But some do quote a package price with a firm airfare; others list the lowest airfare available at the time the brochure was printed—adding that it's subject to change if the airline raises fares.

Charter vs. scheduled airline. You need to know which one you'll get. U.S. regulations are stricter for charters (and tours based on charter flights) than for scheduled airlines. With a charter, a traveler must be given a full refund if the operator imposes any major change before departure: a price increase of 10 percent or more, say, or a switch in departure or return dates. But many important changes aren't deemed "major." A price increase of less than 10 percent, a change in departure time, or a rerouting to pick up passengers in another city, for example, don't entitle you to an automatic refund on a charter-based tour.

Which airline you'll fly. If an airline sponsors a tour, it generally provides the transportation. Independent tour operators may list several airlines (any one of which could be used on a given tour) or a single airline (with the provision that it's subject to change). Whenever there's no promise of a specific airline or if the airline can be switched, you may wind up with below-average (and cramped) economy service.

Types of accommodations. Tour operators generally reserve the right to substitute "comparable" or "equivalent" hotels for those featured in the brochure. Some make specific promises, perhaps limiting substitutions to hotels of at least the same rating as those featured in the brochure. The basis for the rating may also be stated (a government system in Europe, for example). If not, the rating is often taken from the "Official Hotel Guide," a standard industry reference (see Chapter 20). Other brochures promise not only comparable quality but also a similar location within or near a city center or close to a major attraction—a useful plus.

If nothing is said about room quality and location, you're usually assigned a run-of-the-house room, which can be anything with the promised number of beds and bath facilities. When not guaranteed anything better, be prepared for the worst room in the hotel.

Food caliber. Evaluate the meal policy by reading between the lines. Interpret "continental breakfast" to mean self-service coffee, tea, and bread. Unless a brochure specifically promises lunch and dinner choices from a menu, you may face assembly-line, dollop-it-out meals. A few premium operators include alcoholic beverages on some occasions, but most don't.

Itinerary alterations. Usually, the small type says nothing more about routings than the tour description in the front of the brochure. But a few add some specific disclaimers—including the right to make minor adjustments in sightseeing itineraries and to vary the order of cities or attractions visited in a multistop tour.

Tour size. Tours are available in all sizes, from more intimate groups of 10 or so to unwieldy groups of 50. See what size the operator generally books and, more importantly, whether the company reserves the right to cancel the tour without a minimum number of travelers.

Necessary documents. A few operators state exactly when they will send tickets or vouchers to you. Making a reservation within the final month before travel may incur an additional delivery charge. Some operators include a section describing the required documents for the trip (visas, passport, medical certificates, and so forth) and disavow any responsibility for conditions arising from your failure to bring such paperwork with you.

Inclusions and exclusions. Most tour brochures explain policy on specific expenses that might be questioned. Some package prices include services you might consider a given, such as tips to airport and hotel porters. Other items being equal, the more inclusions the better.

Most exclusions are unsurprising: charges for excess baggage, telephone calls, room service, or laundry. Ski-tour operators may disclaim responsibility for lack of snow. Some brochures commit operators to refunds for services that were promised but not delivered. But others allow the operator to make minor changes without a refund—and the operator is the judge of what is minor.

Cancellations and changes. Brochures should spell out the terms. Typically, travelers who cancel well in advance are eligible for full refunds (minus a fee). After a cutoff date (15 to 60 days before departure), there's commonly a sliding scale of penalties. But on many tours, there's no refund at all. A few operators impose especially stringent cancellation provisions for tours during seasonal events at popular destinations—Carnival in Rio, say, or Christmas in Hawaii.

Many operators let you change travel dates or accommodations, subject to availability, for an additional $20 to $100 per change; a few waive the fee for the first change.

Smoking or not? If you want to avoid secondhand smoke, choose a no-smoking tour. No ban in the brochure? You may find a smoking section on the bus. Ask in advance.

Complaints and refunds. Some operators specify a maximum period in which to file complaints and refund requests; they may also delineate the method for resolving conflicts and complaints. Those provisions may not be legally binding—but they're often intimidating.

WHAT WILL IT COST?

Tours come in all price ranges—from budget-oriented "let's all pitch the tent" types running just a few hundred dollars a week to ultra-luxurious tours that skimp on nothing—and cost thousands. Operators Cosmos and Trafalgar specialize in

TOURS &
CRUISES

low-cost, no-frills travel, while operations like Abercrombie & Kent, Mountain Travel Sobek, and Linblad Special Expeditions are known for their premium high-end adventures.

If you spot a tour too pricey for your budget, you might investigate further to find other operators offering similar itineraries for less. However, you usually won't find big discounts on tours—except on cruises, which have become highly promotional in some locations—since margins are thin. At best, you can get a rebate of 5 percent or so through a discount travel agency.

With careful shopping, you can sometimes discover a smaller tour operator that's a real gem. Small firms may specialize in a particular destination, run offbeat tours, or find interesting lodgings that don't accept large groups.

EXAMINE THE ITINERARY

The vast majority of large commercial tours are oriented to two things—sightseeing and shopping—a lot of both, with little free time. Others are specialized, focusing on such areas as history, ecology, architecture, or ornithology. And adventure tours are also gaining in popularity. Whatever type you pick, review the itinerary to be sure you get all you want.

The sights you'll see. Before you book, make sure everything you want to visit is included. Generally, there's little free time to sneak in those spots not covered.

Chances to shop. Many tour operators are under some obligation to stop by certain "shopping" areas—be they markets, tourist shops, or factories. Any time you see a "factory visit" or "handicraft demonstration" listed on an itinerary, you can be certain of a shopping opportunity.

Transportation mode. Will you be traveling by plane, train, bus, or other means? If transport isn't clearly spelled out on the itinerary, ask the operator for specifics.

Evening activities. Some tours include evening activities—

cultural performances, plays, or music. Others leave you to your own devices after dinner.

EVALUATE THE PACE

Trying to cover eight European countries in 21 days, or both Australia and New Zealand in 24, means a hectic schedule with lots of time in transit. Different tours move at different paces, although most try to cram in as much as possible. Check these keynotes to locate a tour that won't require a vacation just to recuperate—or simply bore you beyond words.

Daily schedule. See how much time you actually spend at each stop and judge whether those limits are enough to satisfy you. Most tours linger no more than a day or two in each city—three in some major cities—and just a few hours at each tourist sight.

Morning hours. Unless you're an early riser, you may cringe at typical start times: up, packed, and fed before 8 a.m., so you can hit the sights, then press on to the next destination.

MAKING A PERFECT MATCH

If you're looking for...	Take a tour to ...
Art and European history	Austria, France, Italy, Great Britain, Greece, Russia, Spain, and the Netherlands
Ancient civilization and architecture	China, Egypt, Greece, Japan, Mexico, Peru, and Turkey
Good food	France, Hong Kong, Italy, Montreal, New Orleans, New York, San Francisco/Napa Valley, and Thailand
Wildlife habitats	Africa, Alaska, Antarctica, Australia, Belize, Costa Rica, Galapagos Islands, Indonesia, and the Seychelles
Incredible scenery	Canada, Chile, Iceland, New Zealand, Scandinavia, Switzerland, the U.S. Pacific Coast, and Wyoming
Exotic cultures	The Amazon, India, Morocco, Nepal, South Pacific, Tibet, Tunisia, and Vietnam
Water recreation	Australia, the Caribbean, coastal New England, Fiji, Florida, and Hawaii
Golf	Arizona, Bermuda, California, North Carolina, and Scotland

TOURS & CRUISES

249

Travel time. On some tours, more time is spent in getting to sights than in seeing them. Make sure the pace is such that hours in transit don't become overly tedious. Note, however, that on some tours through extremely scenic regions, travel time can be quite enjoyable.

Physical exertion. Scan descriptions of daily excursions, looking for such phrases as "a short walk," "a hike with some exertion required," or "over challenging terrain." Ask the operator what's involved physically and if any alternative activities are available.

AN ADVENTURE ON THE AGENDA

If your idea of a dream vacation is *not* riding a bus around Rome, but rafting down a river in the Yukon territory, then "adventure" travel might be right for you. If so, you'll be among the tens of millions of U.S. adults of all ages whose quest for less-conventional vacations, from the rough to the plush, has taken the travel industry by storm.

Adventure travel is big business, accounting for $220 billion nationally (about half the nation's entire leisure tourism industry) and getting bigger. Half of all U.S. adults—98 million people—have taken adventure vacations in the past five years, according to a recent study by the Travel Industry Association of America (TIA).

Who's seeking thrills? The swelling ranks of adventure travelers include more than just twenty- and thirty-somethings. Studies show that middle-aged baby boomers and mature adults are also among the adventurous. In fact, the TIA survey found that nearly a million of these adventure travelers are older than 75.

What's available? A wide range of activities falls under the mantle of "adventure travel," from rugged, physically challenging treks to pampered nature excursions. In fact, about 8,000 U.S. companies (most located in the West) offer a variety of domestic and international adventures. (See Chapter 9 for a selection of outfitter web sites.) Tours can be divided into two categories.

Soft adventure. By far the most popular, these trips involve moderately strenuous activities, such as camping, easy day hikes, and casual horseback excursions.

Hard adventure. Anticipate more daring and physically demanding activities, such as mountain trekking and white-water rafting. These trips typically attract the hard-core adventurer but are growing in popularity.

Travel conditions. Some trips require you to share a tent with other travelers, use pit toilets, and eat very basic camp chow. Other operators provide electric-lighted tents and flush toilets as well as gourmet food.

Cost factors. Because adventure travelers don't normally dine in restaurants and sleep between hotel sheets, many prices run fairly low, about $150 a day, including all transportation during the tour in the continental U.S. Because of the added transportation costs, however, travelers to Alaska can expect to pay $300 to $350 a day.

Specialty trips and super luxury trips cost far more. Private jet tours are particularly pricey—from more than $27,000 for the Audubon Society's three-week tour of islands around South America to more than $40,000 for a round-the-world adventure by Abercrombie & Kent.

Risk potential. Perhaps the biggest concern is the risk involved. Though no industrywide statistics are available, anecdotal evidence suggests that most injuries suffered on adventure tours are minor, ranging from cuts and bruises to sprained ankles. But travelers can be seriously hurt or even killed. Some mishaps can be blamed on inexperienced tour operators or travelers who ignore safety warnings. And faulty equipment, poor physical conditioning, dangerous animals, an untamed river, or an unexpected storm can all lead to disaster.

TOURS & CRUISES

Follow some advice to play it safe while still enjoying the thrill of adventure travel:

Judge your limitations. Any reputable outfitter will send you an application that includes important questions about your health and physical abilities. These questions are typical: Have you ever participated in this activity before? What's your fitness level? Do you require a special diet? Are you allergic to bee stings? Are you diabetic? Do you have asthma?

If the outfitter fails to ask an important question, discuss your particular health issues with a company representative. (It's wise to go over these issues with your doctor, too.)

Ask about serious accidents. Any outfitter should be willing to discuss past accidents, how they were handled, and what procedures are now in place to prevent future problems.

Pack your medications. Take not only medications for pre-existing conditions, but those that could protect you from health threats faced on your trip. Your family physician can tell you what shots and pills you'll need; you can also get health information from the Centers for Disease Control and Prevention (see Chapter 36).

Outfitter expertise. To make the right choice among available adventure outfitters, narrow your selection to companies specializing in your kind of tour, then pin down details:

Interview the outfitter before sending a deposit. How long has the company been in business? Exactly what is included in the price? What size is the travel group? How flexible is the tour operator? And will you get any instruction or training?

Ask about the guides. Most outfitters and travelers consider the guides the most important element of a safe and enjoyable adventure. Whether the guide is from the U.S. or a local in your destination country, you'll want to know the person is capable. Find out how long the guides assigned to your trip have worked for the outfitter. And make sure they've had advanced first-aid training.

Get client references. If a tour operator isn't willing to provide you with the names and phone numbers of clients, don't walk away—run away. Any reputable operator should be happy to give you referrals. Then call them yourself.

Read the fine print. Read and understand all the points of your contract. What are the outfitter's refund and cancellation policies? What risks are you accepting—and what rights are you waiving?

Buy trip insurance. Most companies will send you a trip insurance policy, but buy your own policy from an independent insurance company—and make sure you understand all the terms and what the policy covers.

Check for liability insurance and permits. In the U.S., most outfitters have to carry a $300,00 to $500,000 liability policy for biking, horseback riding, river rafting, and other such activities. Such a policy ensures that if the company is grossly negligent, you can sue and collect damages awarded. Also, make sure the tour company is legally in business and that it has required insurance and permits to operate where it does.

CHECK THE AGE RANGE

There's nothing more frustrating than being stuck for a week, two weeks, or even more with a group of people whose interests are very different from yours. Generally, tours appeal to a slightly older crowd, unless otherwise specified.

Everyone welcome. Many tours accept travelers of all ages. If traveling with others your age is important to you, ask the operator about the age range of typical travelers. Too old? Too young? You may want to check with other tour operators to find one with an acceptable clientele.

Seniors. Many tours attract 50-plus travelers due to the convenience of prepackaged travel. Some tour companies, such as Saga and Golden Circle, specify you *must* be 50 or older to take the tour.

TOURS & CRUISES

Younger travelers. Budget- or adventure-oriented packages may welcome all ages, but typically attract a younger crowd. Other excursions have a preset maximum age. For example, Contiki Tours requires that you be 35 or under.

Singles. There are also tours specifically designed for single travelers—companies may concentrate on them or general tour operators may offer special singles-only tours.

Women only. Still other companies cater exclusively to women, which allows female travelers to avoid the couples-oriented world of packaged travel.

Gay tours. An inquiry to a travel agent or a web search will uncover a variety of tours and cruises geared to gay travelers.

Tour Consumer Protection
Save your investment if an operator fails

Several trade associations offer consumer-protection plans. The U.S. Tour Operators Association (USTOA), to which a few of the larger tour operators belong, requires its members to post a surety of $1 million—a useful protection, but not enough to make good on all claims if a big operator fails.

The National Tour Association (NTA) maintains a consumer-protection fund to cover traveler claims if a member tour operator defaults because of bankruptcy. The American Society of Travel Agents (ASTA) offers several forms of consumer protection, but they're all voluntary. It operates an escrow account that tour operators can use to safeguard clients' deposits and lists those operators that offer consumer protection through USTOA or NTA. And ASTA has arranged for umbrella insurance that individual travel agencies can buy to protect clients against supplier default of any kind.

Most operators recommend trip-interruption insurance (see Chapter 34) as a way of hedging your risk and also sell it as a tour add-on. However, we recommend you buy it directly from an independent insurance provider. If you do buy from the tour operator, watch out for unexpected insurance charges added in with other elements of the tour.

VET THE TOUR GUIDES

Guides are a critical tour component—an inexperienced or unprofessional guide can turn even the best itinerary into a bad experience. Ask the tour operator or your travel agent the following questions about the tour guides.

What does the company require of guides? An operator should be able to offer details about their guides' backgrounds and experience as they pertain to the tour's itinerary. For example, are they trained in specific areas, such as history or archeology, that might contribute to their expertise—and your enjoyment?

Is the guide an American? Many U.S. travelers prefer an American guide. Others want English-speaking local guides who might provide a more personal insight into their native country.

If foreign, is the guide fluent in English? Speaking English and being fluent are two different things. If you can't properly understand your guide, you may miss important details or feel frustrated by communication difficulties.

Will you have the same guide for the entire tour? Some fully escorted tours provide a single guide for the entire trip—even if it covers several countries, as many European and some Asian and South American tours do. Others provide a series of guides who meet you at specific destinations, usually at the airport. If you'd rather have one guide for your entire trip, ask the tour operator if this is the plan. However, some tour operators reserve the right to guarantee a single guide only if a minimum number of travelers sign up; if the minimum is not met, they may substitute locals.

A TOUR OPERATOR'S REPUTATION

Reputation can be hard to pin down. But research can help determine whether a tour operator delivers on its promises.

Ask your travel agent. If booking through an agent, see whether other travelers have raved or complained about the tour you're considering.

TOURS & CRUISES

255

Do some digging. Check newspapers and magazines for articles reporting on a tour to learn whether accommodations were acceptable or if there were problems, such as transportation snafus or delays.

Use web "forums." The Internet is a vast source of travel-related information. Forums, particularly helpful, are places where individuals can post questions to be answered by other travelers. If you have any doubts about a tour operator's reputation, you could post a question to those who've taken the tour and see what response you get. Most major travel sites have a forum feature. (See Part Three.)

Check the fine print. Again, those small-type sections can reveal a lot about a tour operator's procedures. For example, you might investigate what happens if a part of the tour needs to be canceled because of some condition like bad weather. Will the operator issue a refund?

CHAPTER 29

What to Expect During the Tour

You've decided to take a tour, whether a week-long excursion to a European city or a three-week journey to a distant land like China. What's ahead?

—————————————— ■ ——————————————

Tour travel is much more predictable than independent travel. On a tour, you exist within a given set of parameters, with itinerary, most meals (and your companions) all preordained. You can generally anticipate the overall structure.

GETTING WITH THE GROUP

Since many tours include the air segment, you may meet fellow traveling companions on the way to your first stop. When you arrive, a company representative (or your actual tour guide) meets you, usually with a sign bearing either the tour name or yours. Once everyone's assembled, you'll claim luggage and be directed onto a tour bus. Depending on the tour, you may be required to wear an identifying name tag, button, or badge.

The tour operator should be able to estimate group size for you when you sign up and then confirm the number prior to your departure.

Small groups. Some operators specialize in small-size tours (of 6 to 10 people), which may cost more than those focusing on larger groups. But they may be worth the extra cost if you want more personal attention from your guide and the atmosphere and advantages of traveling with just a few other people.

Small groups generally travel in small buses or vans, rather than large touring buses, and may stay in hotels not available to larger tour groups. Mealtimes may be less "assembly-line," even allowing travelers to experience more local color. And small groups offer a chance of flexibility—say, deviating from a set itinerary if all group members agree.

Large groups. Most tours consist of at least 20 travelers moving en masse: Everyone assembles at a certain hour, then follows a preset itinerary throughout the day and generally into the evening. A large tour bus is your home base. (Tours covering a large area may use airplanes.) Flexibility is limited and the group generally keeps to the pace of its slowest member. Sometimes guides will split a larger group into two or three smaller groups based on pace and interests.

TRANSPORTATION

Air transportation from one or more U.S. gateway cities (usually those with major international airports, such as New York, Los Angeles, or San Francisco) is usually included in the tour's price. If you do not live near one of those gateway cities, you'll generally need to arrange transportation to get there. Tour operators may also offer pre-arranged add-on airfares, Which are frequently good values. So be sure to ask if this is an option before you go to the trouble of booking your own.

Your tour guide generally makes sure that all transportation and baggage handling are arranged. Baggage is tagged with the tour group name and transported by handlers contracted by the tour company. You just put it outside your hotel-room door at a predetermined time.

ACCOMMODATIONS

You'll usually be told what level of accommodations the tour provides. Many tour brochures list the actual hotels; some offer photos so you know what to expect. Most tours reserve the right to change hotels at any time.

If you doubt that a tour company is up-front about accommodation standards, check guidebooks for hotel evaluations. But many hotel-rating systems in foreign countries are not based on the U.S. standard: A four-star hotel in a country like Turkey may be more like a two- or three-star hotel in the U.S.

The cost of most tours is also based upon double occupancy, which means that if you're a single and opted not to pay a single supplement, you'll share a room with another traveler.

MEAL ARRANGEMENTS

Tours generally include at least two meals a day.

Breakfast. Most tours include all breakfasts. But the meal may simply be a continental breakfast. Other tours list "full American breakfast" or "breakfast buffet." American breakfast generally guarantees familiar breakfast food; a breakfast buffet could feature foods of the country you're visiting.

Lunch. Most lunches are also included. Some are full lunches served buffet style at pre-arranged stops along the route; others are boxed lunches eaten at a sight or on the bus.

Dinner. Policies vary. Some tours include all or some dinners. But often, dinner's on you. (Many travelers prefer the latter.)

When all meals are included, expect them to be mass seatings in the hotel restaurant or a pre-selected restaurant with a few tourist-oriented dinner shows thrown in. If you have special dietary requests, talk to the tour operator *before* you leave.

SINGLE TRAVELERS

Many single travelers take tours to meet other people. You'll pay a premium, however—typically 50 percent more—if you

TOURS & CRUISES

want your own room. There are pros and cons to the single supplement. On the plus side, you're guaranteed a room to yourself, an advantage if you have trouble sleeping or simply value your privacy. But you'll pay more than other travelers for the same trip and services, and you may get the smallest or least desirable room. (Or you might luck out and land a double room all your own.) Still, you may feel isolated from the group without a roommate—and also might miss a chance to find a compatible future travel partner.

SHOPPING

Shopping is an integral part of many classic sightseeing tours, but usually not of more adventure-oriented jaunts. If hitting the stores is important to you, find out how much shopping time you'll get.

DEALING WITH PROBLEMS

Try to resolve any tour problems as they appear. Complain promptly to your tour guide or other company representative (if you're on an escorted tour), to the tour headquarters, or your travel agency back home. Keep your cool, and be specific about the problem and what resolution you desire.

If no solution is possible, bailing out may be best. Admittedly an expensive option, it may strengthen your case for a refund or chargeback (a credit from your charge-card issuer for the disputed amount). To obtain either, you'll have to pursue your complaints in writing, detailing the difficulty and your expected resolution. As a last resort, consider filing a formal complaint with USTOA or NTA (for tour operators) or ASTA (for travel agencies).

CHAPTER 30

How to Choose a Cruise

A cruise may be the most economical way to visit many ports of call. A multitude of options exists already, and new ships are set to join the ever-growing cruise fleet.

———————————————— ■ ————————————————

The cruise market is booming: An estimated 6 million people took a cruise in 1999 and almost 6.4 million are expected to set sail in 2000. Although hotel prices have ballooned, you can still buy a week-long cruise for under $200 a day per couple, little more than you'd have paid 10 years ago.

Several hundred large cruise ships currently ply the seas around the world, and more—especially big ships, à la Grand Princess—are on the way in 2000, and beyond. The Cruise Lines International Association (CLIA) estimates that its member lines plan to add 30 ships to their North American fleets by the end of 2002, some of them 2,000-plus berth behemoths.

No one knows whether cruise lines will fill all these new ships. A constantly swelling capacity may mean potential bargains for consumers—or maybe not. Industry watchers say brochure prices won't drop even though some lines may be faced with excess capacity. Why? Because the biggest cruise lines, like Carnival and Royal Caribbean, are often booked solid, and smaller competing lines can't afford to cut their published rates too deeply.

Still, cruise lines openly promote price cuts for customers who book early and push backdoor discounts through a variety of discount agencies, providing good values for careful shoppers able to navigate the system.

Basically, a cruise is a seagoing package tour with the works thrown in. The price covers almost all your costs—transportation, accommodations, food, entertainment, and sometimes even wine with meals, which means that so many cruises deliver a lot for the money. How do you choose? See what's available—and ask questions.

WHAT WILL IT COST?

The ship. Everything about the vessel, from the operating cruise line to ship size and age, is a factor in pricing. Certain cruise lines (notably Cunard, Norwegian, Seabourn, Silversea, and Windstar), known for top-flight amenities, also command premium pricing. Others (particularly Carnival, Holland America, Premier, and Royal Caribbean) offer a wide range of accommodations, from relatively basic bunkbed-style cabins to luxurious suites.

The itinerary. The longer the cruise, the more expensive. But both the region a ship cruises and its ports of call can also affect pricing. Many Caribbean and Mediterranean itineraries are quite affordable; while cruises to the South Pacific, Alaska, and Antarctica are generally steeper.

The cabin class. Most cruise ships offer about a dozen cabin categories, some even more. The more expensive cabins are larger, outside (with windows), and on the more desirable mid and upper decks. The lowest-priced cabins can be about one-quarter the cost, but may be quite small, inside (no windows), and located on the lowest decks.

The cruise amenities. Everything from food to entertainment to onboard activities can influence a particular cruise's price.

HOW BIG IS THAT SHIP?

The trend in cruise ships these days is big. How big? Colossally so. The Grand Princess and the Carnival Triumph each accommodate more than 2,600 passengers and weigh more than 100,000 tons. Even larger ships are on the way. Carnival, Costa, Norwegian, Princess, and Royal Caribbean all have added or will add megaships with more than 2,000 berths. In late 1999, Royal Caribbean was set to launch its Voyager of the Seas, which weighs in at 142,000 tons and carries 3,100 passengers. This behemoth, three football fields long, has scores of shops, bars, and restaurants, as well as a 900-seat theater, a driving range, and an ice-skating rink.

Some people enjoy being onboard with more than 2,000 strangers; the experience is like visiting a vacation resort with lots of public spaces and facilities to explore.

Others want a smaller ship—and there are some fine small- and medium-sized ships already on the seas or about to join major cruise-line fleets. These days, a small ship carries about 600 to 800 passengers. The advantage of a small ship is that it can get into some ports the biggest ships can't (some giant ships also cannot traverse the Panama Canal). A medium ship carries between 1,000 and 1,750 passengers. Some of the more expensive cruise lines—such as Seabourn and Silversea—also have "intimate" ships that carry just 200 to 300 passengers—for a price, of course. And if sailing appeals to you, a few cruise operators offer "tall-ship" or "windjammer" excursions, carrying fewer than 100 passengers.

WHAT'S THE SHIP'S PERSONALITY?

Each ship has its own onboard atmosphere. For example, Carnival Cruise lines calls its vessels "fun ships." That particular personality can be described as energetic, activity-driven, and often loud.

A cruise line's brochures and web site can give you an idea of the line's personality—and even the character of individual ships. You can also ask your travel agent or a cruise specialist for details on onboard activities and passenger type (couples, singles, older, younger, families). For a look at cruise lines' own descriptions, see "Personality profiles" below.

A cruise line's individual ships also have different personalities, based on such factors as their age (many ships were built in the '90s, but some are 20, 30, even 40 years old, although they've been renovated), the itinerary, the crew and the facilities (such as pools, casinos, cocktail lounges, and spas). Before

Personality Profiles
How the cruise lines describe themselves

Carnival: Fun onboard

Celebrity: Passionate dedication to providing a cruise that exceeds expectations.

Crystal: Charmed universe. Serenity and excitement.

Cunard: Unabashed opulence from the golden age of ocean travel.

Disney: Family fun; a voyage to spark the imagination.

Holland America: Play to your heart's content.

Norwegian: As far from the everyday as a ship can take you.

Premier: Smaller, more comfortable. High vacation value.

Princess: It's more than a cruise, it's the Love Boat.

Renaissance. Great places, great times. Adults-only. Smoke-free.

Royal Caribbean: If you can get it on land, you can get it here, too.

Seabourn: Only 200 pampered passengers. It's not a Seabourn cruise at all; it's a (your name here) cruise.

Silversea: Beautiful, yacht-like ships. Breathtaking in every respect. Excellence in every detail.

Windstar: 180 degrees from ordinary. Time moves slower here. Your personal yacht.

booking a particular ship, make sure it will provide the kind of atmosphere you want on your vacation.

CRUISE ON A SAILBOAT?

A cruise doesn't have to put you aboard a vessel the size of Rhode Island. It can also deliver a more intimate, relaxing, and closer-to-the-water experience aboard a much smaller sailboat. Since there are fewer sailboats than big ships, your choices will be limited. But you can still choose your ambience.

Casual and barefoot. The "windjammer" experience—sailing aboard a restored tall-masted ship—has been around for several decades. These cruises are generally low-cost and casual, with a mix of passengers of all ages. Activities are port-based, including lots of beach and snorkel time. Miami-based Windjammer Barefoot Cruises is one of the largest providers.

Pampered and personal. Several luxury sailing vessels ply the Caribbean, Mediterranean, and South Pacific, operated by, among others, Windstar and Club Med. Ships are sparkling new, rather than renovated, and trips cost much more than those on a traditional windjammer.

Chartered and carefree. A third sailing option is to charter a captain, small crew (usually a mate and cook), and a sailboat accommodating anywhere from six to 12 passengers. Depending on how many people split the cost, chartering can be either expensive or economical. Unless you splurge for a plush yacht, expect relatively basic, cramped cabins and shared shower/toilet facilities.

CRUISE FREIGHTER STYLE?

A 47,000-ton ship, 82 days at sea, hearty meals, ample staff, and only six passengers. Sounds like a royal cruise, but it's actually a container ship, the Pegasus Bay, on a long tour of the South Seas. The cruise is one of several container-ship trips offered by Maris Freighter Cruises (see Resource Guide).

TOURS & CRUISES

265

Freighter cruises offer both pros and cons. You'll have plenty of solitude, if that's what you long for—most freighters carry a maximum of 12 passengers, excluding crew. And freighter travel definitely delivers time to relax and an alternative view of the world.

Accommodations are comfortable. Cabins on Pegasus Bay are usually all located on the top three decks, with private bathrooms, showers, TVs, and VCRs. The ship has a common lounge, videos and books, a small outdoor pool, and an elevator. Passengers dine with the officers and can purchase alcohol and cigarettes onboard.

But trips are generally long and uneventful. Freighters stop in working ports not often on luxury liner itineraries. And there are no casinos, ballrooms, or entertainers.

Freighter travel is also expensive—for instance, $12,900 for two people in a cabin with twin beds ($7,990 for a single traveler). However, that totals only $157 a day per couple for an

Is Your Boat Shipshape?
Know the score on ship sanitation

Under the National Center for Environmental Health Vessel Sanitation Program, all passenger cruise ships arriving at U.S. ports are subject to unannounced inspections. Examiners scrutinize water supplies; food preparation and holding; potential contamination of food; and general cleanliness, storage, and repair. Passing grade is 86—but a score in the 90s is more reassuring.

Scores are published in the Summary of Sanitation Inspections of International Cruise Ships (the "Green Sheet"), updated every two weeks, and available from the U.S. Public Health Service.

To check current scores and/or the actual inspection report, go to *www2.cdc.gov/nceh/vsp/vspmain.asp*. For a fax-back copy, call 888 232-3299 and ask for Document 510051. Or write the Vessel Sanitation Program, National Center for Environmental Health, Centers for Disease Control and Prevention, 1850 Eller Drive, Suite 101, Ft. Lauderdale, Fla. 33316.

82-day trip, comfortably within a $200-per-day standard for cruise bargains. Cost also covers three meals and one snack each day.

A number of companies and travel clubs offer freighter travel as well. For details, ask your travel agent. (Also see the Resource Guide.)

ARE CHILDREN WELCOME?

Some ships (such as Disney, Carnival, Holland America, and Premier) are more family friendly and have extensive onboard kids' programs; others (Renaissance and Seabourn, for example) are strictly dress-for-dinner, adults-only affairs. Whether you're taking children along—or want to avoid them—check with a cruise consultant or travel agent for the ship's policy.

WHAT'S INCLUDED, WHAT'S NOT?

Most cruise rates now include port charges (maybe a few hundred dollars on longer cruises), and some even cover airfare to and from the port city, but count on extras.

What's included. Typically, a quoted cruise price delivers this package: cabin (double occupancy); port charges (since 1997, most cruise lines have included them in advertised rates); taxes (some may be extra, depending on the cruise line and the itinerary); airfare from select gateway cities, but check the fine print; all meals (you can eat all day, if you like); onboard entertainment (daytime music, nightime shows); and certain onboard activities (pools, games).

What's not included. Certain items will cost you extra: shore excursions (easily $30 to $40 per person per port, so shun the cruise line's tours and make your own arrangements once you arrive in port); liquor (almost always extra, though sometimes wine will be served at a special dinner); souvenir photos (a ship photographer will capture you at almost every turn, but these are expensive memories).

You will also be responsible for laundry (prices generally comparable to hotel laundry prices); spa treatments (as high or higher than land-based ones); phone calls (to avoid these costly calls, use a calling card from a pay phone in port); onboard purchases (shopping or gambling can quickly add up); and any gratuities (can easily add $10 a day per person).

IS THE AGENCY RELIABLE?

Cruising remains one of the few travel services usually available only through a travel agent—though a few cruise lines have begun direct consumer sales via the web. Whatever type of agency you choose, deal with someone who has firsthand knowledge of lines, ships, destinations, and ports.

Cruise-only agency. This type of operation can give real advice rather than just take orders. Many cruise-only agencies promote themselves as discounters. But the big discounters sometimes beat their prices.

However, a few big cruise discounters have gone bust in recent years, causing customers to lose both their prepayment and their cruise. You'll find many discounters on the web, but check credentials before you buy. A cruise-only agency should, at minimum, be affiliated with either the Cruise Lines International Association (CLIA) or the National Association of Cruise-Only Agencies (NACOA). Neither has a consumer-protection program, but members must fulfill modest training and financial requirements. Also check the Better Business Bureau in the agency's home city for complaints .

Full-service agencies. The big, multibranch chains can frequently match cruise-only agencies on discounts. Even a small, independent agency should have at least one agent who is current with the cruise industry or has an arrangement with a cruise discounter. If your call yields only an order-taker, try another agency or ask to speak with someone familiar with the cruise that interests you.

WHEN DO YOU BOOK?

For the best deal, the earlier you book, the better.

Early bargains. Check brochures for both early-booking prices (generally a savings of 20 percent or more) and deadlines. Generally "early" means four to six months before departure—and early booking may be the only way to get the best discount (and the best cabins) on some very popular cruises. All the big lines guarantee to refund the difference if they later undercut their early-booking rates.

Early-bird buyers may also find other savings: two-for-one specials; kids-free programs; unpublicized reductions for prior customers; credit for shipboard purchases; and free hotel accommodations before or after the cruise.

Last-minute deals. Still, you don't absolutely have to book early to get a good price, especially if you're flexible. Last-minute bargains are often available one month or less before sailing, when some ships aren't full. Among the best bets for bargain rates are "repositioning" cruises—between-season trips on which a ship moves from one region to another, say, from summer in Alaska to winter in the Caribbean.

CAN YOU UPGRADE YOUR CABIN?

The discount market offers another attraction: the chance to combine a good price with a free cabin upgrade. Upgrades become available when a cruise ship sells a higher percentage of inexpensive cabins than expensive accommodations—a fairly common occurrence. Rather than turn down customers wanting inexpensive but sold-out cabins, the cruise line may offer to upgrade passengers currently holding those accommodations. Upgrades may be either rewards for repeat customers or incentives to entice first-time cruisers who book early. (Cruise lines no longer routinely dangle upgrades as a lure to late buyers.)

However, many travelers who book early want a specific cabin or location and wouldn't consider a change, even to a

TOURS &
CRUISES

larger cabin. So a line won't reassign an early booker unless that traveler really wants an upgrade. If you book early and *would* welcome an upgrade, have your agent add a specific notation in your reservation file.

Cruising for Free
Your talent can be your ticket

Have a talent or expertise to offer? You may be able to cruise for free—if you are willing and able to hold forth in public as what is known as a "destination speaker," giving talks geared to the ship's itinerary.

For example, art historians or authorities on ancient civilizations or architecture can lecture aboard ships sailing the Mediterranean or Aegean. Other experts in demand include ornithologists and archaeologists for South America and the South Pacific. In fact, even doctors, psychologists, lawyers, and others can parlay their talents into a free trip. However, talent is the operative word. Impressive academic credentials are not enough. You must have a flair for public speaking and be able to give a 55-minute presentation each day at sea.

What are your chances of being hired? It depends. Some lines have been known to hire as many as 1,200 speakers a year. But even if you're a pro, you'll be vying with thousands of would-be speakers for these plum assignments. Cruise lines are very picky about who preaches from their podiums; just a tiny fraction of the proposals received each month are actually considered. Want to give it a go? Here are some tips.

Don't call, write—via mail, as faxes and e-mails are frowned upon—and type all correspondence.

Along with your proposals, include a bio, color photo, two or three references, and any newspaper or magazine articles written about you.

If possible, send a videotape showing three to five minutes of your presentation.

Don't expect your materials to be returned or to hear from the cruise line unless you're selected for further screening.

If you're available for last-minute assignment, say so because this will improve your chances.

But remember that most people who get these assignments are accomplished academics, authors, or art historians.

CHAPTER 31

What to Expect Onboard

Ahoy, first-time cruisers! Learn what you'll likely experience as you board your ship and set sail on a journey from island to island, through a canal, or around the world.

——————————— ■ ———————————

As you shop around for a cruise, the lines will try to dazzle you with brochures filled with lavish promises: The voyage will be "pure magic," the accommodations "first class," and the food "the finest you've ever tasted." How much is true and how much is hype varies from line to line and ship to ship.

What you need instead of puffery is a full picture of cruising realities—some wonderful, some not so wonderful.

GETTING THERE AND BOARDING

Take first things first: Before you can cruise, you must get to the ship. Unless airfare is included in the cost of the cruise (in which case you may be traveling with other passengers, on either a charter or a commercial flight), you are responsible for reaching the port city and the correct pier. (See "Port cities," on the next page). And as you make your get-to-the-ship travel arrangements, remember these hassle-saving tips.

Arrive early. When scheduling your flight, always allow plenty of time—at least six hours, preferably more—between your arrival in the port city and your ship's departure. If your flight is delayed, the ship will leave without you. Some cruise lines recommend that you arrive a day ahead and spend a night at a hotel in the port, especially wise in the winter, when bad weather can cause flight delays and even cancellations.

Know your pier. Large ports like Miami and San Juan have literally dozens of cruise ships docked, an overwhelming and confusing sight. Don't expect to simply tell a cab driver, "The Sea Princess, please." Some drivers may know exactly where certain ships are docked—most won't. Give the driver the pier number; if you're leaving from a foreign port where English isn't spoken, write down the pier number to show the driver.

Board early. You'll avoid major lines as 1,000 to 2,000 passengers try to clear immigration (if required) and board. Most cruise lines offer a boarding period of several hours and make the process as easy as possible. If you arrive early, you simply

---

Port Cities
Who docks where?

Before you take your cruise, you've got to get to your ship. Depending on the itinerary, here's where it might be docked.

Caribbean: Miami, Fort Lauderdale, or San Juan
Alaska: Vancouver
Mexico: Los Angeles (Pacific) or Miami (Gulf)
Mediterranean: Athens or Barcelona
Aegean/Adriatic/Baltic: Venice or Istanbul
Transatlantic: New York, Fort Lauderdale, or Miami
South America/Panama Canal: Miami, Fort Lauderdale, or San Juan
Hawaii: Honolulu or Los Angeles
South Pacific: Hong Kong, Sydney, or Papeete
Scandinavia: Amsterdam, Copenhagen, or Southampton
Antarctica: Buenos Aires or Ushuaia, Argentina

sign in and hand over your bags. Then you can sightsee for a few hours before reboarding and wishing yourself bon voyage.

CHOOSING ACCOMMODATIONS

Accommodations on newer ships are generally a bit bigger and better than those on their older counterparts; some small to medium-size ships now feature outside-facing, suite-only cabins. Most ships, however, offer a variety (as many as 15) cabin categories ranging from very small interior cabins with bunk beds to windowed, multiroom suites.

Which type should you choose? First, ignore the misleading brochure pictures, taken with a wide-angle lens. Follow basic guidelines, based on what you can spend.

If you're on a budget, you'll find plenty of cabins in your price range, but they'll be small and situated on a low deck. Budget cabins usually measure either 9 by 12 or 10 by 13 feet and, on most ships, they're inside, with no portholes or windows. Bathrooms can be quite tiny; they generally have a drain in the center of the floor and a shower that sprays the entire bathroom if you're not careful.

You must pay more to get more. Some expensive cabins are quite large, maybe even a suite of two or three rooms. Many have windows facing a deck, somewhat like motel rooms on an outside corridor; so you can enjoy your privacy or the view—just not both at the same time. Also note that few cabins have a double bed. Book early if you want one.

MEALS AT SEA

Take a cruise, gain five pounds—or more. That's the commonly held belief (and often the reality) of today's eat-around-the-clock cruise ships. If a calorie-laden midnight buffet suits your tastes, most ships oblige. Watching your weight? Some offer low-cal spa menus, too.

Most cruise specialists and some travel agents should be

TOURS & CRUISES

able to steer you in the right food direction. And some cruise line web sites offer morsels of menu information.

For dinner, you'll typically be asked to choose the first or second sitting; if you don't like to eat after 8 p.m., sign up for first. You may also have the option of sitting with the same table mates the entire cruise or switching night after night. Some cruises also offer private seating (one couple per table).

COPING WITH SEASICKNESS

After cabins and food, the possibility of seasickness seems to be the top concern for cruisers—first-timers and veterans alike. Mal-de-mer occurs when your middle ear is affected by the ship's movement and in turn sends signals to the brain, triggering vertigo (loss of balance), nausea, and vomiting.

You cannot tell if you will fall victim. You might be prone to seasickness, however, if you ever experience motion sickness when in a car, plane, or other moving vehicle; or have middle-ear problems.

Today's large, modern ships are equipped with stabilizers, making them less prone to provoke this trip-spoiler than traditional sailing ships and smaller vessels. But rough seas can result in more shipboard motion than desirable. So you may want to pack one of several preventive treatments, or get medication from the ship's doctor at the first sign of trouble.

Anti-seasickness pills. Meclizine (Bonine) and diphenhydramine (Dramamine) are two commonly used over-the-counter drugs. Side effects include drowsiness, so they should be taken with care.

Anti-seasickness patches. Small patches containing scopolamine worn on the neck (good for 72 hours) are available by prescription only. However, studies have shown that their use may contribute to glaucoma, so discuss risks with your doctor first.

Wrist bands. A metal ball in a terrycloth band exerts pressure on an acupressure point that affects equilibrium. Some cruisers swear by these bands, donning them a few days before sailing and wearing them throughout the cruise. There's no scientific proof that they work, however, and some find them useless.

Ginger root. Taken 12 to 24 hours before sailing, these capsules are said to have a positive effect on equilibrium and stave off seasickness. (Some people wear a wrist band, too.) But this approach doesn't work for everyone.

Wellness tips. If seasickness strikes, some easy-to-follow tips can help: Drink plenty of water after vomiting has stopped (avoid alcohol); avoid cramped spaces (like below-deck cabins); stay active in the fresh air; breathe deeply; look at the distant horizon (not down at the water); and avoid reading.

SHIPBOARD AMENITIES

Today's modern cruise ships have been called "floating cities," and that's no misnomer. You'll find almost everything onboard that you might encounter in a small town or resort community.

Entertainment opportunities. Most ships have at least a few bars and lounges—some of the biggest ships may have a dozen—and gambling facilities are a possible attraction too. You may also find a theater showing first-run movies and/or documentaries about your ports of call, plus a library providing books to read by the pool.

Exercise and relaxation. Gym facilities are increasingly common (you can work off those midnight buffets); outdoor tracks for walking or running are a possibility. There may be one or more pools, although not Olympic-size. Ships do provide enough deck chairs to go around, but the prized locations—near the pool, in a spot sheltered from the wind—will be snapped up first. Some ships have a spa featuring massages, facials, and wraps.

Shipboard commerce. Expect a variety of boutiques, just like those at major resort hotels, selling apparel and souvenirs. You

TOURS & CRUISES

can get money or exchange currency at the ship's bank, and buy stamps and mail letters and postcards at the shipboard post office. A hairdresser or barber will be handy for touch-ups and trims.

Medical facility. All ships are required to have a trained medical staff. If you have a serious medical condition, ask the cruise line if it has sufficient and correct onboard equipment and adequately trained personnel to handle it. See Chapter 36 for additional information.

YOUR FELLOW PASSENGERS

There will be lots of them—from about 100 on a windjammer cruise to over 2,000 on the new megaships. You certainly won't meet all of them. Most cruisers get to know only a few of their fellow passengers, usually acquaintances from the pool, a shore excursion, or their particular dinner seating. The other passengers can make the trip more—or less—enjoyable. Personalities are easily exaggerated by the vacation mindset and alcohol consumption.

Different cruises cater to different age groups and personalities. Before you reserve, be sure that the ship and/or itinerary traditionally appeals to the type of people you'd enjoy as fellow passengers. Then if you want to meet others, make an effort to mingle, favoring locations (pools, lounges) and activities (group games, shore excursions) that allow you to get to know your cruising colleagues.

PORTS OF CALL

The itinerary indicates which ports the ship will enter, and there is usually little deviation. But unforeseen circumstances, such as bad weather or localized conflicts, can necessitate skipping or a substitution.

How much time will you have in each port? Again, the brochure itinerary is generally followed. Most ships stop for just a day (sometimes two on longer cruises). You usually arrive in the middle of the night, then have a full or half day to explore before the ship sails again in the evening.

SHORE EXCURSIONS

Part of the allure of cruising is the chance to sample a few different islands or cities during one journey. But you'll want to make the most of the time in each port. Virtually all cruises have pre-arranged tours, generally priced higher than tours you can arrange yourself once ashore.

You'll probably want to bypass the ship's excursions in all but a few cases: during peak tourist season in very popular ports (onshore tours could be booked); when time is very limited (say, a half day) and the ship's trip includes many sights you want to see; or if stopping in a non-English-speaking country or one where travel warnings have been issued to lone tourists.

Outside these instances, your own plans will probably be more satisfying. You have several options.

Rent a car—or a car and driver. Depending on the port, this approach is quite affordable or quite overpriced. If cost is an issue, try to find another person or couple to split the costs.

Go by taxi or public transportation. Most cities have navigable and affordable buses or underground transport. You can also make your way on foot.

Take a tour. If you like the security of a structured tour—a few hours in a bus with stops at the top tourist sights—you should be able to book at one of many tour operations located dockside. (Reputable tour operators are generally listed in major travel guidebooks.)

Book a guide. Individual guides, available for hire, will approach you as you leave the ship. Some are quite personable and provide a unique insight into a city or island. But before you head off with someone, ask to see his or her credentials (local tourist offices often issue IDs to reputable guides). And

TOURS & CRUISES

if a port is known for hustlers or scam artists, ask the ship's shore-excursion coordinator whether other passengers have had bad experiences with local guides.

But whatever route you choose, know when the ship sails and give yourself enough time to get back to the dock. Remember, the ship will leave without you.

DISEMBARKATION

Cruise over, it's time to tend to your shipboard expenses, get your bags ready, and clear customs and immigration. Individual ships operate differently, but usually an announcement is made or distributed the day before the cruise ends outlining procedures: how to clear up onboard charges (for alcohol, shore excursions, or purchases); when and where to leave your luggage so it can be taken off the ship; and what the customs/immigration drill will be.

Expect to wait in a few lines. You can simplify by having all your paperwork filled in. Once off the ship, you will be asked to claim your luggage and proceed through customs. Typically, there are lines of taxis waiting to ferry passengers from the pier to the airport for the flight home.

PART TEN

Travel Savvy

CHAPTER 32

Your Pretrip Checklist

Want to enjoy a smooth, hassle-free journey? These trip-preparation tips can help you avoid the most common travel missteps and mistakes.

■

The world of international travel is so alluring—exotic destinations, romantic ports of call, exciting adventures—that many people easily forget that travel is also highly dependent on myriad details: tickets, vouchers, reservations, passports, visas, flight schedules, and on and on. And overlooking any one of those details can mean canceled plans, hassles or delays at customs, or a scramble to find new accommodations—not exactly the stuff of dream vacations.

CONFIRMATION AND DOCUMENTATION
Anyone who's ever arrived at the airport only to realize that a ticket or passport is still at home will do everything possible to avoid such a disaster again. This troubleshooting timetable helps avert major frustrations later.

Two months ahead. If traveling abroad, take care of your passport, visas, and immunizations.

Confirm your passport expiration date. U.S. passports are good for 10 years. Unless you pay an extra fee, renewal generally takes four to five weeks.

Be sure you have all necessary visas. Guidebooks should tell you whether Americans need a visa for your destination. (Your travel agent should also know.) Doublecheck for yourself by calling the country's embassy. Embassies are located mainly in Washington, D.C., with outposts in many major U.S. cities.

Get all needed immunizations. Chapter 36 has general guidelines, plus sources for further information.

One month ahead. See to potentially time-consuming details.

Check tickets. Always examine your tickets when they arrive. See that the listed flights—and airports—are the ones you booked and look over airport arrival and departure information.

Reconfirm hotel and rental-car reservations. Be sure you have solid reservations—a reservation confirmation number from a rental-car company and a mailed or faxed confirmation from your hotel. (Your travel agent, if you're using one, should provide this information.) Confirmations are especially important if you're traveling during peak season, when hotels may be sold out and equivalent accommodations scarce.

If traveling by car, have it tuned up. Don't wait until right before you leave. Tune-ups can uncover other problems that need fixing—or even create new ones.

One week before. Put together a travel packet.

Consolidate documents. Recheck that you have all necessary confirmation numbers and vouchers for rental cars, hotels, and cruises. By now, these documents should be in a neat package, put together by either you or your travel agent.

Type an itinerary. Include all relevant information: flight numbers and arrival times; hotel names, addresses, phone numbers, and rates; rental-car confirmation numbers and rates. This detailed day-to-day itinerary acts as an at-a-glance

TRAVEL
SAVVY

guide for you as you travel and also as a "tracking memo" in case anyone needs you in an emergency. Make several copies: Give one to relatives, then slip one into your bag and each piece of luggage, in case a copy is lost or a bag stolen.

Photocopy your passport. Should your passport be lost or stolen, a photocopy will greatly speed up the replacement process. Make two or three copies and keep one in each bag.

Bring trip-related documents home from the office. Many people plan trips during working hours, leaving important or helpful documents in a desk drawer. Bring everything home ahead of time.

Three days before. Small steps now can prevent last-minute panic on your day of departure.

Gather all trip-related documents in one place. You should have all your tickets and vouchers by now. So put them in a place where they will not be disturbed or accidentally thrown out in the pretrip mayhem—but not somewhere where they'll be forgotten. A leather or plastic document holder is ideal. You can keep it in a secure pouch or in hotel safes as you travel.

Confirm all international flight connections. If you are flying on an international carrier then transferring as soon as you land to a local carrier (say, to Papeete, Tahiti, on United, then on to Bora Bora on Air Tahiti), confirm your connecting flight 72 hours in advance (that is, two to three days before your international flight).

Exchange a small amount of money into foreign currency. You'll congratulate yourself when you arrive at your destination and see the lines at the airport exchange booths. Usually, $20 to $50 will get you to your hotel. You can then cash traveler's checks or ask about a nearby ATM.

One day before. It's packing time—so look over your luggage.

See that luggage is properly tagged. When you pull your luggage out to begin packing, be sure that luggage tags are secure and contain enough, but not too much, information. Include a first initial and last name (if your name is very common, use both first and last names and even a middle initial) and a hometown and contact phone number. As for the address, a business address or post office box number can thwart would-be burglars, such as unscrupulous airport workers who might take advantage of your absence.

Confirm carry-on guidelines. You'll want to keep all your documents in a carry-on bag so they're safe and accessible. Make sure that bag meets the airline's size requirements. If the size is wrong, you'll want to switch now.

As you leave the house. Take time for a last-minute review.

Check your tickets and passport. As you start the car or get in the cab, check that you do indeed have your tickets and all other necessary documentation.

Double-check airport and terminal information. You want to be absolutely certain you head to the right airport. As for terminals, with the increasing use of code-sharing you may have booked on United and have a ticket with a United flight code, but you'll actually be flying Lufthansa, and therefore must go to the Lufthansa terminal. (Your ticket *should* indicate the terminal or the flight operator or both.)

Stow documents in an accessible place. You'll be asked to show documents several times—at check-in, at security points, and at the gate—so make sure they're easy to reach.

SUITCASE SAVVY

These days, there is little reason to "lug" anything. The new wheeled luggage has morphed into every shape and size—duffels, garment bags, suiters, uprights, compact carry-ons, even convertible backpacks—from numerous manufacturers at all prices. (See the luggage Ratings on page 288.)

Gazing at an aiport luggage carousel, you may think that all bags look alike—most are black fabric, with wheels and handles. But a closer look will reveal big differences, which can

10 WAYS TO TRAVEL LIGHT

1. Wear bulkiest items in transit.
2. Pack lightweight washables.
3. Layer clothing.
4. Choose several base colors.
5. Choose dirt-deflecting dark colors.
6. Think Polartec, Gore-Tex and CoolMax.
7. Bring just two pairs of shoes.
8. Use travel-size toiletries.
9. Forget the tux.
10. Buy T-shirts there, rather than pack them.

affect long-term wear, toting comfort, and how well your luggage (and your clothes) survive the trip.

Fabric. Your choices are generally nylon, polyester, or a blend. Nylon with a high "denier" number (check the label) is thicker, coarser, and takes longer to wear through.

Pockets. Large, soft-sided bags have at least one pocket outside and at least one inside. Also look for a "wet pouch," handy for damp bathing suits.

Seams. You'll usually find plastic-covered wire piping around corners. Flexible piping is less damage-prone.

Zipper. The bigger and farther from the edge, the less likely it is to be damaged. Those that open the bag like a book are more convenient than those that open a big, U-shaped tongue of fabric.

Pull-handle. On a large bag, expect it to extend 38 to 44 inches from the ground. If you're tall, get a longish handle or the suitcase may nip your heels as you pull it.

Locks. Most are too small to foil a determined thief. But they might discourage casual pilferage and prevent accidental opening.

Carry-handles and feet. Large bags have additional handles on the side and top, so you can carry them like conventional suitcases. You'll want the feet positioned opposite the side handle, to keep the bag from getting wet or dirty when you put it down.

Frame. Though soft-sided, a large bag will have a hard frame, made of metal, wood, plastic, or a combination. No material has a clear advantage, but a full frame, which surrounds the cargo compartment, will likely protect contents best and prove most durable. To check, read the bag's literature, or open the bag and run your hands around the perimeter, squeezing the sides. A full frame will feel uniformly thick, and the sides won't flex much.

Skids. Plastic shields near wheels can make it easier to drag

Safeguarding Your Film
Don't expose yourself to ruined photos

Ever wonder whether it's safe to expose undeveloped film to the ever-more-powerful X-ray machines at airport security checkpoints? In 1999, photography and film experts formed an advocacy group called Film Safety for Traveling on Planes (FSTOP) to alert travelers to the potential hazards posed by new airport X-ray screening equipment used for checked baggage. The new high-dosage security scanners can ruin undeveloped film by leaving a stripe or line across it; processed slides and prints are not affected.

FSTOP has this advice for travelers:

• Do not pack unprotected film or loaded cameras in checked baggage without protective pouches specifically designed for high-dosage scanners. These lead-lined film bags are made by Sima Products Corp. in two "strengths," each designed to protect different types of film: FilmShield XPF 8 for slow-speed film (below ISO 200), and FilmShield XPF 20 for faster film (ISO 400 and above). Both types are available in photo-supply stores. They come in two sizes, at $10 to $40, depending on strength.

• Unprotected film may also be packed in carry-on baggage. Ask that film be hand-inspected. Or pack it in a low-dosage protective pouch and send it through airport screening equipment in a carry-on. The Federal Aviation Adminstration guarantees hand inspection at domestic airports when requested, but international travelers may not have the same option.

• You may buy and develop film at your destination—but that is often expensive.

• If you're traveling with a lot of film (20 rolls or more) or with motion-picture film, FSTOP advises giving advance notice so a hand-inspection appointment can be scheduled with local airline officials before the flight.

For more information, contact FSTOP (888 301-2665, *www.f-stop.org*).

TRAVEL SAVVY

a bag up a curb or stairs without damage. (If the bag has very large wheels, you probably won't need skids.)

Wheels. If you buy a smaller bag with wheels—such as a convertible backpack—try it on first. On some, wheels are positioned so the packs are uncomfortable.

Decoding new carry-on rules. As domestic airlines continue to crack down on carry-on bags, more passengers have more problems. In July 1998, in response to industry and consumer requests, the Federal Aviation Administration (FAA) asked the

Laptop Warning
Take precautions to protect your equipment

Always carry on your laptop. Rough baggage handling can damage notebooks, even those buried deep among clothing. Choose a briefcase or carrying case designed to house a notebook and its accessories.

Avoid the metal detector. Do not put the laptop through or anywhere near it—metal detectors can damage or even erase your hard drive.

Decide whether to have it X-rayed. Although the FAA says checkpoint X-ray machines will not harm computer hard drives or diskettes, you can ask to have your laptop hand inspected, (an especially good idea in some third world and Eastern European countries where X-ray equipment is generally older). When you get to a security checkpoint, alert security workers that you have a laptop and would like it hand-inspected.

If they comply, give it to a security person before passing through the metal detector. Claim your carry-ons as they come through on the belt and follow security personnel to a nearby table. You'll be asked to turn on the laptop, so make sure your batteries aren't dead. If the security officer asks that the carrying case be put through the X-ray machine, remove all floppy disks first.

Once aboard, stow the laptop carefully. When placing a laptop in the overhead bin, make sure it's resting securely on the bottom of the bin, below the lip of the door. If stowed on top of another bag, it could fall out when the bin is opened. Alternatively, fit the case under the seat in front of you.

airlines to clarify their carry-on rules. By late 1998, most major carriers had either introduced, or begun to enforce, limits on the number of bags that can be schlepped aboard.

But there's a big catch: Carry-on rules and maximum allowable sizes differ from airline to airline. And airlines have done only a so-so job of conveying rules to passengers. A survey by CONSUMER REPORTS TRAVEL LETTER of 12 airlines turned up these guidelines.

What's allowed? Every major domestic airline except Northwest now has a two-bag carry-on rule, although several carriers reserve the right to limit passengers to just one bag on full flights.

Exceptions. If you're a first-class, business-class, or elite frequent flier, you may not have to comply with such rules. Four airlines—Alaska, American, Northwest, and TWA—have developed more generous guidelines for their VIPs, either permitting one extra bag or increasing the allowable size limit.

What size qualifies? Most airlines use total-linear-inch guidelines (adding the length, height, and depth of a bag), but some also require carry-ons to fit into their "sizer boxes" at ticket counters and gates. If your bag won't slide in easily, or if it has protruding handles or wheels, you'll have to check it. (Air Canada and Canadian Airlines permit two carry-ons, but both bags *combined* equal the dimensions allowed by U.S. carriers, meaning they allow half the baggage volume. One purse, laptop, or briefcase, however, is exempt from the restrictions.)

Exempt items. In general, briefcases, laptops, and purses confuse the carry-on count, since some airlines consider them exempt and others don't.

"Reasonably sized" purses are exempt on most airlines, although American, Southwest, United, and US Airways count larger purses toward the two-bag limit. Alaska and TWA count all purses as one piece of the carry-on limit.

(Text continued on page 290)

TRAVEL SAVVY

Ratings *Luggage*
& Recommendations

The tests behind the ratings

Overall score is based on **ease of use** as determined by panelists who led the suitcases through our obstacle course; on **features and construction;** and on **durability** as determined by our tumbler tests. Even a bag rated fair in durability may withstand moderate abuse. In the **Details on the models,** capacity includes external pockets and is rounded to the nearest quarter-cubic-foot. **Price** is suggested retail unless marked with *. (Prices marked with * are estimated average based on national survey.) Discounts are often available.

Typical features for these models

• A retractable pull-handle on top. • Fixed carry-handles on top and side. • At least one lock to keep the main zipper from opening. • Two wheels on the back. • A latching "piggyback" strap that lets you attach a small bag. • A garment carrier.

Recommendations

Any of the models would be a fine choice. The Tumi Wheel-A-Way has a large capacity and many useful features. The Samsonite model was somewhat less durable but was much easier to pull. The Ricardo Beverly Hills bag, at only $160, is a **CR Best Buy**.

Source: Consumer Reports December 1998 and November 1999

Overall Ratings

Listed in order of overall score

Key no.	Brand and model	Price	Overall score	Ease of use	Features and construction	Durability
1	**Tumi** Wheel-A-Way 2245	$625		⊖	⊖	⊖
2	**Samsonite** 700-Series Silhouette 6 26 Piggyback Suiter	420		⊖	⊖	○
3	**Andiamo** Valorosa VJ25	495*		⊖	⊖	⊖
4	**Hartmann** Intensity Expandable Mobile Traveller 318	625		⊖	⊖	⊖
5	**Impuls** Targa 3692-26	230*		⊖	⊖	⊖
6	**Pathfinder** by Paragon 8002-B	190*		⊖	⊖	◐
7	**Ricardo Beverly Hills** Big Sur 1825 **A CR Best Buy**	160*		⊖	⊖	○
8	**Briggs & Riley** U-26WG	350*		⊖	⊖	◐

Details on the models

1 Tumi Wheel-A-Way 2245 $625
Excellent; lots of features, but expensive.
• 3¾ cu. ft. • 16 lb.
FEATURES: • Handle extends to 40 in.
• Wraparound plastic frame. • Three inside,
two outside pockets. • Garment carrier, which
can't be used separately. *PERFORMANCE:*
Fabric binding on the edges came free in the
tumbler test; bag was still usable.

2 Samsonite 700-Series Silhouette 6 26 Piggyback Suiter $420
**Excellent; extremely easy to pull, but some-
what less durable than the other two.**
• 3¼ cu. ft. • 18½ lb.
FEATURES: • Handle extends to 43 in.; locks
in two positions. • No feet on the side opposite the carry handle, which is messy if you
put the bag down on wet ground. • Three inside, two outside pockets. • Padded garment
carrier can be used separately, and it's less
likely to wrinkle a garment folded into it.
PERFORMANCE: • Suitcase was badly worn
but usable after our tumbler test.

3 Andiamo Valorosa VJ25 $495*
**Excellent and extremely durable, yet
pricey and short on features.**
• 2¾ cu. ft. • 14½ lb.
FEATURES: Handle extends to 39 in. and
locks in two positions. One large pocket outside and one inside, plus small detachable
bag inside. • No garment carrier. *SIMILAR:*
Tuxedo TJ25, $485; *VJ25 LS,* $595, with
garment carrier.

4 Hartmann Intensity Expandable Mobile Traveller 318 $625
Excellent; extremely durable and roomy.
• 4¼ cu. ft. • 14½ lb.
FEATURES: Handle extends to 39 in.
• Wraparound frame. • Three inside, three
outside pockets and a "wet pouch."
• Expansion gusset adds 3 in. to bag's depth.

• Garment carrier can be used separately, but
it isn't padded and may wrinkle a garment
folded into it. *SIMILAR:* • *323,* $595; *316,* $525.

5 Impuls Targa 3692-26 $230*
Excellent.
• 3¼ cu. ft. • 13 lb.
FEATURES: Handle extends to 40 in. and
locks in two positions. Two pockets outside
and two inside. • Padded internal separator
serves as a garment carrier.

6 Pathfinder by Paragon 8002-B $190*
**Excellent and carries a lot of cargo for its
weight, but not as durable as many. The
lightest bag tested.**
• 2¾ cu. ft. • 11½ lb.
FEATURES: Pull-handle extends to 44 in.
—good for tall people. • Three pockets
outside and six inside. • No garment carrier.
• One of the most popular bags with
panelists.

7 Ricardo Beverly Hills Big Sur 1825 $160*
**Very good performance at a very good
price. A CR Best Buy.**
• 2½ cu. ft. • 13 lb.
FEATURES: Pull-handle extends to 40 in.
Three pockets outside and five inside;
detachable "wet pouch." Garment carrier in
bag's lid.

8 Briggs & Riley U-26WG $350*
**Very good and full of features, but pricey
and very heavy for what it holds.**
• 2½ cu. ft. • 17 lb.
FEATURES: Pull-handle extends to 43 in. and
locks in two positions. Two pockets outside
and three inside; "wet pouch." Unlimited lifetime warranty. Very popular with panelists.
SIMILAR: U-26, $290, *BRX-U66N,* $270.

TRAVEL SAVVY

Continental is the only line not classifying briefcases and laptops as carry-ons; the other airlines all consider each a carry-on item. Although Northwest allows just one carry-on, passengers are also allowed one exempt purse, laptop, or briefcase.

Other items. Assistive devices for the disabled, an overcoat, an umbrella, a reasonable amount of reading material, and a camera are exempt from limits on all airlines.

Childcare gear. Policies vary widely. Strollers are usually checked at the gate, but in a few cases may be brought onboard and counted as one piece, subject to size and space restrictions. All carriers exempt child safety seats for ticketed children, but only Northwest, Southwest, and United exempt safety seats for an unticketed child who sits on an adult's lap. (During the flight, the safety seat is stored in an overhead bin or under the seat.) On full flights, carriers that usually allow strollers and unticketed child safety seats may make passengers check them at the gate. And diaper bags may be counted as a carry-on, so be ready.

CHAPTER 33

Travel Smart Overseas

Many international destinations have very different customs, health concerns, social/political situations, and currencies. Know what to expect.

———————————————— ■ ————————————————

A smooth trip abroad begins with knowing what you might potentially encounter. Doing your homework helps you avoid frustration—and danger.

AVOIDING HAZARDS ABROAD

Prudent travelers always take many potential risks into account when planning a trip. After all, enterprising criminals and even rickety buses and crazy drivers can turn a dream vacation into a nightmare. But until recently, getting complete and important information hasn't always been easy. Luckily for travelers who want to know, a growing army of experts is tracking the risks and making information on travel hazards easily accessible. Investigate these key topics.

Travel warnings. The U.S. State Department provides travelers with two forms of information about areas around the globe. The countries consistently ranking among the riskiest for

American travelers are listed at web sites maintained by the State Department, which posts daily warnings and updates on such risks as state-sponsored terrorism. (As of early September 1999, the agency cautioned against travel in about 30 countries.) The basis for such warnings includes unusual security and/or travel conditions, such as the potential for unexpected detention, unstable political conditions, or serious health problems.

Consular information sheets. Available for every country of the world, these include such details as the location of the U.S. embassy or consulate, unusual immigration practices, health conditions, minor political disturbances, entry regulations, crime and security information, and drug-possession penalties. Any instabilities in a country not severe enough to warrant a warning may be included in an optional section of the consular information sheet called "Areas of Instability."

Highway peril. Traffic constitutes a very significant travel risk, one not often considered by tourists. Road accidents are the second leading cause of death for Americans abroad, after illness, according to statistics from the Maryland-based Association for Safe International Road Travel (ASIRT), a nonprofit organization that tracks road conditions and accidents in 54 countries.

Anyone can be a victim. Travelers are urged to find out about road safety *before* setting out on a trip, particularly to developing countries, where the hazards can be significant. Be informed not only about a country's accident rates and trouble spots but also about its "road culture," such as its acceptance of speeders and stop-sign runners.

Air safety. The FAA lists foreign governments that don't comply with established safety in their oversight of civil aviation. You can check their web site at *www.faa.gov/avr/iasa/ index.htm*.

Crime toll. You're more likely to be a victim of a petty crime while traveling than to be caught in a terrorist attack. These tips can help you gauge a country's criminal activity:

Assess economic conditions; troubled regions often have

high crime rates. Watch for news reports on criminal activities in your projected destination. Consult guidebooks for warnings on specific regions or neighborhoods prone to danger. Once at your destination, keep a low profile; don't flash money, jewelry, or expensive electronic equipment. Travel with

Where To Get The Facts
Plan ahead to ensure your safety

The U.S. State Department. The agency maintains warnings on global terrorism and countries to avoid at *www.state.gov/www/global/terrorism* and *http://travel.state.gov/travel_warnings.html*. Similar information is available on recorded phone messages at 202 647-5225. You can order specific reports via automated fax-back service; call 202 647-3000.

Association for Safe International Travel (ASIRT). The group provides road-safety data for each of 54 countries in its publication "Road Travel Reports," available for donations starting at $5. ASIRT's web site offers free travel tips and a sample report. Call 301 983-5252, fax 301 983-3663, or visit *www.asirt.org*.

National Business Travel Association (NBTA). Contact this organization for a free 10-page tip list, "General International Travel Advice," which includes commonsense counsel on how to act in strange surroundings, avoid threats, and stay safe in a foreign country. Call 703 684-0263, or fax 703 716-3487 and request Document 2000, or go to *www.nbta.org*.

Pinkerton Global Intelligence Services. Besides rating countries from low to extreme risk on a four-tier scale on its World Status Map, the security organization also provides summary reports for each country. The back of the map lists such items as immunizations and documents required for travel. A year-long subscription to the map (six editions) is $36; single issues sell for $6.95. Call 703 525-6111, fax at 703 525-2454, or visit *www.pinkertons.com*.

Kroll Associates. Kroll Travel Watch City Updates are available for $19.95 per report, each including the latest news, currency exchange rates, airport and transportation information, practical how-tos, plus useful phone numbers. The reports are short but include current information on trouble spots. Contact Kroll at 800 824-7502 or visit *kins.kroll-ogara.com*.

TRAVEL SAVVY

293

a companion, if possible. Change your routine frequently, so criminals can't lie in wait.

Natural disasters. As more travelers journey to far-flung and underdeveloped locales, the threat of harm from natural disasters such as floods, severe storms, earthquakes, and avalanches looms larger. Such phenomena are almost impossible to predict. Nevertheless, be alert to potential danger whenever you plan to travel overseas.

Stay informed and avoid traveling when disasters are apt to strike. For example, bypass hurricane season in the Caribbean and Atlantic (August through October) or flood season in Southeast Asia (July through September).

• Heed warnings, such as those posted in ski resorts and other alpine areas about risk of avalanches.

• Should a disaster be predicted, listen to evacuation warnings and have your escape route planned out.

KEEP CURRENT ON CURRENCY

Developing a foreign-currency strategy is an essential aspect of trip planning wherever you go.

Maximize your exchange rates. Preparing now can get you more for your dollar later.

Learn the exchange rate before your trip. This will give you a fairly accurate idea of your probable expenses.

Exchange a small amount of money in the U.S. You won't need much: Just $20 to $50 will allow you to bypass the lines and lousy rates at most airport exchange booths. If you have no time before you leave, exchange only $20 to $50 at the airport. Look for a bank-affiliated ATM, increasingly common at airports.

Put big expenditures on a charge card. Items such as tickets, hotels, car rentals, and the like are best paid for with plastic. You'll save the percentage point or two in price that you'd otherwise lose in currency conversion (although the new surcharges being levied by some cards might negate the savings). You will also gain the protection of the card's chargeback provisions and (with some credit cards) an extra guarantee on your purchases.

Use an ATM card for incidental cash. Remember, it's always a good idea to carry a small amount of local currency with you at all times for transportation, phone calls and incidentals. But also tote along some traveler's checks as backup. They may be your only option if an ATM rejects your card.

The ATM option. If your ATM card works in the Cirrus or Plus network at home, you may be able to withdraw cash from foreign-bank ATMs belonging to the same network. Your withdrawal will be converted at the interbank exchange rate—the "wholesale" rate that banks use for large-scale financial transactions.

That rate confers quite an advantage. If you exchange currency or traveler's checks at a bank exchange counter, you get a retail rate that's often 3 to 5 percent less favorable. At many banks, an additional fee—per transaction, per check, or a percentage of the transaction—can add another 2 to 5 percent.

Cirrus and Plus overseas work exactly as ATMs work at home: You insert your card, then punch in your personal identification number (PIN) followed by the amount of withdrawal (in local currency). The machine issues the currency, and your home account is automatically debited. As in the U.S., the foreign bank may or may not impose a fee. The other possible extra is a per-use fee your bank may impose for using an ATM elsewhere on the network (usually $2 to $3 per transaction, $5 at a few banks). Those fees can add up, so plan ahead to minimize the number of transactions.

Follow these pointers to minimize ATM hassles.

Check your PIN! ATMs outside North America often do not accept PINs longer than four digits. If your PIN is longer, ask your bank for a different number. And keypads on many foreign ATMs have numbers only. So if your PIN contains letters, use

Make Way for the Euro
Europe rolls out its universal currency

The euro is the new universal currency of 11 participating countries in Europe's Economic and Monetary Union (EMU), the product of one of the largest currency consolidations in history. Here are the vital statistics:

Timetable. The euro debuted January 1, 1999, as a "virtual" currency, meaning it can be used only in noncash situations, such as credit-card purchases and traveler's-check transactions. During a three-year transitional period (until December 31, 2001), the paper money and coins of the 11 EMU countries listed below will remain in use. On January 1, 2002, the first euro notes and coins will enter circulation. The coins will carry a common European face on the "heads" side, but the "tails" side will have a different design in each member nation. The notes will be uniform throughout the EMU. For the first six months of 2002, euro notes and coins will coexist with the currency of each country, as these national currencies are phased out. Finally, on July 1, 2002, only the euro will be accepted as legal tender in the 11 EMU countries.

Who's who. Austria, Belgium, Finland, France, Germany, Ireland, Italy, Luxembourg, the Netherlands, Portugal, and Spain are the first to participate in the introduction of the euro. Three other members of the EMU—Great Britain, Denmark, and Sweden—may eventually join the currency program. Greece has not been able to meet the EMU's financial criteria for participation.

What it means to you. The euro will eventually have wide-ranging effects on American travelers, who'll soon be able to skip the hassles and costs of changing money in each country as they travel through Europe. And no more calculating new exchange rates every few days. You'll also find it easier to compare prices among different destinations—which could lead to greater price competition among the EMU countries.

What it's worth. At its debut on January 1, 1999, the euro was worth about $1.10, and 10 months later, it was holding at about $1.05. During the transition period, the exchange values of local currencies against the dollar will be determined by dollar-euro fluctuations. For example, if the euro declines 4 percent against the dollar, the franc, deutschmark, and lira would also decline 4 percent.

the standard letter-number correspondences from U.S. phones to convert. (By the way, don't worry about a language problem: Most foreign ATMs affiliated with Cirrus or Plus provide instructions in English.)

Stock your account. Overseas ATMs may not give you a choice of accounts to tap. Make sure you have adequate funds in your primary checking account.

Have other money sources. Finding a participating ATM may be difficult, and your card may not work in all locations. And banks in a few important tourist countries still aren't set up to handle ATM debit withdrawals—our standard "cash card" transactions. So travelers from the U.S. can get cash only by using a credit card (and paying interest on the withdrawal as a cash advance). But the situation is improving, as both Cirrus (MasterCard) and Plus (Visa) extend their ATM networks. Both systems now publish directories of overseas locations, which should be available from the issuing bank.

However, don't rely solely on ATMs to replenish your cash supply while you're traveling, unless you're sure (from a prior trip) that your card will work.

Since conversion surcharge policies keep changing, travelers should check their monthly statements for changes to cardholder agreements, or call the company's toll-free customer-service numbers before taking a trip. It may even pay to ask your credit-card company for its current policy in writing.

But remember, it's still smart to charge your purchases overseas rather than exchanging currency or traveler's checks, because the exchange rate is better. Credit-card companies typically grant consumers the same favorable rates banks give each other for bulk transactions—essentially a daily wholesale rate plus a 1 percent fee. By contrast, travelers can lose 5 to 10 percent of their money when converting cash.

Traveler's checks. Widely accepted in hard-currency countries, traveler's checks offer protection against loss or theft.

TRAVEL
SAVVY

Most provide worldwide refunds and emergency services if your checks are lost or stolen.

Other money options. The following choices are convenient and may also help you get a good exchange rate.

Plastic checks. The Visa TravelMoney card, available at U.S. banks, is meant to compete with traveler's checks. You prepay the selling bank as much as you want, plus a 1.5 percent fee, then use the card just like an ordinary debit card at Visa/Plus ATMs throughout the world.

The 1.5 percent fee is more than you typically pay for traveler's checks, but with TravelMoney you get a much better exchange rate than you do with paper checks. So overall, you probably come out ahead. The big advantage is that you're getting cash from a specified fund, not dipping into your bank account or building up credit-card debt through cash advances. Order an extra card or two, then keep the cards in different places in your wallet or luggage, in case one is lost or stolen.

Hotel money exchange. Holders of Diners Club cards can exchange up to $1,000 a week for local currency at

Credit-Card Surcharges
Watch your exchange rate

In 1999, travelers encountered an irritating new trend that chipped away at their expected exchange rates. Credit-card issuers began imposing currency-conversion surcharges of 1 to 2 percent on foreign purchases. As of late 1999, here's how the major credit-card companies stood on the issue:

- **American Express:** 2 percent (up from 1 percent in mid-1999)
- **Diners Club:** 1 percent
- **First USA:** 0 percent (reversed earlier charge of 2 percent)
- **MasterCard:** 1 percent
- **Providian Bank:** 5 percent
- **Visa:** 1 percent

participating Inter-Continental hotels around the world. You nab the bank rate, less a service charge of 4 percent. The handy service is relatively inexpensive if you're in a country where ATMs won't accept your card or if you need to pick up some foreign currency when banks are closed.

Foreign payment. These services are available through large banks, exchange services, and travel agents. Upon receipt of your U.S. payment (in check or money order), a bank draft or wire transfer is issued in local currency to the foreign hotel, air, rail, or other travel company you specify. (By making your deposit or even prepaying the full amount in the local currency, you may be able to save if the dollar's exchange rate weakens by the time the bills are rendered.) Ruesch International and Thomas Cook both offer check and wire-transfer services for modest fees.

HOW TO CASH IN ON VAT REFUNDS

Travelers who shop abroad may be entitled to a refund of the value-added tax (VAT) added to the retail price of merchandise in most European countries. You can potentially save a lot: VAT can account for as much as one-fourth of an item's retail selling price. But you'll encounter minimum-purchase requirements.

Global Refund (formerly Europe Tax-free Shopping, or ETS), run by Europe's largest tax-refund specialist, helps American tourists reclaim VAT. (The new name reflects an expansion to Canada and Singapore, with several other Asian countries targeted for future expansion.)

VAT basics. Participating merchants will display a blue-and-silver "Tax Free for Tourists" sign or sticker in English in the window or on the door. (The new Global Refund logo is similar to the old ETS logo.) When you finish shopping in each store, you ask for a tax-free shopping check for the amount of the tax refund.

You have the refund check stamped by a customs officer when you leave the country. (Since you must show your purchases to

TRAVEL SAVVY

a customs official, keep them handy in your carry-on baggage.) Then you redeem the check at a Global Refund desk, located at most major gateway airports. You can usually request the refund in local currency or U.S. dollars, or as a credit to your charge card.

For countries within the European Economic Community (EEC), you get your refund at a Global Refund desk after you've cleared departure customs in the final country you visit before returning to the U.S. In countries other than those belonging to the EEC, you receive your refund as you leave each country. You may also request your refund when you return home, either by mail or as a charge-card credit.

VAT pitfalls. In almost all countries, you must make a minimum purchase in each transaction to be eligible for a refund. The minimum is usually under $100. However, minimums are high enough in Switzerland ($340), France ($210), Italy ($180), Singapore ($172), the Netherlands ($160), Canada and Greece ($150), and Belgium and Hungary ($145) to mean that many tourists may not qualify for a refund. For more information, call Global Refund, 800 566-9828, or visit their web site, *www.globalrefund.com*.

Also, take note of three more reasons why VAT refunds are less generous than they first appear.

• The minimum purchase you must make to qualify for a refund typically applies to all the goods you buy during one shopping session (one visit to one store). If you go to more than one store or revisit a store, the minimum applies separately to each shopping session. And in Italy and Luxembourg, it applies per individual item.

• Global Refund deducts as much as 20 percent of the refund as a handling fee (the percentage may go down on large refunds).

• Many of the goods you might be tempted to buy in Europe are cheaper in the U.S.

Any visitor to Europe can potentially receive VAT refunds

on merchandise. Tourists aren't eligible for VAT refunds on the travel services used while vacationing. But people who travel on business can get refunds of the VAT charged on hotel, restaurant, and rental-car bills in some countries.

BAGGAGE LIABILITY

Lost luggage is the nightmare of every traveler, novice or experienced. And compensation may not equal the true value if your baggage ends up in luggage limbo.

Domestic. If an airline loses or damages your checked or carry-on baggage on a domestic trip, the liability is limited to $1,250 per person (American Airlines, however, raised its liability limit to $2,500). The limit applies both to flights on a plane seating more than 60 and to those on a smaller plane included on the same ticket with a flight on a larger plane. The limit of $1,250 covers luggage packed for a short trip or with casual clothes. But if you're off on a long or more formal trip, it may not balance out your loss.

International. On international trips, maximum baggage compensation is set by treaty at $20 a kilogram of checked baggage weight (about $9 a pound). The airline is liable only for depreciated value, not replacement value or original purchase price. The international limit is grossly inadequate. For example, the claim allowance of $270 for a typical 30-pound suitcase would hardly begin to cover the possessions in the average traveler's baggage.

But the U.S. Department of Transportation (DOT) says that claims are seldom based on actual weight. Most carriers serving the U.S. have filed tariffs stating that rather than weighing every bag at check-in, they will assume that every lost or damaged bag equals their maximum weight limit, usually 32 kilos (around 70 pounds). Thus the international liability limit for most airlines serving the U.S. (both U.S. and foreign carriers) is a flat $640 per bag (32 kilos times $20), regardless of what a bag weighs.

TRAVEL
SAVVY

301

Insurance. To protect yourself, cover the difference between the value of your personal effects and the maximum airline payment with insurance. You may use a year-round personal-property policy, a separate baggage insurance policy, insurance

Tax Barometer Rising
Travel can be taxing

An index of transportation and travel-related taxes in 52 high-traffic destinations worldwide shows 17 cities boosted taxes on transportation and tourist services during late 1998 and early 1999.

The World Travel & Tourism Council (WTTC), a coalition of travel industry executives, monitors the impact of taxation on business and vacation travel. Its mid-1999 "Tax Barometer" shows that travelers continue to be a tax target of governments. Since 1994, 43 of 52 destinations have raised travel-related taxes; only six cities have lowered taxes. Take a look at trends by category:

Air. Taxes and surcharges on air travel (arrival and departure taxes, surcharges for passenger service and security measures, and various inspection and immigration fees) have had the biggest impact on the increased cost of travel, according to the WTTC. Between June 1994 and February 1999, 46 of the 52 destinations posted increases, with a dozen cities doubling flight-related taxes.

Hotel. Lodging taxes have risen at 42 percent of all destinations during the same five-year period. Based on a four-night stay, five destinations charge lodging taxes that equal or exceed 20 percent of the final bill: Copenhagen (25 percent), Prague (23 percent), Buenos Aires (21 percent), and Bombay and Delhi (both 20 percent). Six destinations— Athens, Helsinki, Hong Kong, Manila, Nairobi, and New York—decreased their lodging taxes during this period.

Rental car. Car-rental taxes increased in more than half of the destinations during the same period. The highest car-rental taxes were found in Delhi (49.4 percent), Brussels (25.9 percent), Prague (25.8 percent), Vienna (24.9 percent), and Paris (23.9 percent).

Food. Meal taxes have increased in 21 of 52 destinations surveyed since June 1994, most notably Nairobi (up 500 percent), Manila (up 194 percent), Osaka and Tokyo (both up 167 percent).

offered by your credit card, or excess-valuation coverage available for purchase from the airline

Enforcement. The DOT cannot force airlines to reimburse you for lost luggage. The law only states the liability limit; it doesn't provide for enforcement. Most airlines voluntarily accept valid claims up to the maximum amount.

Delays. Baggage is delayed far more often than it's lost. Though the airlines aren't required to give you anything if that happens, some offer free kits of supplies to tide you over. (As a precaution, pack whatever you need for 48 hours, including small valuables, keys, travel documents, and medicines, in your carry-on luggage.)

An airline may also offer to reimburse you for the cost of personal-care products plus a few basic clothing items (shirts, underwear). But don't buy anything without authorization from the airline, and save all your receipts. If the delay drags on a day or more, ask the airline to authorize additional purchases.

Always negotiate your baggage problems with the airline on which you arrived. Even if another airline is involved—either in tracing the baggage or paying for it—the airline on which you arrived will initiate the necessary procedures.

GETTING THROUGH CUSTOMS

A lot of travelers like to shop, but few know the rules and regulations as to what (and how much of it) they are allowed to bring back into the U.S. Brush up on customs guidelines for overseas travel.

Purchased goods. If you've been abroad for at least 48 hours and are returning to the U.S., you may bring $400 worth of personal or household articles with you duty-free ($800 if you are coming from American Samoa, Guam, or the U.S. Virgin Islands; there is no time limitation if returning from Mexico or the Virgin Islands). Beyond that, you must pay a flat 10 percent duty on the next $1,000 worth (5 percent from U.S. possessions)

TRAVEL
SAVVY

303

and various duty rates for any additional items.

Duty-free goods. You can bring in no more than 100 cigars (non Cuban); 200 cigarettes (one carton); or one liter of wine, beer or liquor (none if you're under 21), without paying duty.

Restricted items. You may need a permit or license—or may not be allowed to bring the following in at all: food; drugs; certain products not approved by the U.S. Food and Drug Administration; fruits; plants; vegetables and their byproducts; and meat and poultry. Also restricted are pets and wildlife; trademarked items (certain cameras, watches, perfumes); lottery tickets; firearms; ammunition; and hazardous materials.

Receipts. Keep receipts for anything you purchase. If you've spent more than $1,400, you must list in writing all items acquired on your trip and what you paid for them. To avoid hassles on your return, you'd be wise to carry receipts for any foreign-made articles you take with you, to prove that you didn't buy them on the present trip.

Gifts. Gifts under $200, except for perfume and tobacco, may be mailed duty-free to friends and relatives (the limit is also $200 from U.S. possessions). However, postal laws don't allow you to ship alcoholic beverages.

Currency. Take out or bring in more than $10,000 in currency and you must file a form with U.S. Customs.

Multicountry trips. Items designed for personal use, including souvenirs purchased in other countries, can be brought duty-free into most foreign countries (a verbal declaration may be required). Other items may be restricted or prohibited; if you have questions, check with the appropriate consulate before departure.

More information. You can write to the Department of Documents, P.O. Box 371954, Pittsburgh, PA 15250-7954, for the booklet "Know Before You Go." Regulations for Canada are similar; for details, write to Canada Customs, Inquiries Unit, First Floor, 333 Dunsmuir Street, Vancouver, B.C. Canada V6B 5R4, or call 604 666-0545 and ask for the booklet "I Declare."

CHAPTER 34

Facts About Travel Insurance

Having to cancel or cut short a trip due to illness, accident, or emergency can be not only disappointing but financially devastating. Travel insurance can protect you.

———————————— ■ ————————————

If sickness, accident, or even death strikes before or during a tour or cruise, you could face two major financial penalties: the loss of nonrefundable prepayments and the heavy expense of emergency transportation home. Either one can total thousands of dollars. Fortunately, travel insurance can shield you against both—but it's the most overpriced of all travel services.

TYPES OF COVERAGE

Travel insurance offers two types of coverage.

Trip cancellation/trip interruption (TCI). These policies cover losses incurred if you cancel a trip before you leave home or cut the trip short. They reimburse you for whatever portion of your payment cannot be recovered from the travel supplier.

Emergency medical evacuation (EME). This coverage pays if you must be rushed to a medical facility far from the site of the accident or illness.

Policy types. TCI/EME is sold in several versions.

Bundled policies. Most major travel insurance companies now feature their bundled (or cruise/tour) policy options as their primary product. The better examples include as much TCI as you want to buy (typically subject to a $10,000 maximum), a moderate amount of EME, plus a handful of other coverages. The price is based on the amount of TCI you buy—but travel insurance is grossly overpriced. The wholesale price of flight insurance is approximately 17 cents for $100 of coverage. Insurance companies, however, take a huge markup.

Custom policies. Several major insurance carriers also sell custom policies, allowing you to assemble your own travel-insurance package from a selection of options, each priced separately. Once popular, custom policies are losing ground to bundled options that often provide much or more coverage. A custom TCI policy typically sells for about $6 per $100 of coverage. The EME components and other options are usually priced according to the duration of your trip.

Wholesale policies. Many big cruise lines and tour operators sell wholesale policies under their own names (although the insurance is actually issued by an insurance company noted in the brochure's fine print). Wholesale policies are typically a bit cheaper than retail bundled policies, but not always; the cruise line or tour operator, not the insurance company, sets the selling price. But these policies don't cover some important risks, notably operator or cruise-line failure. The risk of tour-operator failure has been a long-standing problem, and some cruise lines are now wobbly as well.

Some wholesale policies do have an offsetting advantage: If the underwriting insurance company rejects a claim for an aborted trip, the line usually offers partial compensation in the form of a substantial discount on a future cruise.

Cancellation waiver. Usually the cheapest form of trip-cancellation coverage, this is also the weakest. In fact, it's not *really* insurance. Instead, for a price, the issuing cruise line or tour operator agrees to waive its own cancellation penalties if you cancel your trip for a covered reason, typically only pre-departure contingencies that occur more than 24 hours before departure. Waivers don't cover mid-trip interruption at all, and compensation is nil if the tour operator or cruise line fails.

WHY YOU NEED INSURANCE

The wide array of travel insurance policies available will usually add an extra 5 to 10 percent to your total bill. But the investment in insurance is smart for two big reasons:

Cancellation penalties. Cruises, package tours, and airline tickets typically require 100 percent payment in advance, sometimes months before departure. If you're forced to cancel 60 days before the trip, the penalty may amount to pocket change. However, closer to departure time, cruise and tour companies impose stiff penalties for cancellations. Worst case, you could lose your entire prepayment. Even after you start your trip, your own illness or a problem at home could force you to abandon your journey.

Evacuation. If you suffer a severe accident or illness in a remote area, you might have to be evacuated to a medical facility. Just rescheduling your ticket or paying for a conventional flight could be expensive; evacuation by helicopter or private jet —unlikely though that might be—could cost a small fortune.

WHAT'S COVERED

Coverage for big financial risk falls into three broad categories.

Illness/injury/death. TCI and EME cover different aspects of dire travel situations.

TCI policies. Such policies reimburse you (or your heirs) for extra costs you might incur should either you or a traveling companion fall sick, suffer an injury, or die either before

TRAVEL SAVVY

307

departure or during your trip. (They won't reimburse you for the companion's expenses unless the companion is also insured.) The policies also provide reimbursement if illness, injury, or death of a close family member at home forces you to cancel or interrupt your trip.

Most TCI policies now waive any exemptions for preexisting medical conditions, provided you insure the full value of your trip within seven days of making your initial deposit or prepayment.

However, some TCI policies won't cover any preexisting condition, controlled or not, for which the insured person received

When You Don't Need Insurance
Some coverage doesn't pay

TCI and EME policies often include other benefits. Most aren't worth buying separately, especially since travel insurance coverage is usually secondary, meaning it only picks up what you can't recover from your own insurance or from a supplier. So don't be pressured.

Medical/hospital. Chances are your own medical insurance or HMO covers you even when traveling, as do some Medicare-supplement policies. Go for travel-insurance coverage only if you aren't otherwise covered.

Baggage loss. Your homeowner's or renter's policy probably covers personal effects, even when you travel. Some travelers, especially those on cruises, bring along valuables that may not be covered. But even those people are probably better off with a year-round floater policy than with by-the-trip baggage insurance.

Trip and baggage delays. Many policies pay up to $1,000 reimbursement for minor hassles. If coverage is bundled at no extra cost, you might as well take it, but don't bother buying it separately.

Accidents. Some policies include accident insurance, either for the entire trip or just as airline flight insurance. That coverage cynically plays on an irrational fear of flying: You're more likely to die of a bee sting than in an airplane crash.

medical treatment or advice within 90 to 180 days before buying the policy. In theory, that means the company could deny a claim if you so much as took an aspirin on a doctor's advice within the exclusionary period. So read the fine print.

Typically, rules on preexisting conditions apply to any person—you (the traveler), a traveling companion (insured or not), or a family member at home—whose medical condition causes a trip to be canceled or interrupted.

EME insurance. Either a straight EME policy, or the EME component of a bundled policy, provides for emergency transportation in the event of serious illness or injury.

Exclusions. However, both TCI and EME policies exclude a long list of medical conditions, and typically won't cover you if, for example, your trip is spoiled by a self-inflicted injury; an injury resulting from hazardous activities, such as mountain climbing; a medical problem that results from the use of illegal drugs; or a war injury.

Operator failure. All too often, a tour operator fails, leaving customers stuck with worthless (but completely prepaid) air tickets and hotel vouchers or stranded abroad without return transportation. TCI can cover those losses, too.

Most policies reimburse you if your operator or cruise line "fails," "defaults," or "ceases operations." But the application can be tricky, so study terms before you buy. Several policies pay off only if the operator ceases all operations for 10 days or more, although a much briefer failure could seriously disrupt your trip. Even worse, some policies pay off only in case of "bankruptcy," which could render the coverage useless. Tour operators that hit the skids seldom actually file for bankruptcy; many simply close their doors and disappear.

To guard against losses caused by tour-operator failure, see that your cruise or package tour operator belongs to the U.S. Tour Operators Association (USTOA), or participates in an escrow program recommended by the American Society of

Travel Agents (ASTA). Then purchase your TCI directly from an insurance company—if you buy from a tour operator who subsequently fails, the coverage would be worthless.

However, if protection against supplier failure is your only concern, you don't need to buy TCI. Instead, use a credit card to buy your tour or cruise. If the supplier fails, you can get a chargeback that removes the charges from your account. (You can't get a chargeback for any of the other cancellation risks.)

Unforeseen emergencies. TCI covers a wide range of accidents and unpleasant surprises that might abort or interrupt a trip: a fire or flood in your home; a call to jury duty; an accident that makes you miss a flight or sailing; an airplane hijacking; a natural disaster (fire, flood, earthquake, or epidemic); terrorism; or a strike.

Recently, TCI policies have generally become more liberal on covered risks. In fact, many now include the catchall term "unforeseen emergencies" rather than providing a long list of specifics. Still, TCI isn't a blank check. Even the most liberal policies usually exclude personal financial circumstances, business or contractual obligations, or "change of plans."

INSURANCE PAYOFFS

Should you be hit with a travel problem, TCI or EME offers relief for specific expenses.

Cancellation fees/penalties. In the event of a predeparture cancellation or postponement, TCI reimburses you for the fraction of your prepayments or deposits you can't recover from the supplier. You must first apply for whatever refund may be available from your tour operator, cruise line, or airline, under the terms of the ticket. TCI then pays the difference between your original price and that settlement.

Double/single adjustments. As a rule, you buy a tour or cruise at a per-person, double-occupancy rate. Should your traveling companion suddenly be unable to leave on a trip (for a covered reason, of course), TCI pays the single supplement so you can take the trip alone. Similarly, TCI covers adjustments required if your companion has to return home early.

Transportation adjustments. Typical coverage stipulates a payoff in a variety of scenarios:

• When a covered reason forces you to postpone a trip, TCI pays the cost of switching your airline ticket to a later flight, or the extra cost of alternative transportation to join a trip in progress, say, airfare to your cruise's first port of call.

• If a problem arising during your trip forces you to return home early, TCI covers the extra costs. But you must first find the best deal your airline will give you, then apply for TCI to pay for any additional fare or replacement ticket reissuing fee.

• In the event you suffer an illness or accident, most TCI policies pay for a family member to travel from home to the location of your accident or hospital confinement.

• Should your sickness or accident be severe enough, EME insurance (or the EME component of a bundled policy) typically will cover getting you to the nearest adequate medical facility—even a special evacuation—as well as your eventual transportation home. Generally, EME services are provided at the discretion of the insurance company's medical adviser.

• Most TCI/EME policies include some form of worldwide assistance: a number to call for referral to a doctor, lawyer, or

Finding the Insurers
Compare companies and rates

Access America: 800 284-8300, *www.worldaccess.com*
CSA: 800 348-9505, *www.csatravelprotection.com*
Travelex: 888 457-4602, *www.travelex-insurance.com*
Travel Guard: 800 826-1300, *www.noelgroup.com*
Travel Insured: 800 243-3174, *www.travel-insured.com*
Universal Travel Protection: 888 795-1561, *www.utravelpro.com*

TRAVEL
SAVVY

other person or service valuable in a pinch. But if you're look-ing for help with anything other than a covered medical emer-gency, although the insurance program will provide a referral, *you* must pay. And similar referral services are widely available as free benefits on some premium charge cards.

BUYING TRAVEL INSURANCE

The safest way to buy TCI is directly from an insurance com-pany. That way, you're protected even if your travel provider should fail. Be cautious if a travel agency pushes one company's policy. Agents usually get big commissions from policy sales. Most agencies are allied with the large, reputable insurers, so they're unlikely to steer you to a bum deal. But travel agents aren't insurance specialists, and consumers should consider what coverage they need—and what exlusions are unaccept-able—before buying anything. See "Finding the insurers," at left, for company names and contact numbers.

Regardless of which supplier you choose, don't overbuy TCI. You can't recover more than your actual loss, so insuring for an amount beyond your total financial exposure is a waste. Cover only the risks you can't afford to absorb.

CHAPTER 35

Phoning Home for Less

Staying in touch while traveling can be a challenge—and expensive, too. Some smart telephone tactics can help you get the most talk for your money.

■

Most people want to phone home when traveling, either to share incredible experiences or just check in. But when long-distance calls are placed from hotel phones or public phone booths, you can face an outrageous phone bill at trip's end. These tips can mean less-expensive calls.

AVOID HOTEL SWITCHBOARDS

Overseas hotel switchboards are the worst by far, so grossly overcharging for calls made from a hotel room that a single call sometimes costs more than the room. Savvy travelers avoid the gouge with two options:

Use a calling card. Most hotels will allow you to access the international calling codes provided by the major calling cards. Just dial into the provider's network to get the calling card's agreed-upon rates. But make sure the hotel doesn't levy a heavy surcharge for letting you access the network.

Use a public phone. You can use a carrier-based calling card that will bill to your home phone, or in some countries, a calling card in the local currency to access international numbers. The card is also sometimes a thrifty option for short (under five minute) calls.

COMPARING CALLING CARD FEATURES

The calling cards and international access numbers doled out by the leading U.S. phone service providers—AT&T and MCI—are certainly convenient. But their call-home-from-abroad service may not be the most economical choice.

Even within the U.S., you can easily overpay. The big-company calling cards are among the most expensive. Fortunately, a number of other companies operate calling-card programs with rates much lower than those of the big-three carriers. Comparing these factors can help you evaluate calling cards:

Calling area. Cards typically charge the same amount per domestic call, regardless of distance. However, intrastate long-distance calls and calls to or from Alaska, Hawaii, and Puerto Rico may be charged at different rates. Generally cards have at least one option to let travelers call overseas from the U.S., and most provide for calls from overseas locations back to the U.S. Charges for calls from abroad to the U.S. may well be more important to you than calls from the U.S. to overseas phones, in view of the sky-high rates charged by some foreign hotels when guests call home (or phone any other country).

Rate plan. With flat-rate cards, you pay one set amount per call; neither time of day nor day of the week matters. Peak/off-peak cards assess different charges. Typically, peak times mean normal business hours where the call originates; off-peak times are evenings, weekends, and holidays. Some cards use peak/off-peak pricing in some areas, flat-rate pricing in others. Many companies also offer a per-minute rate.

Long-distance surcharge. Many cards impose a surcharge on each call (at least in some calling areas), an initial charge that's added to the per-minute charge, something like the flag drop in a metered taxicab. But several cards have low rates and no surcharge. Surcharges are especially high (some over $2.50 a call) on international calls.

Pay-phone surcharge. Early in 1998, a new pay-phone rule allowed owners of public pay phones to collect a charge for toll-free calls originating from their phones. Those 800 and 888 calls remain nominally free to callers, but not to the phone companies that use pay phones for access. Most calling-card operators pass some or all of that charge along to users. And prepaid-card phone services deduct a charge equal to the cost of an additional one to three minutes for each call that originates at a pay phone.

Billing increment. Some companies bill in increments of six seconds (usually with a 30-second minimum charge); some bill in one-minute units. Those quirks can make a big difference. On a call lasting just over a minute—say, 1 minute, 3 seconds—some companies bill for a full two minutes, while others charge for just 1 minute and 6 seconds. When rates are comparable, a short billing increment is clearly preferable.

Foreign-to-foreign calls. Several cards permit you to call from one foreign country to another. Using a U.S. company's calling card is often cheaper than dialing direct on a local public phone and much cheaper than calling from your hotel room.

CALLING CARDS

You can buy prepaid calling cards in local currency, anywhere from the U.S. equivalent of $5 to $50 or more. In countries where they're popular, you'll find phones that show a digital-display countdown of the value remaining on the card as you use it. Consider prepaid cards if you'll make calls within a given city or country—setting up tour or hotel reservations, for example—or for making quick calls home. (The time you get for your money depends on the country's international rates.)

CALLBACK SYSTEMS

People who make many international phone calls from foreign locations might save with a callback phone system, which capitalizes on low international rates from the U.S. Rather than dialing directly from a foreign country, you call a dedicated number in the U.S., let it ring once or twice, then hang up. The "switch" in the U.S. is programmed to dial your overseas number right back and offer you a U.S.-based dial tone. You then make your calls.

If you hang up quickly, there's no charge for the unanswered call to the U.S. switch: You are billed only for the callback from the U.S. to your foreign location, plus the subsequent calls you make using the U.S. dial tone. Even though you pay two tolls, the sum is often less than what you'd pay for a single direct call from a foreign country.

Callback may not always work for all travelers. With most systems, you must call from a phone that the U.S.-based switch can dial directly—which precludes service to travelers in hotel rooms. A few callback systems provide a computer-generated voice that can be programmed to request a specific extension, but such a system might not work with every hotel switchboard.

So callback probably isn't feasible for individual overseas travelers moving from place to place and staying in hotels. But if you're renting an overseas accommodation for several months, callback might work for you.

CHAPTER 36

Health Tips for Travelers

No one likes to think about getting sick or injured while on vacation. But it can happen, and being informed can be the best medicine.

■

All the details for a perfect trip to an exotic locale are in place. You're all set, right? But have you had the necessary inoculations and packed the recommended medications?

You'll find basic health preparations for travelers, plus smart precautions to take at your destination, outlined here. But every traveler, particularly those with special health problems or needs (including pregnant or breast-feeding women, older persons, those with lowered immunity or chronic diseases, and anyone traveling with infants and young children), should consult physicians or other professionals for specific advice or treatment.

BASIC PRECAUTIONS

Illness—from common traveler's diarrhea to something more serious, such as malaria or hepatitis—can not only ruin a trip but impair your long-term health. So wise travelers prepare for health risks before they pack.

Study health conditions at your destination. Most American tourists traveling abroad don't need to be too anxious about health. In larger European cities, the health environment is very similar to that in the U.S. However, if your itinerary takes you off the beaten path—particularly to Asia, Africa, and parts of South America—you may need special protective measures.

Read up on the diseases commonplace in the region you'll visit. Most guidebooks contain general recommendations and precautions, which you can use as a starting point. You can also go to the U.S. Public Health Service's Centers for Disease Control and Prevention web site (*www.cdc.gov*.) The CDC's International Travelers' hot line (404 639-8105) presents programmed responses to questions 24 hours a day (with a touch-tone phone). Operator assistance is available 8:00 a.m. to 4:30 p.m. EST, Monday through Friday.

Schedule doctor and dentist visits. A month or two before your trip, ask your doctor to review your immunization status, to help you plan the full course of vaccinations you'll need and to be sure they're appropriately spaced and timed. Allow at least one or two weeks before departure for possible reactions to subside. You may require even more time because of the need to space certain combinations of vaccines.

If you're planning a long trip and/or your last routine physical was more than a year ago, schedule an exam. Anyone suffering from a chronic disease or on long-term medication needs a more complete check-up.

Before any extended trip, see your dentist far enough in advance to allow time for necessary work. And do have your eyes checked. If you wear corrective lenses, pack an extra pair, plus a copy of your lens prescription.

Get required immunizations. Some countries require certain immunizations before you can enter. For current information, call your county or state health department or the CDC. If you plan to be abroad for more than a month, particularly in a rural area, check with those agencies about any recommended precautions.

Travelers' health information and international vaccination requirements and recommendations are also available from the U.S. Public Health Service Quarantine Station in your area (see the CDC listing in the Resource Guide). And the following guidelines can also help you prepare:

International Certificate of Vaccination. To avoid hassles where immunizations are required, take a written record. This certificate—Form PHS-731—is available from many travel agencies and transportation companies, from your local health department, or from the Superintendent of Documents, U.S. Government Printing Office (Stock #017-001-004405; $2 a copy). Some physicians keep a supply of the forms on hand. All immunizations can be given and recorded on your certificate by any licensed physician.

Keep your completed vaccination certificate with your passport. Each traveler in your party needs a separate certificate.

Yellow-fever vaccination. Yellow-fever vaccine and the certification of yellow-fever vaccination must be obtained at an officially designated Yellow-Fever Vaccination Center, where the certificate is validated by the authorized physician or health department. Your own physician can get the vaccine for you under a special license. Boosters are needed every 10 years.

Some African countries require a certificate of yellow-fever vaccination from all travelers who enter; other countries in Africa, and some in South America and Asia, require evidence of vaccination from travelers who have come from or traveled through areas where yellow fever is present. If your physician is not licensed to give it, contact your county or state health department.

Omissions. If your physician advises you to omit a required immunization for medical reasons, have the doctor record the omission on your certificate and attach a signed and dated statement on letterhead stationery specifying the reasons.

Exemptions. Infants are often exempt from vaccination requirements for foreign countries, and some countries require no certificates for very young children. Before traveling, check with the foreign embassy or consulate for exemption requirements.

Routine vaccinations. Whether traveling or not, everyone needs these immunizations, typically given in early childhood, to protect against common illnesses such as measles and mumps. But adults without an adequate vaccination history should consult a doctor for the safest immunization strategy, considering age, medical condition, and travel plans.

Individual decisions. When your destination country does not *require* immunizations, your physician can help you decide which are still a good idea by evaluating your destination, time of year, trip duration, living arrangements, plus personal risk factors such as age, current health and immunization status.

Which immunizations? Few if any travelers would need all the immunizations available. Following is an overview of 10 immunizations and one preventive drug treatment (for malaria). Ask your physician if you fall into a high-risk group (infants, pregnant women, and those with lowered immunity); for such people, the risk from the vaccine may be greater than the health risks of the disease itself.

Many diseases are spread by contaminated food or water or by insect bites. Even if you have had required shots, you must still take precautions. Food and water safety, as well as protection against insects, are discussed later in this chapter.

Cholera. Still a possibility in parts of Asia, Africa, and Latin America, this illness causes intestinal cramps and diarrhea. In severe cases, dehydration can be fatal unless vigorously treated with intravenous fluids and salt replacement. Antibiotics can also help.

Since the risk of cholera to tourists is now very low, the CDC advises that routine use of the vaccine is questionable. At this writing, no country officially requires vaccination against it (though local authorities may occasionally require documentation of such). The cholera vaccine can cause a reaction and is effective less than half the time, so the best precaution is to avoid potentially contaminated food and drink. For those who must travel into cholera-infested areas, new oral vaccines (Mutachol, Orachol) seem more protective than the injectable type.

Hepatitis A. Like cholera, this disease is transmitted by contaminated food and drink, or by human carriers of hepatitis A virus (HAV). Consider immunization if you are traveling anywhere *besides* Japan, Australia, New Zealand, Northern and Western Europe, Canada, or the U.S.

Hepatitis A vaccine has replaced gamma globulin as the preferred hepatitis A preventative. There are two available: Merck's VAQTA and Smith Kline Beecham's Havrix. Both provide protective antibodies from two weeks after injection; a booster dose is given six to 18 months later. Virtually 100 percent immunity is believed to last for 10 to 20 years.

Hepatitis B. The transmission agent is contaminated blood or sexual contact with carriers of hepatitis B virus (HBV). Consider immunization with Recombivax-HB or Energex-B (both genetically engineered in yeast) well in advance—you'll need three injections over a six-month period. For those needing more immediate coverage, there is a short course (three injections over three weeks) that provides partial (68 percent) protection. Shots should be given in the arm, not the buttocks. Areas where the disease is common include sub-Saharan Africa, southeast Asia, South Pacific islands, and parts of the Caribbean. It is also present in other regions of Africa and Asia, as well as Japan, Eastern and Southern Europe, the Commonwealth of Independent States (former republics of the U.S.S.R.), and most of Central and South America.

The risk of hepatitis B infection is generally low for most travelers. But it rises dramatically for those who have sexual contact with residents of infected areas (or come into contact with their blood). Condoms can lessen the chance of infection.

Japanese encephalitis. Vaccines against this disease should be considered by anyone intending to spend extended periods of time in rural Asia. The specific areas of risk include Bangladesh, Cambodia, China, India, Indonesia, Korea, Laos, Malaysia, Myanmar (Burma), Nepal, Pakistan, the Philippines, Singapore, Sri Lanka, Taiwan, Thailand, Vietnam, and eastern parts of Russia. But the threat is slight for short-term travelers.

Malaria. Malaria is transmitted by the female anopheles mosquito. Consider preventive treatment if you're traveling to areas where malaria is known to exist, generally in Central and South America, Haiti, sub-Saharan Africa, South and Southeast Asia, the Middle East, and a few South Pacific island nations. In addition to the drug regimen, travelers to those regions should try to avoid being bitten by mosquitoes by using insect repellent and staying indoors during peak mosquito time—dusk.

Antimalarial drugs help prevent or suppress malaria, but they don't immunize against the disease. Should you develop a high, spiking fever, which can happen as early as a week after you arrive in a malarial area, or as long as six months after you return home, seek medical help immediately.

Drug treatment begins before departure. Weekly doses of one 500-mg tablet of chloroquine (Aralen), a commonly prescribed malarial drug, may be taken beginning one week before you leave for a malarial area, then continued while you're away and for four weeks after you return home. (But you may begin drug treatment as early as two weeks before departure and continue for six weeks after return.)

Children's weekly dosages are determined by body weight.

The carefully calculated amount can be ground up and put in gelatin capsules, to be mixed with food or drink.

All doses *must* be taken once each week. Missing even a single dose will reduce protection.

However, chloroquine-resistant strains of the malaria parasite are now common. In areas infested with these resistant strains—which includes *all* malarial areas except for parts of Central America and the Middle East, Haiti, and the Dominican Republic—mefloquine (Lariam) is increasingly recommended as the antimalarial suppressant. One 250-mg Mefloquine capsule is taken starting one week before departure and continued weekly for four weeks after return.

Mefloquine shouldn't be taken by people taking beta-blockers—propranolol (Inderal) or atenolol (Tenormin)—or calcium-channel blockers such as verapamil (Calan), diltiazem (Cardizem), or nifedipine (Procardia); any cardiac or hypertension medication (check with your doctor); by children weighing under 30 pounds; or in areas where chloroquine is still effective.

If you intend to travel in isolated malarial areas, ask your doctor to consider prescribing three pyrimethamine/sultadoxine (Fansidar) tablets to take along, strictly as a backup. (Fansidar should be avoided by persons with a history of sensitivity to sulfa drugs and by infants under two months.) The drug should be taken only if you begin to have malarialike symptoms (high fever, chills, sweating, headache, and muscle ache) and you can't get medical help. Take the pills—but get to a medical facility as soon as possible.

Bring along enough of the prescribed drug(s) to cover four to six weeks *after* your stay in malarial areas. (Warning: Overdoses of antimalarial drugs can be fatal; observe the prescribed dosages carefully and store out of the reach of children. In all malarial areas, it's also a good idea to protect yourself against mosquito bites.)

TRAVEL
SAVVY

Plague. This vaccination is recommended only for travelers to rural or highland areas of Africa, Asia, and South America who may be unable to avoid contact with infected rodents, rabbits, and fleas, but is not necessary for travelers visiting urban areas with modern accommodations.

Poliomyelitis (polio). The disease is transmitted by water and food contaminated by the feces of human polio-virus carriers. Consider having an additional single dose of vaccine (beyond the immunization you probably received as a child) if traveling to tropical or developing countries or to most states of the former Soviet Union. Ipol (enhanced-potency inactivated polio vaccine) is given by injection. It should be taken only once as an adult.

Spinal meningitis. Frequently fatal, spinal meningitis is caused by a bacterium known as meningococcus and transmitted by contaminated food and drink and by human carriers. Get the vaccine if you're going to sub-Saharan Africa, Nepal, or Northern India, especially if you'll be in close contact with locals or present during the dry season (December to June). The vaccine is expensive but fairly effective; immunity typically lasts for three years.

Typhoid fever. This is another disease spread by contaminated food and water. Consider immunization if you're traveling to Africa, Asia, or Central and South America (especially rural and tropical areas) and plan to spend at least six weeks there. An oral typhoid vaccine, Vivotif (one capsule every other day for four doses), is just as effective as injectable vaccine, with fewer (if any) side effects, and protects for five years. Even with vaccination, however, take strict precautions against contaminated food and water.

Yellow fever. Transmitted by mosquitoes, yellow fever is reported in Africa, South America, and South and Southeast Asia, especially in rural or forested areas within about 15 degrees of the equator. The Public Health Service still strongly recommends vaccination for those traveling to yellow-fever areas, although it isn't required to re-enter the U.S. Even with vaccination, travelers should guard against mosquito bites in yellow-fever areas.

Other precautions. Adult travelers should be sure they've had a tetanus-diphtheria shot within the past 10 years. If over 65, also consider getting a flu shot and perhaps a pneumonia shot as well. Travelers born in or after 1957 should also see about a second dose of measles vaccine before traveling abroad.

MEDICAL SUPPLIES

Just as important as preparing to stay healthy before a trip is maintaining a good defense while abroad.

Pack a medical kit. Buying unfamiliar drugs abroad, where safety standards for pharmaceutical products may not be as rigorous as those in the U.S., can be risky. In many countries, medicines sold over the counter (including some available only by prescription here) may have serious side effects.

Refuse any unfamiliar remedies that friends or pharmacies urge upon you during your travels. Instead, take your own medications and supplies. (See "Medical kit checklist.")

Carry a medical history. A brief medical record can provide information helpful to a physician in an emergency. Your own doctor can help you create a form, or you can photocopy (and enlarge if needed) the sample in this chapter. Also include copies of current prescriptions, and, if pertinent, a copy of your most recent electrocardiogram.

If you have a medical condition that could be life-threatening, you may want to wear a warning. For a one-time, $35 membership fee (annual renewals are $15), the nonprofit Medic Alert Foundation International provides a special necklace or bracelet engraved with your medical condition and a 24-hour toll-free telephone number for access to your medical history and the names of your physicians and close relatives. Call 800 763-3428 for more information.

INSURANCE COVERAGE

No matter where you travel, some emergency services may already be covered by your existing health insurance (check with your carrier). In addition, coverage is available for travelers who become ill or suffer a serious accident anywhere in the world. For more information on emergency medical insurance (EME), see Chapter 34.

HEALTH-WISE TRAVELING

Once you've had your shots, should you feel absolutely secure? Immunization can never guarantee 100 percent protection

Health Reference
An invaluable book for travelers

The 10th edition of "The International Travel Health Guide" ($19.95) is an exhaustive, 480-page compendium of health information for travelers. Author Stuart R. Rose, M.D., addresses everything from pretrip shots to help in identifying mysterious illnesses that can plague travelers months after they return home.

The volume covers health-care items to pack, travel insurance, food and drink safety, medical care abroad, and emergency medical transport, as well as common complaints such as motion sickness, altitude sickness, jet lag, traveler's diarrhea, and insect-borne diseases.

Most impressive is the World Medical Guide, a continent-by-continent and country-by-country catalog of disease-risk summaries for more than 200 countries. Each country's profile includes its visa requirements, the locations and telephone numbers of U.S. embassies or consulates, and locations of major hospitals. A useful appendix features a directory of more than 700 centers and physicians that specialize in travel medicine in the U.S. and some other countries.

"The International Travel Health Guide" is available at bookstores or from the publisher, TravelMedicine (800 848-2793).

Medical Kit Checklist

What you pack can save headaches later

The more remote your destination and the longer you'll be there, the more medications and supplies you'll want to take along. Pack all drugs safely away from heat, light, moisture, and children. Keep over-the-counter drugs in their original containers.

Should you need any prescription drugs, have your doctor prescribe or record them by generic names (brand names vary from country to country). Make sure that the name and strength of each medication are clearly identified on the pharmacy's original label. If you take a prescription drug containing a narcotic (such as codeine), carry a copy of the prescription to satisfy customs officials.

Here are some candidates for your traveling medical kit (not all are applicable for every person and destination):

Medications
Any prescription drugs
Pain medication (aspirin, acetaminophen)
Altitude-sickness medication
Motion-sickness medication
Antacid
Multipurpose antibiotic
Cold remedies
Diarrhea remedy
Hydrocortisone cream
Laxative
Nausea remedy
Sedative
Fungicidal preparation

Supplies
Ace bandage
Adhesive bandages and tape
Rubbing alcohol
Clinical thermometer
Corn pads
Scissors
Tweezers and needle
Facial tissues
Packaged moist towelettes
Flashlight
Condoms/contraceptives
Menstrual pads/tampons
Water heater/electric immersion*
Water purification solutions or tablets
Paper coffee filters*
Insect repellent
Snakebite kit
Sunblock

*To aid in purifying water

TRAVEL SAVVY

against typhoid fever or other intestinal diseases. Wherever you go, a smart defense is to avoid possibly contaminated food and drink.

The main culprits are untreated water, unpasteurized dairy products, unpeeled raw fruits and vegetables, and cooked

EMERGENCY MEDICAL RECORD

This information supplements, but does not replace, the International Certificate of Vaccination, which may be required for entrance into certain countries.

Name _____

Address _____

Blood type_____ **Rh Factor** _____

Date of birth _____

Tetanus and Diphtheria Immunization:

Primary series _____ **Date** _____

Last booster dose_____ **Date** _____

I have these medical conditions:

I am allergic to:

I take these drugs (generic name, U.S. trade name, dosage schedule):

My medical insurance plan is:_____

My doctor is: _____

Address: _____

Phone: _____

In an emergency please notify:_____

Address: _____

_____

Phone: _____

foods that are improperly handled—touched by unclean hands or contaminated utensils, or spoiled by inadequate cooking, poor storage, or careless serving. (Maintaining your own good personal hygiene, including frequent hand-washing, is also essential.) Health hazards vary from place to place. The U.S. Public Health Service considers most developing countries of Africa, Asia, Latin America, and the Middle East to be high-risk areas. Most of Southern Europe and a few Caribbean islands pose intermediate risks. The following sections detail necessary precautions in these areas.

WATER SAFETY

In the U.S., we take our safe water supply for granted. But since contaminated water is a common source of infection, pay close attention to the water you ingest while traveling abroad —as a beverage, frozen into ice cubes, or streaming from the tap as you brush your teeth.

Drinking water. Although often safe in large cities, drinking water may be contaminated in rural regions by bacteria, viruses, or parasites. If chlorinated tap water is not available, or if local conditions are questionable, stick to bottled water or other beverages or purify the water yourself.

What's safe. Generally, carbonated drinks (canned or bottled), beer, and wine are safe. So are citrus fruit juices, either bottled or made from frozen concentrate with purified water (water that has been boiled or treated).

What's risky. Glasses and cups may be contaminated. Drink from disposable paper containers, or quaff directly from the can or bottle—after wiping it clean. Noncarbonated, bottled fluids aren't necessarily safe; it depends on how and where the drink was bottled. If in doubt, steer clear. Use ice cubes *only* if they're made from purified water.

Purification. If you must drink or brush your teeth with suspect water, treat it first. First choice: Boil the water for one minute (three minutes at altitudes above 6,500 feet), then allow to cool. While chemical treatment may prove more convenient and practical than boiling, it's less reliable. Iodine or tetraglycine hydroperiodide tablets (Globaline, Potable-Agua) are both available at pharmacies and camping stores. (Chlorine may be used as well, although it's less dependable than the two other chemicals.) Be especially wary of cloudy water: If possible, boil it.

For swimming. Bathing or swimming in contaminated water can lead to skin, eye, ear, and intestinal infections. Fresh water—especially warm, dirty water in the tropics—is the most hazardous. Chlorinated pools are usually safe. So is salt water, though some beaches are contaminated by streams, sewage outlets, or animal feces. Inquire locally before you venture into any waters.

One of the leading dangers of fresh-water exposure is schistosomiasis, a disease that occurs sporadically throughout the tropics. You can get it by swimming or bathing in freshwater streams, ponds, or lakes containing snails harboring the infectious form of the schistosoma parasite (cercariae). Cercariae can penetrate intact skin to cause an itchy eruption known as swimmer's itch. They then enter the bloodstream and can lodge and grow in the liver or other organs. Adult worms inflict serious damage on the liver, intestines, or urinary tract.

While schistosomiasis can be treated with drugs, it's obviously better to avoid swimming in suspect water. If you do come in contact with contaminated or doubtful water, strip immediately and towel off vigorously to prevent the cercariae from penetrating your skin as water evaporates.

FOOD CAUTION

A general rule for all travelers: Where hygiene and sanitation are poor, view every food source with suspicion.

Meat, fruit, and vegetables. If you think food handling may be questionable or refrigeration lacking, avoid cold cuts and potato or egg salads. Order any meat, poultry, fish, or shellfish dishes thoroughly cooked and served piping hot.

In tropical areas, don't eat raw fruit unless it has an unbroken skin (like oranges or bananas) that you can peel yourself (after washing it with purified water). Otherwise, only freshly prepared, thoroughly cooked foods are safe. Be especially wary of salads and leafy vegetables.

Milk and dairy products. In large European cities, milk and other dairy products labeled as pasteurized can usually be considered safe. Outside urban areas, however, dairy hygiene may not be as strict as in the U.S. or Canada. Where sanitation, food handling, or refrigeration are a problem, avoid raw egg mixtures, cream, milk (even if pasteurized), and milk-containing foods such as cream sauces and certain pastries, ice cream, frozen desserts, whipped-cream confections, and any other dairy products.

In risky regions, canned, evaporated, or condensed milk is safe only if used straight or reconstituted with boiled water. Consider bringing powdered milk to mix with boiled water.

To be free of contamination, cheese must either be made from pasteurized milk or be cured for at least 60 days. In Europe, most cheeses are cured for at least that long to improve flavor. Fresh and special native cheeses similar to our cream cheese, which are not cured, are best avoided unless you're sure they've been made from pasteurized milk.

For infants not being breast-fed, the safest and most practical food is ready-to-use formula.

TRAVELER'S DIARRHEA

Of the millions of people who travel to developing countries, about one-third get traveler's diarrhea at least once during their stay. The usual cause is a pathogenic variant of a common bacterium that normally lives in the intestine. You can help prevent traveler's diarrhea by scrupulously observing the precautions against contaminated food and drink previously discussed.

Symptoms. Typical symptoms are frequent watery bowel movements and abdominal cramps, sometimes accompanied by weakness, muscle aches, dizziness, and loss of appetite. Severe chills, high fever, nausea, vomiting, bloody stools, and dehydration usually indicate a more serious condition, so seek medical care promptly.

Prevent dehydration by drinking lots of fluids. (Infants, toddlers, and older people in particular may become dehydrated rapidly.) Canned soup and fruit juices help offset sodium and potassium loss. Avoid alcohol and coffee.

Treatment. As uncomfortable as it is, traveler's diarrhea is rarely life threatening. Most cases last just one to three days. But recurrences are possible, so before heading to a high- or intermediate-risk area, ask your doctor to prescribe an antidiarrheal product (loperamide or Imodium A-D) for mild traveler's diarrhea, plus an antibiotic, in case a more serious case develops.

Bismuth subsalycilate (Pepto-Bismol, for example) can prevent diarrhea in travelers who take two tablets four times a day. However, it turns stools black, and can cause mild ringing in the ears. No one should take it for more than three weeks. Those allergic to aspirin, taking anti-clotting drugs, or who have diabetes or gout should check with their physician first.

INSECT PERILS

Insects—mosquitoes, flies, fleas, ticks, mites, and others—are not only annoying to travelers, but in tropical climates can be quite dangerous. Malaria is the most common insect-borne disease; others are yellow fever, dengue fever, and Lyme disease.

A country-by-country report on the risk of diseases spread by insects can be found in the latest edition of the CDC's "Health Information for International Travel," published annually and available for $20 from the Superintendent of Documents, U.S. Government Printing Office. The report is also available via the CDC web site (*www.cdc.gov*).

These precautions can help protect against insects:

• Avoid insect territory from dusk until dawn. When you go out, cover your skin, including feet. Avoid dark colors, which attract some insects. Wear long pants and tuck them into your socks and/or boots. Don't use scented toiletries in insect-infested areas.

• Apply insect repellent to clothing and exposed skin. The most effective insect repellents contain DEET (diethyltolu-amide, or N,N-diethylmeta-toluamide). However, CONSUMER REPORTS' medical consultants advise against using DEET-based repellents on children under age 6. For older children, adolescents, and adults, it's usually unnecessary to use any product that contains more than 30 percent DEET on the skin; if needed, higher concentrations can be used on clothing. Spraying clothing with permethrin (Duranon, Permanone) and using permethrin-impregnated mosquito netting can also provide some protection.

• Sleep in an air-conditioned or well-screened bedroom, or under mosquito netting. Shower at least daily, and check for lice and ticks.

• Store food in insect-proof containers. Dispose of garbage immediately and properly.

SEXUALLY TRANSMITTED DISEASES

With the increased prevalence worldwide of many sexually transmitted diseases (STDs), among them hepatitis B and C and acquired immune-deficiency syndrome (AIDS), choosing a new sexual partner while traveling can be dangerous.

Before AIDS appeared, techniques for preventing STDs were not often discussed openly, and public awareness of the risks involved in unprotected sexual contact was low. Things have changed. Because there is not yet a cure or vaccine for AIDS, prevention is the only way to control its spread. Other types of STDs can be successfully treated if detected early, but prevention is always better than treatment.

By observing the safe-sex practices described here, one can reduce the chance of contracting any STD—those mentioned above, as well as syphilis, gonorrhea, chlamydia, herpes simplex II, and venereal warts.

• Avoid multiple, casual, or anonymous partners, prostitutes, and others who may have had multiple sex partners, as well as sexual contact with anyone having genital warts, sores, or discharge.

• During intercourse (including oral-genital and anal-genital) use a latex condom and a spermicide. Use a water-based lubricant, not petroleum jelly, with the condom. Don't trust contraceptive products available abroad; bring your own.

• Consider a vaccination against the hepatitis B virus if you're traveling to an area where it's common and you anticipate sexual contact with local residents.

• If you engage in any high-risk sexual behavior, seek prompt medical advice.

COPING WITH CLIMATE

Everyone hopes to have favorable weather when traveling, but climatic conditions aren't always on your side. Your best defense is to be prepared.

Heat dangers. Always take it easy in oppressive heat. Overexertion can lead to heat exhaustion or heatstroke. Watch for warning signs: headache, weakness, dizziness, blurred vision, cramps, and sometimes, nausea and vomiting.

Immediate care. For heat exhaustion, stop what you're doing, get out of the sun, sip cool water, and lie down with your feet elevated until symptoms subside; if they don't, seek professional medical help.

Heatstroke shares many of the above symptoms, but is also marked by hot, dry, flushed skin; disorientation; racing pulse; mental confusion; rapid breathing; and high fever. Have the victim lie down in the shade, and place cold, wet towels on the body. Seek medical care immediately.

Protective measures. Don't exercise during peak heat hours (generally 10 a.m. to 3 p.m.). Avoid the hot sun.

Drink plenty of fluids (but none that contain caffeine or alcohol, which can promote dehydration). Shower once or even several times a day (not in very hot or very cold water).

Wear a broad-brimmed hat and lightweight, light-colored, loose-fitting clothing. Cotton and linen are preferable to synthetics. Choose cotton socks and lightweight shoes or open sandals.

Sunburn. The sun can wreak havoc anywhere but is most dangerous in tropical zones and at high altitudes. The fair-skinned are most vulnerable. Ultraviolet (UV) rays can also cause skin reactions in anyone taking certain drugs, including some antibiotics, diuretics, and anti-hypertension medication.

Prevention. Sunscreens, containing one or more chemicals that absorb rays before they can harm the skin, are the best defense against UV radiation. Each sunscreen carries a "sun protection factor," or SPF number, indicating the degree of protection. An SPF of 15 to 30 effectively blocks most UV rays.

Apply sunscreen liberally, making sure all exposed areas are covered. Reapply every three to four hours, and after swimming or sweating profusely. Wear a hat and UV-protective sunglasses during midday.

Treatment. Treat sunburn as you would other burns. First-degree sunburn can be soothed by cloths dipped in cool water or by a cool bath with baking soda. Hydrocortisone creams and ointments may help decrease the inflammation; moisturizing lotions can rehydrate skin. Aspirin can also be used to calm the inflammatory reaction (within the first 24 hours) and for pain relief, but take no more than one or two every four hours. A severe sunburn can cause fever, chills, and blistering. Should these occur, seek professional care.

Extreme cold. Frigid conditions present the twin dangers of frostbite and hypothermia (abnormally low body temperature). Anyone underdressed and inadequately prepared for the cold is vulnerable. Older people are especially at risk.

Frostbite. Frostbite results from exposure to subfreezing temperatures; the colder the temperature, the quicker and more severe the frostbite. Frostbitten skin progresses from painful to numb, turns white or bluish, and becomes firm and stiff. Do not rub the skin or thaw it with intense heat. Rather, gently wrap frostbitten areas in a blanket, clothing, or newspaper. Find shelter immediately, preferably in a hospital.

Otherwise, go indoors and start the thawing process immediately by immersing the frostbitten parts in tepid (not too warm and never hot) water for up to an hour. Function, feeling, and color should return gradually. Do not touch any blisters that might appear during the warming process. Take acetaminophen, aspirin, or ibuprofen for pain. A hot, nonalcoholic beverage may also be beneficial, as long as the victim is awake. After the initial thawing treatment, cover affected skin with sterile gauze. The victim should go to a hospital.

Hypothermia. This life-threatening condition can result from overexposure to cold alone, and not necessarily to below-freezing temperatures. A combination of cold and wet can dramatically hasten its onset.

Mental confusion is one of the most ominous symptoms of hypothermia. At the first signs—violent shivering, difficulty walking, slurred speech—seek warmth and shelter. In a more advanced state, marked by progressive disorientation or even unconsciousness, the victim requires immediate medical help.

Frostbite and hypothermia prevention. Dress to preserve body heat and stay within reach of shelter in case of emergency or sudden weather changes. Wear loose-fitting layers of clothing that trap insulating pockets of air. Wear thin liners under fur-lined or down- or synthetic-filled mittens to keep hands protected. Shoes or boots should be loose enough to accommodate wool socks over cotton socks with a little room to spare. Choose a hat that covers the ears, a scarf, and, if needed, a face mask.

Winter sun. The snow-filled landscape poses two other risks: sunburn and snow blindness. Sunlight reflected off snow can burn even more quickly than summer sun, so wear sunscreen. Dark glasses or goggles can prevent snow blindness.

Altitude hazards. Until you become acclimated to high altitudes, you may experience mountain sickness. Symptoms include headache, nausea, shortness of breath, insomnia, fatigue, poor appetite, and mental confusion. Acetazolamide (Diamox), a prescription drug, can be used to prevent mountain sickness, though people with allergies to sulfa drugs should avoid it. Anyone with a history of heart or lung problems should consult a doctor before traveling to altitudes over 5,000 feet. Above that point, oxygen levels may be dangerously low.

MEDICAL CARE ABROAD

When you're sick, the last thing you want to worry about is the caliber of available medical care. But care quality is a real issue for travelers, especially those visiting developing regions, where substandard hygiene and medical practices can have long-term health implications. However, well-trained physicians and well-equipped hospitals can be found in most large cities worldwide, even in some of the economically underdeveloped countries of Africa, Asia, and Latin America.

Consider the following guidelines to help locate medical care abroad.

In an emergency. When minutes count, take fast action.

Go to the nearest hospital. You can always transfer to a better-equipped facility once an acute situation is stabilized.

TRAVEL
SAVVY

But protect yourself. Be aware of the instruments and procedures used—and ask questions. Are hypodermic needles (preferably disposable) sterilized and prepackaged? Do medical personnel wear sterile gloves and change them between patients? If there's a language barrier, request an English interpreter before you agree to any procedure not clear to you.

Blood-screening policies (for HIV and other diseases like

Cruise Ship Medical Care
Staying healthy on the high seas

When it comes to onboard medical care, is there trouble in paradise for the 6.4 million people who take cruise vacations each year? It's estimated that about 5 percent of passengers (or about 320,000 people) seek medical attention on cruise ships. While the vast majority suffer only seasickness or sunburn, thousands of cruisers will turn to the ship's infirmary to treat serious, even life-threatening, illnesses or injuries.

That in mind, you might be surprised to learn there are no international standards for medical care on passenger cruise ships, not even a regulation requiring that a physician be onboard. Although most ships generally do carry doctors, many of them are not U.S.-trained or licensed to practice medicine in the United States, critics charge.

Among the concerns: Some doctors and nurses are not certified in advanced trauma life support; doctors are not board-certified in their areas of practice; and onboard equipment may be lacking or not properly maintained.

Before booking a cruise, take steps to assess both your own health and the ship's ability to deal with potential emergencies:

Consult with your doctor. Travelers with chronic medical conditions should discuss travel plans with their regular physician before booking the trip. Is it safe to travel? Should any activities be avoided?

Are there special precautions? Check with the cruise line. Facilities, staff, and services vary from ship to ship, so get the details on the one you're sailing. What are the doctor's qualifications? Does the medical staff speak English? Is there equipment such as cardiac defibrillators to handle specific emergencies?

hepatitis B) are not as stringent in some developing countries. Should you require a blood transfusion, ask if your spouse or traveling partner can donate, if feasible.

When you are traveling extensively in a high-risk region, consider packing a medical kit containing sterilized needles and other sterile medical items.

Finding a doctor. With time less critical, you have more

Also notify the cruise line of any special medical needs you have. And check the ship's most recent sanitation scores from the Centers for Disease Control and Prevention's Vessel Sanitation Program.

Pack extra medication. Your supply should outlast the duration of your trip (in case you're delayed). Be sure all containers have dosage information clearly indicated on the label, and stow them in your carry-on luggage.

Carefully choose your itinerary. If there's a chance you'll need medical care, avoid cruises to undeveloped areas.

Bring a medical information sheet. The sheet should detail your medical history and a list of allergies, current medications, blood type, and immunization status. Also include recent test results (such as an electrocardiogram if you have a heart condition).

Designate an emergency contact. This should be a person back home familiar with your medical history. Write out specific contact information on your information sheet.

Carry physician contact information. Have your doctor's office and emergency numbers, pager number, fax number, and e-mail address.

Consider comprehensive insurance. Buy coverage for trip cancellation and medical care (scrutinize the policy for limitations on preexisting conditions), including emergency air evacuation.

Be realistic about your health and available care. Shipboard medical facilities, and many onshore clinics and hospitals, may not be up to your accustomed standards.

Source: Consumer Reports Travel Letter

TRAVEL
SAVVY

options. Check with a hospital affiliated with a medical school or operated by the government.

In areas where physicians aren't connected with community or medical-school hospitals (as in Great Britain), your hotel manager may be able to direct you to a group practice medical center or, in more remote areas, a general practitioner. If you need a specialist, these physicians can refer you to a qualified (usually hospital-based) consultant.

If you're sick enough to require a house call, ask your hotel manager for help. Many hotels keep lists of English-speaking physicians willing to make a hotel-room call. Or you may be able to get reliable medical care or advice from the physicians assigned to a nearby American military base. In more remote areas, Peace Corps volunteers may also provide referrals.

Prepare in advance. Consider joining the International Association for Medical Assistance to Travelers before you leave home. This nonprofit organization provides members with a worldwide directory of English-speaking physicians adhering to a set fee schedule. IAMAT also distributes helpful charts and publications on immunizations, diseases, climactic and sanitary conditions, and more.

ONCE YOU'RE HOME

Continued vigilance is necessary long after the trip is over. Fever or intestinal problems that develop after you return home—sometimes even weeks or months later—may have their origins abroad. Delayed-onset symptoms can be caused by malaria, schistosomiasis, typhoid fever, hepatitis, sexually transmitted diseases, and certain parasitic infections. Any symptoms that occur up to six months or even 12 months after your return should alert you to the possibility of travel-related illness. Consult your doctor for a thorough evaluation.

Resource Guide

The following is a list of phone numbers for domestic and foreign airlines, charter airlines, cruise lines, hotels and motels, car-rental companies, and domestic and international travel advisories.

NAME	PHONE	WEB SITE (WWW.)

CHARTER AIRLINES AND TOUR OPERATORS

Name	Phone	Web site
Adventure Tours USA	800 999-9046	atusa.com
Ah Wee WorldTravel Agency	718 584-2100	
Airhitch	800 326-2009 / 888 AIRHITCH (CA)	airhitch.org
Amber Travel	800 262-3701	
DER Travel Services	800 782-2424	dertravel.com
Euram Flight Centre	800 555-3872	flyeuram.com
Fantasy Holidays	800 645-2555 / 516 935-8500	fantasyholidays.com
France Vacations	800 332-5332	france-vacations.com
Funjet Vacations	800 558-3050	funjet.com
GWV International	800 225-5498	gwvtravel.com
Homeric Tours	800 223-5570	homerictours.com
Hot Spot Tours	800 433-0075 / 212 421-9090 (NY)	hotspottours.com
Marcus Travel	800 524-0821 / 973 731-7600 (NJ)	
Martinair	800 627-8462	martinair.com
New Frontiers/Corsair	800 677-0720	newfrontiers.com
Pleasant Holidays	800 242-9244	pleasantholidays.com
Rebel Tours	800 732-3588	travel@rebeltours.com
Sceptre Tours	800 221-0924	sceptretours.com
Skytours Travel Agency of San Francisco	800 246-8687 / 415 228-8228 (CA)	skytours.com
SunTrips	800 786-8747 / 408 432-1101	

NAME	PHONE	WEB SITE (WWW.)

DOMESTIC AIRLINES

NAME	PHONE	WEB SITE (WWW.)
Air Canad	800 776-3000	aircanada.ca/home.html
Air North	800 764-0407 800 661-0407 (Can.)	airnorth.yk.net
AirTran	800 825-8538	airtran.com
Alaska Airlines	800 252-7522	alaska-air.com
Aloha Airlines	800 367-5250	alohaair.com
American Airlines	800 433-7300	americanair.com
American Trans Air (ATA)	800 225-2995	ata.com
America West Airlines	800 235-9292	americawest.com
Canadian Airlines	800 426-7000	cdnair.ca/cpi
Continental Airlines	800 525-0280	flycontinental.com
Delta Airlines	800 221-1212	delta-air.com
Eastwind Airlines	800 644-3592	eastwindairlines.com
Frontier Airlines	800 432-1359	frontierairlines.com
Hawaiian Airlines	800 367-5320 800 882-8811 (HI)	hawaiianair.com
Horizon Air	800 547-9308	horizonair.com
Laker Airways	800 432-2294	
LTU International Airways	800 888-0200	ltu.com
Midway Airlines	800 446-4392	midwayair.com
Midwest Express Airline	800 452-2022	midwestexpress.com
Myrtle Beach Jet Express	800 386-2786	
Northwest/KLM	800 225-2525	nwa.com
ProAir	800 939-9551	proair.com
Southwest	800 435-9792	flyswa.com
Spirit Airlines	800 772-7117	spiritairlines.com
Sun Country	800 752-1218	suncountry.com
Tower Air	800 348-6937	towerair.com
Trans World Airlines (TWA	800 221-2000	twa.com
United Airlines	800 241-6522	ual.com
US Airways	800 428-4322	usairways.com
Vanguard Airlines	800 826-4827	flyvanguard.com

FOREIGN AIRLINES

Name	Phone	Web Site (www.)
ACES Airlines	800 846-2237	acescolombia.com
Aer Lingus	800 223-6537	aerlingus.ie
Aerolineas Argentinas	800 333-0276	aerolineas.com.ar
AeroMexico	800 237-6639	aeromexico.com/start.html
Air Aruba	800 882-7822	interknowledge.com/air-aruba
Air Caledonie/Solomon	800 677-4277	pacificislands.com
Air France	800 237-2747 800 667-2747 (Can.)	airfrance.com
Air Jamaica	800 523-5585	airjamaica.com
Air Littoral	800 237-2747	
Air Nauru	310 670-7302	airnauru.com.au
Air New Zealand & Ansett Australia	800 262-1234 800 663-5494 (Can.)	airnz.com
Air Niugini	949 752-5440	airniugini.com.pg/
Air Pacific	800 227-4446	airpacific.com
Alitalia Airlines	800 223-5730	alitalia.it
ANA - All Nippon Airways	800 235-9262	fly-ana.com
Ansett Australia	800 366-1300	ansett.com.au
AOM French	800 892-9136	aom.com
Asiana Airlines	800 227-4262	asiana.co.kr/asiana.co.kr
Austrian Airlines	800 843-0002	aua.com
Austral Lineas Aereas	800 333-0276	austral.com.ar
Avianca	800 284-2622	avianca.com.co
Aviateca	800 327-9832	grupota.com
Braathens SAFE	800 548-5960	
British Airways	800 247-9297	british-airways.com
British Midland	800 788-0555	iflybritishmidland.com
Cathay Pacific Airways	800 233-2742	cathay-usa.com
China Airlines (Taiwan)	800 227-5118	china-airlines.com
City Bird Airlines	888 248-9247	citybird.com
Condor German Airlines	800 524-6975	condor.de
Copa	800 359-2672	copaair.com
CSA - Czech Airlines	800 628-6107	csa.cz
Easy Jet	0870-6-000-000 (UK)	
El Al Israel Airlines	800 223-6700	elal.co.il
Emirates	800 777-3999	ekgroup.com

NAME	PHONE	WEB SITE (WWW.)
EVA Airways	800 695-1188	evaair.com.tw
Finnair	800 950-5000	finnair.fi
Garuda Indonesia	800 342-7832	
Gulfstream International	800 992-8532	flycontinental.com
Gulf Air	800 553-2824	gulfairco.com
Iberia Airlines of Spain	800 772-4642	iberia.com
Icelandair	800 223-5500	icelandair.is
Japan Airlines (JAL)	800 525-3663	jal.co.jp
KLM	800 225-2525	nwa.com
Korean Air	800 438-5000	koreanair.com
Kuwait Airways	800 458-9248	travelfirst.com/sub/kuwaitair.html
Lacsa Airlines	800 225-2272	flylatinamerica.com/ing
LanChile	800 735-5526	lanchile.com/english
Lloyd Aereo Boliviano	800 327-7407	labairlines.com
LOT Polish Airlines	800 223-0593	lot.com/english
Lufthansa	800 645-3880 800 563-5954 (Can.)	lufthansa.com
Malaysia Airlines	800 552-9264	malaysiaair.com
Mexicana Airlines	800 531-7921	mexicana.com.mx
Nica	800 831-6422	flylatinamerica.com/ing
Olympic Airways	800 223-1226	olympicair.com
Pakistan International Airlines	800 221-2552	
Philippine Airlines	800 435-9725	philippineair.com
Polynesian Airlines	310 830-7363	polynesianairlines.co.nz
Qantas Airways	800 227-4500	qantas.com.au
Royal Jordanian Airline	800 223-0470	rja.com.jo
Sabena Belgian WorldAirlines	800 955-2000	sabena.com
SAS	800 221-2350	sas.se
Saudi Arabian Airlines	800 472-8342	saudiairlines.com
SilkAir	800 742-3333	singaporeair.com
Singapore Airlines	800 742-3333	singaporeair.com
South African Airways	800 722-9675	aa.co.za
Swissair	800 221-4750 800 267-9477 (Can.)	swissair.com
Taca	800 535-8780	flylatinamerica.com/ing
TAP Air Portugal	800 221-7370	tap-airportugal.de
Thai Airways	800 426-5204 800 668-8103 (Can.)	thaiair.com

NAME	PHONE	WEB SITE (WWW.)
TransBrasil Airlines	800 872-3153	transbrasil.com.br
Turkish Airlines	212 339-9661	turkishairlines.com
Varig Brazilian Airlines	800 468-2744	varig.com.br/english/ rghome-p.htm
VASP	800 732-8277	
Virgin Atlantic Airways	800 862-8621	fly.virgin.com

CRUISE LINES

NAME	PHONE	WEB SITE (WWW.)
American Canadian Caribbean Line	800 556-7450	accl-smallships.com
American Hawaii Cruises	800 513-5022	cruisehawaii.com
Carnival Cruise Lines	800 327-9501	carnival.com
Celebrity Cruises	800 437-3111	celebrity-cruises.com
Clipper Cruise Line	800 325-0010 314 727-2929 (MO)	clippercruise.com
Costa Cruises	800 462-6782	costacruises.com/home.html
Crystal Cruises	800 446-6620	crystalcruises.com
Cunard Line	800 528-6273	cunardline.com
Delta Queen Steamboat Co.	800 458-6789	deltaqueen.com
Discovery Cruises	800 937-4477	www.discoverycruiseline.com
Fantasy Cruises & Tours	800 798-7722	
Holland America	800 426-0327	hollandamerica.com
Maris Freighter Cruises	800 996-2747	freightercruises.com
Norwegian Cruise Line	800 327-7030	ncl.com
Premier Cruises	800 327-7113	premiercruises.com
Princess Cruises	800 421-0522	princesscruises.com
Renaissance Cruises	800 525-5350	renaissancecruises.com
Royal Caribbean International	800 327-6700	rccl.com
Royal Olympic Cruises	800 221-2470	epirotiki.com
Seabourn Cruise Line	800 929-9595	seabourn.com
Windjammer Barefoot	800 327-2601	windjammer.com
Windstar Cruises	800 258-7245	windstarcruises.com
World Explorer Cruises	800 854-3835	wecruise.com

NAME	PHONE	WEB SITE (WWW.)

HOTELS AND MOTELS

Name	Phone	Web Site (www.)
Adam's Mark	800 444-2326	adamsmark.com
Admiral Benbow Inns	800 451-1986	admiralbenbow.com
AmericInn	800 634-3444	americinn.com
AmeriSuites	800 833-1516	amerisuites.com
Aston Hotels	800 922-7866	aston-hotels.com
Baymont	800 428-3438	baymontinns.com
Best Inns & Suites	800 237-8466	bestinn.com
Best Western	800 528-1234	bestwestern.com
Bradford Homesuites	888 486-7829	bradfordsuites.com
BridgeStreet Accommodations	800 278-7338	bridgestreet.com
Budget Host Inns	800 283-4678	budgethost.com
Canadian Pacific	800 441-1414	cphotels.com
Candlewood Suites	800 946-6200	candlewoodsuites.com
Choice Hotels	800 221-2222	choicehotels.com
Circus Circus	800 634-3450	circuscircus.com
Clarion	800 424-6423	clarioninns.com
ClubHouse Inn & Suites	800 258-2466	clubhouseinn.com
Club Med	800 258-2633	clubmed.com
Coast and WestCoast	800 663-1144	coasthotels.com
Colony	800 777-1700	
Comfort Inns & Suites	800 424-6423	comfortinns.com
Concorde Hotels	800 888-4747	concorde-hotels.com
Country Hearth Inns	888 443-2784	countryhearth.com
Country Inns & Suites	800 456-4000	countryinns.com
Courtyard by Marriott	800 321-2211	courtyard.com
Cross Country Inn	800 621-1429	crosscountryinns.com
Crossland Economy Studios	800 398-7829	crosslandstudios.com
Crowne Plaza Hotel	800 227-6963	crowneplaza.com
Days Inns	800 329-7466	daysinn.com
Delta Hotels & Resorts	800 877-1133	deltahotels.com
Doral Hotels	800 223-6725	arrowwood.com
DoubleTree	800 222-8733	doubletree.com
Downtowner	800 251-1962	reservahost.com
Drury Inn	800 325-8300	drury inn.com

NAME	PHONE	WEB SITE (WWW.)
Econo Lodge	800-424-6423	choicehotels.com
Economy Inns of America	800 826-0778	innsofamerica.com
Embassy Suites	800 362-2779	embassysuites.com
Exel Inns of America	800 356-8013	exelinns.com
Extended Stay America	800 398-7829	extstay.com
Fairfield Inn by Marriott	800 228-2800	fairfieldinn.com
Family Inns	800 362-1188	familyinnsofamerica.com
Fiesta Americana	800 343-7821	fiestaamericana.com
Forever Resorts	800 255-5561	foreverresorts.com
Forte Hotels	800 225-5843	forte-hotels.com
Four Points	800 325-3535	fourpoints.com
Four Seasons	800 332-3442	fshr.com
Friendship Inn	800 424-6423	choicehotels.com
Golden Tulip	800 344-1212	goldentulip.com
Grand Heritage Hotels	800 437-4824	grandheritage.com
Guest Quarters Suites by DoubleTree	800 424-2900	doubletree.com
Hampton Inns & Suites	800 426-7866	hamptoninn.com
Harley	800 321-2323	
Harrah's	800 427-7247	harrahs.com
Hawaiian Hotels & Resorts	800 222-5642	hawaiihotels.com
Hawthorn Suites	800 527-1133	hawthorn.com
Heartland Inn	800 334-3277	heartlandinn.com
Helmsley	800 283-3824	helmsleyhotels.com
Hilton	800 445-8667	hilton.com
Holiday Inn	800 465-4329	holiday-inn.com
HomeGate Studios & Suites	888 456-4283	homegate.com
Homewood Suites	800 225-5466	homewood-suites.com
Howard Johnson/HoJo Inn	800 446-4656	hojo.com
Hyatt Hotels and Resorts	800 233-1234	hyatt.com
Innkeeper	800 466-5337	
Inns of America	800 826-0778	innsamerica.com
InnSuites	800 842-4242	innsuites.com
Inter-Continental Hotels & Resorts	800 327-0200	interconti.com
ITT Sheraton	800 325-3535	sheraton.com
Jameson Inns	800 526-3766	jamesoninns.com

NAME	PHONE	WEB SITE (WWW.)
Keddy's	800 561-7666	keddys.ca
Knights Inns/Arborgate Inn	800 843-5644	knightsinn.com
Kimpton	Call local property	kimptongroup.com
La Quinta	800 531-5900	laquinta.com
Leading Hotels of the World	800 223-6800	lhw.com
Lexington Suites	800 537-8483	lexres.com
Loews Hotels	800 235-6397	loewshotels.com
MainStay Suites	800 660-6246	mainstaysuites.com
Manhattan East Suite Hotels	800 637-8483	mesuite.com
Marc Resorts	800 535-0085	marcresorts.com
Marriott	800 228-9290	marriott.com
Masters Economy Inns	800 633-3434	masters-inns.com
Master Hosts Inn	800 251-1962	masterhosts.com
Meridien Hotels & Resorts	800 543-4300	forte-hotels.com
Microtel Inn & Suites	888 771-7171	microtelinn.com
Milner Hotel	800 521-0592	milner-hotels.com
Moat House Hotels	800 641-0300	hotelbook.com
Motel 6	800 466-8356	motel6.com
National 9 Inns	800 524-9999	
Nendels Inns	800 547-0106	
Nikko Hotels International	800 645-5687	nikkohotels.com
Oakwood Corporate Housing	800 888-0808	oakwood.com
Omni Hotels	800 843-6664	omnihotels.com
Outrigger Hotels & Resorts	800 622-4852	outrigger.com
Pan Pacific Hotels & Resorts	800 327-8585	panpac.com
Park Inn and Plaza	800 437-7275	parkhtls.com
Passport Inn	800 251-1962	reservahost.com
Preferred Hotels	800 323-7500	preferredhotels.com
Prince Hotels	800 542-8686	princehotels.co.jp
Quality Inns Hotels & Suites	800 424-6423	qualityinns.com
Radisson	800 333-3333	radisson.com
Ramada	800 272-6232	ramada.com
Red Carpet Inn	800 251-1962	reservahost.com
Red Roof Inns	800 843-7663	redroof.com
Regal Hotels International	800 222-8888	regal-hotels.com
Renaissance Hotels & Resorts	800 468-3571	renaissancehotels.com
Residence Inn by Marriott	800 331-3131	residenceinn.com
Ritz-Carlton	800 241-3333	ritzcarlton.com/splash.htm

NAME	PHONE	WEB SITE (WWW.)
Rodeway Inn	800 424-6423	rodeway.com
Scottish Inns	800 251-1962	reservahost.com
Sheraton	800 325-3535	sheraton.com
Shilo Inns & Resorts	800 222-2244	shiloinns.com
Shoney's Inn	800 222-2222	shoneysinn.com
Sierra Suites Hotels	800 474-3772	sierra-orlando.com
Signature Inns	800 822-5252	signature-inns.com
Sleep Inn	800 424-6423	sleepinns.com
Small Luxury Hotels of the World	800 525-4800	slh.com
Staybridge Suites by Holiday Inn	800 238-8000	staybridge.com
Sofitel, Hotel	800 763-4835	sofitel.com
Sonesta	800 766-3782	sonesta.com
Studio PLUS	800 646-8000	studioplus.com
Suburban Lodges	800 951-7829	suburbanlodge.com
Summerfield Suites Hotels	800 833-4353	summerfieldsuites.com
Super 8	800 800-8000	super8.com
Susse Chalet	800 524-2538	sussechalet.com
Swissotel	800 637-9477	swissotel.com
Thistle Hotels	800 847-4358	thistlehotels.com
Tokyu Hotels	800 428-6598	tokyuhotel.com
Towne Place Suites by Marriott	800 257-3000	towneplace.com
Travelers Inns	800 643-5566	travelersinn.com
Travelodge/Thriftlodge	800 578-7878	travelodge.com
Vagabond Inns	800 522-1555	vagabondinns.com
Villager Lodge	800 328-7829	villager.com
Viscount	800 527-9666	viscountsuite.com
Vista International	800 445-8667	hilton.com
Walt Disney World	800 786-1766	disneyworld.com
Wellesley Inns	800 444-8888	
Westin	800 228-3000	westin.com
Westmark	800 544-0970	westmarkhotels.com
Wilson Hotels	800 945-7667	wilsonhotels.com
Wingate Inns	800 228-1000	wingateinns.com
Woodfield Suites	800 338-0008	woodfieldsuites.com
Woodfin and Chase Suites	800 237-8811	woodfinsuites.com
Wyndham Hotels & Resorts	800 996-3426	wyndham.com

NAME	PHONE	WEB SITE (WWW.)

RAIL PASSES

Name	Phone	Web Site
Amtrak	800 USA-RAIL	amtrak.com
Australian Tourist Com.		aussie.net.au
BritRail Travel Int	888 274-8724	britrail.com
CIE Tours International	800 243-8687	cietours.com
CIT Rail	800 223-7987	
DER Travel Service	800 421-2929	dertravel.com
Forsyth Travel Library	800 367-7984	forsyth.com
Japan Nat. Tourist Org.	212 757-5640 (NY) 312 222-0874 (Chicago) 213 623-1952 (LA)	jnto.go.jp
New Zealand Tourism Board	800 388-5494	nztb.govt.nz
Orbis Polish Travel Bureau	800 223-6037	orbis-usa.com
Rail Europe	800 438-7245	raileurope.com
Rail Pass Express	800 722-7151	
Scandinavian American World Tours	800 545-2204	scanamtours.com
Scantours	800 223-7226	scantours.com
Viarail	888 842-7245	viarail.ca

RENTAL-CAR COMPANIES

Name	Phone	Web Site
Alamo	800 327-9633	goalamo.com
Auto Europe	888 223-5555	autoeurope.com
Avis	800 331-1212	avis.com
Rob Liddiard Travel	800 272-3299	
Budget	800 527-0700	budgetrentacar.com
DER Travel Services	800 782-2424	dertravel.com/dercar.htm
Dollar	800 800-4000	dollar.com
Enterprise	800 325-8007	pickenterprise.com
Europcar	800 800-6000	europcar.com
European Car Reservations (ECR)	800 535-3303	
Europe by Car	800 223-1516	europebycar.com
Hertz	800 654-3131	hertz.com
International Travel Services (ITS)	800 521-0643	its-cars-hotels.com

NAME	PHONE	WEB SITE (WWW.)
Kemwel Holiday Autos	800-678-0678	kemwel.com
Kenning	800 227-8990	
National	800 227-7368	nationalcar.com
Payless	800 237-2804	paylesscar.com
Renault Eurodrive	800 477-7116	eurodrive.renault.com
Thrifty	800 367-2277	thrifty.com
Town and Country International	800 248-4350 (Eng., Scot., Wales)	its-cars-hotels.com
Ugly Duckling	800 843-3825	uglyduckling.com
Woods Car Rental UK/ British Network	44-1293-658888 (UK)	woods.co.uk/index.html

TRAVEL ADVISORIES

NAME	PHONE	WEB SITE
Centers for Disease Control International Travelers' Hot Line	404 639-8105	cdc.gov
International Assoc. for Medical Assistance toTravelers	716 754-4883	sentex.net\~iamat
Medic Alert Foundation International	800 432-5378 800 763-3428	medicalert.org
U.S. Dept. of State Travel Advisory Service	202 647-5225	state.gov
U.S. Public Health Service Vessel Sanitation Program	888 232-3299 (Doc. # 510051 fax back)	cdc.gov/nceh/program/ sanit/vsp/scores/scores.htm
World Health Organization Publications Center	518 436-9686	who.ch

Index